Oxford Socio-Legal Studies

Corporate Regulation

OXFORD SOCIO-LEGAL STUDIES

Oxford Socio-Legal Studies is a series of books exploring the role of law in society for both an academic and a wider readership. The series publishes theoretical and empirically-informed work, from the United Kingdom and elsewhere, by social scientists and lawyers which advances understanding of the social reality of law and legal processes.

CORPORATE REGULATION

Beyond 'Punish or Persuade'

FIONA HAINES

CLARENDON PRESS · OXFORD
1997

Oxford University Press, Great Clarendon Street, Oxford OX2 6DP
Oxford New York
Athens Auckland Bangkok Bogota Bombay Buenos Aires
Calcutta Cape Town Dar es Salaam Delhi Florence Hong Kong
Istanbul Karachi Kuala Lumpur Madras Madrid Melbourne
Mexico City Nairobi Paris Singapore Taipei Tokyo Toronto Warsaw
and associated companies in
Berlin Ibadan

Oxford is a trade mark of Oxford University Press

Published in the United States by
Oxford University Press Inc., New York

A catalogue record for this book is available from the British Library

Library of Congress Cataloging in Publication Data
Haines, Fiona.
Corporate regulation : beyond "punish or persuade" / Fiona Haines.
p. cm.
Includes bibliographical references.
1. Criminal liability of juristic persons. 2. Corporation law—Criminal provisions. 3. Liability for industrial accidents.
I. Title.
K5069.H35 1997 97–24346
346.03'1—dc21
ISBN 0–19–826572–7

Typeset by Graphicraft Typesetters Ltd., Hong Kong
Printed in Great Britain by
Biddles Ltd., Guildford and King's Lynn

Dedication

To Bruce, Chris and Tim

General Editor's Introduction

REGULATION only established itself as an important focus for socio-legal research in the 1980s, with the publication of a number of studies of regulatory enforcement. These early analyses provided evidence of some of the realities of regulatory practices for a number of scholars who were becoming increasingly dissatisfied with traditional command-and-control approaches in regulation. The result was a number of publications, many by researchers at work in Australia, addressed to the question of how regulatory systems might be better designed to achieve greater effectiveness and efficiency.

Fiona Haines' book is the most recent work of this kind to have been produced in Australia. As its subtitle suggests, it reaches beyond earlier studies of regulation to rethink strategies of regulatory control. The work's starting point is the current dissatisfaction with command-and-control regulation and it goes on to consider the economic and political conditions under which compliance with regulation can be achieved. Taking the example of occupational safety as the basis for her analysis, Dr Haines shows how companies respond differently to fatalities in the workplace, analysing comparatively how large and small firms react to regulatory control, and showing how organisations behave in the social context of the everyday pressures routinely affecting firms.

This book is, however, much more than another empirical analysis. It is theoretically innovative. One of its concerns is to explore the extent to which regulatory institutions can be designed to encourage "virtue" in the business community, while retaining the ability to act more stringently when this approach fails. To do this, the author develops the virtue-based literature on regulation in various ways and combines this approach with broader theoretical perspectives. She considers how the changing character of contemporary capitalism relates to the capacity of regulatory systems to encourage virtuous corporate behaviour, with an analysis informed primarily by those theorists who have been concerned with the nature of capitalism, particularly Marx, Weber, and David Harvey.

Fiona Haines' works is important because it enhances our understanding of regulatory processes in a number of ways. It confronts the question of what it is that encourages organisations to take responsibility for their actions and to improve safety. It builds on literature which is concerned with the origins of corporate responsibility, and in particular explores further the idea of corporate virtue, seeking to move away from a concern to punish for the harm done by organisations to one which encourages good corporate behaviour through the development of relationships of trust between business and regulator. Indeed, this book takes the recently-published literature on the importance of corporate virtue as a regulatory tool to a new level. This study does not simply explore the changes taking place in regulatory systems but sets them in the context of changes in the nature of late 20th-century capitalism.

It is also, from the point of view of public policy, a timely book. Dr Haines shows us that the design of regulatory institutions and the development of regulatory policy can only be properly conducted when we have a clear understanding of the springs of organisational action. Ideas of command and control regulation tend to sit awkwardly in the current political and economic climate in which forms of deregulation are regarded as important and where it is deemed desirable to harness market forces at the expense of potentially highly interventionist governmental regulation. The push towards deregulation is occurring at a time in which organisational structures and relationships have themselves become increasingly complex with the development of privatisation, contracting out and the like. In short, the book considers in detail the implications of the changing nature of contemporary capitalism for the reformulation of regulatory policy and for the analysis of regulatory systems. Dr Haines has placed the regulatory debate in a much broader political and economic context. She has written a book rich in interesting ideas, one which will be an important addition to the socio-legal literature.

Keith Hawkins

Preface

My interest was sparked in this research when I was at the Victorian Coroner's Court going through files of people who had been killed at work, for a project funded by the Australian Research Council (Polk, Haines and Perrone, 1995). It was emotionally draining work, but over time there was a growing anger that the same sort of 'accidents' seemed to occur with unfailing regularity, construction workers falling from heights, loggers killed by falling branches, forklifts crushing operators and so on. Yet there was also complexity, since in many of the cases there was not one company involved, but two or more. In each case the file ended the same way, a finding (either with or without inquest) with a series of recommendations. The recommendations seemed eminently sensible, but at that point the file ended. I wondered what happened after the investigation took place. Did companies take any notice? Did they ignore the findings? When more than one company was involved, did they try and 'pass the buck' or accept their share of responsibility? These seemed obvious questions, yet ones that were rarely asked. This omission was repeated in the literature, which was reasonably comprehensive when dealing with the *causes* of death and tragedy, but little dealt with the effect. Both the files and the research literature seemed to stop at the same point; an analysis of the causes of the deaths, followed by recommendations concerning future action.

The research findings into organizational responses surprised me. First, contrary to my fears many companies welcomed my interest, managers, safety officers and company owners went to great lengths to explain their side of the story, the effect the death had on them, and how they and their organizations responded to the death. There were exemplary responses in terms of safety (what I called 'virtuous' responses), and others which took a narrow view of their responsibilities, for a range of reasons (the 'blinkered' responses). At every turn there were complications; companies going out of business, being taken over, or changing their identity.

There was a rich mine of information, yet when I returned to the academic literature, little seemed to capture the essence of what I had found. A focus on the actions of the regulator, in terms of their punitive or persuasive response went only a very small way to explain the motivations and actions of the companies I researched. Further, recent appeals to corporate virtue as a regulatory tool appeared somewhat naïve, even though there were instances of corporate virtue in my data. What concerned me was this debate seemed to deal with regulatory strategies in a vacuum, precisely when the pressures each firm faced in their daily life explained so much. Understanding the way organizations behave, and the way they respond to their regulatory responsibilities only made sense when the social context (what I call the 'regulatory space') was taken into account.

Analysing this space required a re-reading of theorists who were acutely concerned with the construction of this space, and the nature of capitalism, in particular Marx, Weber and David Harvey. Armed with their insights the data made sense, and so did the task of regulation. When this analysis was tied back to the regulatory debate in terms of punish or persuade, the strengths and weaknesses of current literature became clear. Further, the inherent dangers in the pursuit of competition as a solution to economic woes, evident in the broader political debate, were clarified. The answer though was not simple, the current economic and political emphasis on competition *can* enhance compliance with regulations (in this case concerning safety), but can also be antithetic to that aim. Again the context within which competition takes place is central to understanding the conditions under which competition enhances or undermines compliance. What is clear though, is that the debate concerning regulation cannot usefully progress without taking account of both the economic and political debate. This book represents a tentative step in linking the regulatory debate to economic and political realities, by way of social theory.

Acknowledgements

THIS book has benefited immeasurably from the assistance of many people. First and foremost my thanks go to Ken Polk and Adam Sutton. Initially my supervisors for my Ph.D., both contributed expertise and support well beyond the bounds of that task. Ken Polk introduce me to the area of health and safety, which has become an abiding interest. He is also a stickler for clarity, much to the reader's benefit! Theoretically I owe a considerable debt of gratitude to Adam Sutton, who introduced me to the work of major social theorists and convinced me of the importance of reconnecting my work with this broader literature. The work of Weber, Marx, Harvey, and others formed the basis of many long and fruitful discussions which found their way either directly or indirectly into my book.

Secondly, I would like to thank my husband Bruce. As well as being a great emotional support, Bruce as a mechanical engineer working both in private industry and the public service has given me understanding of technical issues associated with the data. As important, however, were his stories of the way technical and management issues become translated into action in everyday business and organizational life, an invaluable resource.

There are many others whose insight and assistance have been invaluable. In particular I would like to thank John Braithwaite for his enthusiastic interest in my work, and for his many insights into issues raised by this book. Also many thanks go to Richard Johnstone, Amanda Sinclair, Graeme Johnstone, Peter Grabosky, Michael Quinlan and Santina Perrone. Both the book and my enjoyment of the academic enterprise have been enhanced greatly by these people. Thank you. I am grateful for the assistance of the Victorian Institute of Forensic Medicine in accessing the Coronial material.

Finally, I would like to thank my children Christopher and Tim. Many times they would rather I had played with them, or picked them up early from school than work on 'Mum's Book'. This book owes much to their sacrifices.

F.H.

Contents

List of Tables

List of Figures

1 Introduction

> *Between January 1990 and August 1991, six bulk carriers are 'lost' in rapid succession after leaving ports in Western Australia. In three of these sinkings the entire ship's crew—a total of 77 people—perishes.*
>
> *(Morris, 1992)*

> *In 1987 a team of nine engineers, supervisors and workers is installing and checking a massive open cut dredge for a mining firm in Victoria. During tests a component in the hydraulics system fails. Three men are thrown nine metres to the ground. One dies, two are seriously injured.*
>
> *(Summary from records of the Victorian Coroner)*

> *On May 10, 1993 fire breaks out in a Thai factory making 'Bart Simpson' and other soft toys, mainly for Western markets. 189 female workers are burned to death, crushed or asphyxiated, and more than five hundred injured, as they try to escape from a building whose windows had been locked and doors guarded, allegedly to stop 'employee pilfering'.*
>
> *(Chua and Wei Ling 1993)*

THESE three accounts of death at work were gleaned from newspaper, coronial and government records. They illustrate why crime in the suites has been argued to extract greater harm than crime on the streets (Pearce, 1973; Geis and Meier, 1977; Clinard and Yeager, 1980; Fisse and French, 1985). Apart from the huge financial losses which result from white collar crime such as the estimated 20 billion dollars lost during the 1980s in Australia (see for example Sykes, 1994), abuses perpetrated by those of high social status can wreak great physical harm. The impact of such incidents are immediate and long lasting. In light of this many have argued that they need to be treated as unequivocally criminal, with penalties certain and severe (Glasbeek and Rowland, 1979; Sutherland, 1983; Grabosky, 1983; Wettenhall, 1988; Pearce and Tombs, 1990).

Against this backdrop, recent theorizing by one major group of commentators and academics on how to eliminate, or at least minimize such harm appears incongruous. Rather than condemning business élites out of hand, it is argued that what is needed is to 'nurture virtue', to support and encourage good business practice by giving them the freedom to be trustworthy. A prominent example is work by the Australian criminologist John Braithwaite:

> Instead of institutions that economise on virtue, we need institutions that give actors space to be virtuous. Regulatory institutions can be designed to nurture rather than destroy civic virtue in the business community. At the same time, we need tough-minded regulatory institutions that can shift to a hard headed approach when virtue fails, as it often will. [Braithwaite, 1993:85]

This apparent new found optimism concerning the possibilities of corporate virtue is echoed in recent writings by Grabosky (1994a and b). Grabosky explores how organizations regulate themselves within the market. In doing so, he looks beyond the relationship between regulator and organization for insight into effective regulation. Grabosky argues the intervention of the market is both more effective and encounters less resistance than the actions of government regulators. In this 'brave new market' regulators are set at a distance from the major thrust of the regulatory impetus of market forces, 'they [the regulators] may simply stand to one side and rely on the markets to do their work for them' (Grabosky 1994a:196).

The ability of the market, or individual corporations to act to improve safety is echoed in the recent report on health and safety by the Australian Industry Commission (Industry Commission, 1995). The Commission complained that there was 'too much legislation' (page xxiv). Further, it argued regulation was too inflexible that it does 'not allow for different capabilities of employers to develop their own safety management' (page xxv). While the commission saw a role for effective law enforcement, the ultimate aim is for organizations to take responsiblity and 'do the right thing' when it comes to safety. This book asks the question, 'what motivates organizations to take responsiblity for their actions and improve safety?'

In answering this question the book aims to explore the shift in the literature on business regulation towards corporate responsiblity, and the new possibilities this holds for regulatory theory. The implications of such theorizing are of importance, since changes in the area of regulation are proceeding at a rapid pace, encouraged primarily by pressure from governments both nationally and internationally for 'deregulation', i.e. the removal of constraints on industry to enhance competitiveness in the international market (INDECS, 1992). The book explores how organizations behave with regards to deaths at work, as an illustration of regulatory theory, and the usefulness of that theory's predictions regarding organizational behaviour.

Tracing the Regulation Debate: From Corporate Condemnation to Corporate Virtue

Our initial task, and the purpose of this chapter, is to understand why this shift in attitude towards organizations has occurred. The move from punitive responses to the harm caused by organizations, to ones which seek to maximize good behaviour through emphasis on building trusting relationships with business warrants close attention. This chapter raises questions which must be answered if this shift is to be effective in reducing harm. It certainly does not appear in keeping with much writing and analysis of white collar crime, whether historical or contemporary. Many writers, particularly in the area of health and safety, point to the enormity of the harm wrought by death at work, and correlate such harm with homicide (Glasbeek and Rowland, 1979; Reasons, Ross and Paterson, 1981; Wells, 1988; Reiner and Chatten Brown, 1989a and b; Bergman, 1991; Slapper, 1992). In light of the harm which results from these incidents, they argue strongly that such events can only be considered criminal.

Condemnation of major corporate citizens for the enormity of the harm they perpetrate is clearly present in Edwin Sutherland's seminal work on white collar crime. The central issue which struck Sutherland in his theorizing about organizational harm was the apparently arbitrary way harm perpetrated by persons of wealth and power or high status often failed to be labelled as deviant. Whereas taking money which belonged to others would be defined as theft when perpetrated by someone of low status, when it was undertaken by a person of high status in the course of their (white collar) occupation, the same result would be considered a regulatory matter (Sutherland 1940, 1983). As well as being defined differently, the two examples of theft also receive different responses from authorities. Once apprehended for theft, a low status offender would be likely to be charged with a criminal offence, and if convicted, faced the possibility of prison. White collar offenders on the other hand tended to be exposed to an entirely different enforcement and sanctioning agency. Regulatory agencies used regulations, not criminal laws, and would take a persuasive approach, attempting to encourage organizations and the individuals within those organizations back to the 'straight and narrow' (Sutherland, 1983; Grabosky and Braithwaite, 1986).

Sutherland (1983) called for a fundamental change. Pointing out that harm perpetrated by those of high status was as great, if not greater than, street crime he argued that it should be treated as unequivocally criminal. Greater use should be made of the criminal law against those of high status. Sutherland's work was a watershed in criminology in that it heralded a 'loss of innocence' by mainstream sociologists and criminologists regarding the benign nature of industrial activity. His work led to a range of analyses in the area of workplace health and safety which argued that similar disparities arose when death and injury occurred at work, rather than in the context of conventional street crime (Carson, 1970; Glasbeek and Rowland, 1979; Reasons, Ross and Paterson, 1981; Wells, 1988; Reiner and Chatten Brown, 1989a and b; Bergman, 1991; Polk, Haines and Perrone, 1993).

The increasing scepticism regarding the beneficial effects of corporate activity resulted in greater calls for accountability for both private and public companies. Following Sutherland, the most consistent demand was for use of the criminal law. In the case of death at work arresting and convicting negligent employers for manslaughter was considered the optimal outcome (Glasbeek and Rowland, 1979; Wells, 1988; Bergman, 1991). Others called for a 'recriminilization' of existing health and safety laws (Hopkins, 1989a; Carson and Johnstone, 1990; Haines and Polk, 1990; Haines 1990), with emphasis still being on the need to recognize and label such events criminal.

Implicit in these demands for greater use of the criminal law was re-evaluation of what constitutes criminality. Given the enormity of the harm resulting from 'normal' organizational activity, criminality became progressively associated more with the harm resulting from an act or omission, as opposed to the traditional definition which is premised upon a narrow definition of intent (Von Ebers, 1986; Bucy, 1991). Society could be seen to be demanding a redefinition of what constitutes 'normality' in business relations. These demands in Australia reached their public zenith in 1981. Calls from Bob Hawke, then Prime Minister, made front page news in major Australian newspapers for the offence of manslaughter to be used against a company when two young apprentices were asphyxiated (Hawke, 1981 cited in Carson and Johnstone, 1990).

However, academic arguments for criminalization of corporate actions go beyond demands for retribution. Some theorists view the criminal law as an uncommonly efficient tool for curbing corporate harm. Corporations, it is argued, are uniquely sensitive to the criminal law, and therefore use of such law against those of high status is both an effective and efficient deterrent. It deters not only the company directly punished, but also sends clear messages to the wider business community (Pearce and Tombs, 1990, 1992). This unique sensitivity on behalf of corporations is seen to arise from two attributes. First, the fear of a fall from grace, loss of prestige which results from a criminal conviction. Secondly, organizations act rationally, unlike most typical offenders, and according to strict cost-benefit calculations. Use of the criminal law against corporations would greatly increase the cost of harmful behaviour. A rational calculation of the costs involved, therefore, would lead the corporation to desist from perpetrating harm (Sutherland, 1983; Pearce and Tombs, 1990).

Despite this call, the record of criminalizing (or recriminalizing) death at work remains limited. While prosecutions for death at work have increased in most Australian states, including Victoria (Polk, Haines and Perrone, 1995; Hopkins, 1994a) the rationale of magistrates and judges in sentencing reflects their quasi-criminal understanding of the status of that law (Johnstone, 1994). The net result is that despite the increase in prosecutions and fine levels, fines often remain below levels which could be expected to influence a rational cost-benefit calculation averaging a little over $10,000 in Victoria in 1991 (Hopkins, 1994a).

Use of manslaughter provisions representing the 'hard end' of the criminal law remains minimal. With the exception of certain states in the US, such as California (Reiner and Chatten Brown, 1989a and b), use of manslaughter provisions remains largely a purely theoretical possibility. Reasons for this lack of enthusiasm for deploying the criminal law to curb corporate harm are multifaceted and reflect both theoretical and practical difficulties. There is consistent and continuing resistance to criminal prosecution by the state, and those prosecutions which do occur can sometimes be seen to be politically motivated rather than purely determined by the degree of harm or negligence involved (Sutton, 1983; Perrone, 1993). On a practical level, it is clear that mounting a prosecution for manslaughter requires a very different enforcement and investigatory strategy than that historically undertaken by health and safety inspectorates (Reiner and Chatten Brown, 1989a and 1989b). Training personnel and gathering of sufficient evidence to support such prosecutions remains a major hurdle (Polk, Haines and Perrone, 1993). Also there are real problems in determining who to hold accountable for the harm, individuals or organizations. Those who argue for prosecuting of individuals do so as they see only people, not organizations, as ultimately deterred (for a theoretical debate see Fisse and Braithwaite, 1993, chapter 2; for a prosecutor's perspective see Reiner and Chatten Brown, 1989a and 1989b). Others argue that organizational structures and defences make it unlikely that those ultimately responsible can be convicted (see for a discussion Fisse, 1990:591–4; Fisse and Braithwaite, 1993: chapter 3). Policies which emphasize prosecution of individuals bring a high likelihood of scapegoating within the target organization (Braithwaite, 1984; Stone, 1987; Jackall, 1988; Foerschler, 1990). However, the law itself, particularly manslaughter provisions, does not lend itself easily to prosecution of organizations as opposed to individuals (Fisse, 1990; Field and Jorg, 1991; Polk, Haines and Perrone, 1993). Major cases costing the state considerable resources have failed, due to the inadequacy of the law (Von Ebers, 1986; Fisse, 1990; Foerschler, 1990; Bucy, 1991; Polk, Haines and Perrone, 1993).

Legal mechanisms have long been recognized as problematic as the source of change in organizational behaviour. Macaulay and others point to the separation between the intention of law, and the way law is received and used. His and other research (Macaulay, 1969; Sitkin and Bies, 1994a; Van Maanen and Pentland, 1994) essentially point to the Weberian distinction between formal and substantive justice. To understand how regulation works, or can be derailed, we need to explore how the organizations themselves react to the imposition of law and the methods of formal accountability it imposes. Formal accountability is primarily about written records, statements which show the 'outside' how a particular event was dealt with. Van Maanen and Pentland nicely capture the impetus behind formal accountability:

> Records are not neutral, factual, technical documents alone, although when serving legitimate ends they must appear this way, and when serving illegitimate ones even more so. They are designed—implicitly or explicitly—to produce an effect in some kinds of audience, which itself actively uses records to interpret events. [Van Maanen and Pentland, 1994:53]

The demand for formal accountability in regulation may then result in record keeping for the purpose of being **seen** to comply in order to prevent the organization from being prosecuted or sued. The relationship these formal records have with the reality of organizational life is entirely a separate issue. The use of law and law enforcement by regulators to exact compliance may force changes in formal accountability which can improve procedures, but are equally likely to produce little or counter-productive real effects on behaviour.

Contemporary researchers are not alone in finding that the law seems ineffective against corporations and high status individuals. Writing nearly a century ago Ross (1907 reprinted 1977) pondered on the apparent immunity those in power seemed to have from traditional measures of accountability:

> The Edda has it that during Thor's visit to the giants he is challenged to lift a certain grey cat: 'Our young men think it nothing but play'. Thor puts forth his whole strength, but can at most bend the creature's back and lift one foot. On leaving, however, the mortified hero is told the secret of his failure. 'The cat—ah! we were terror stricken when we saw one paw off the floor; for that is the Midgard serpent which, tail in mouth, girds and keeps up the created world.'
>
> How often today the prosecutor who tries to lay by the heels some notorious public enemy is baffled by a mysterious resistance! The Thews of Justice become as water; her sword turns to lath. Though the machinery of the law is straining askew, the evildoer remains erect, smiling, unscathed. At the end, the mortified champion of the law may be given to understand that, like Thor, he was contending with the established order, that he had unwittingly laid hold of a pillar of society and was

Ber

therefore pitting himself against the reigning organisation in local finance and politics. [Ross, 1907:29]

Such reflections have more than a degree of resonance with the scant record of prosecutions for the excesses of the 1980s (Sykes, 1994). Similarly the absence of prosecutions for deaths at work and the failure of high profile cases such as the case against the *Herald of Free Enterprise*[1] suggests we should reassess how to tackle major social harm perpetrated by organizations.

In addition to the practical difficulties of using criminal prosecution and other legal measures against corporate actors, the possibility of renewed determination in the area of prosecutorial activity is currently politically problematic. Deregulation and simplification of regulations have achieved paramount political importance. Reflecting on this, it is not surprising that shifts in the regulatory debate should be towards encouraging trustworthiness and enforced self-regulation (Stone, 1975, 1987; Braithwaite, 1982; Ayres and Braithwaite, 1992) and enhancing market forces in the regulatory endeavour (Grabosky, 1994a and b). Rebuilding government bureaucracies which are highly interventionist in relation to business practice goes against the current tide of economic and political thinking.

Instead of renewed determination to prosecute, the key concept in this latest shift in the regulatory debate is a perceived need to encourage trust between regulator and regulated. The traditional criminological role of wholesale condemnation of corporate activity in the analysis of white collar crime is seen as ultimately unproductive:

> . . . what is most evidently missing in our corporate/social relations today, and needs to be restored, is a measure of mutual trust and respect. As things stand, we are settling into a self defeating cycle in which the anti-corporate sentiment is increasingly shrill and ill-informed, and the corporate response is too often self defensive, unheeding and unconstructive. [Stone, 1987:34]

[1] The *Herald of Free Enterprise* was a car ferry which sank in the English Channel in March 1987 killing nearly 200 people (Wells, 1988). A manslaughter prosecution brought against seven employees collapsed after Turner J concluded that 'there was not evidence that reasonable prudent marine operators would or should have recognized that the system gave rise to an obvious and serious risk of open-door sailing' (cited in Wells, 1993:555).

A judicious mix of persuasion and punishment is needed to harness the virtue within organizations. Braithwaite (1993) and Bardach and Kagan (1982) argue that excessive focus on prosecution creates an ultimately counter-productive distrust and distance between companies and regulators. Distrust and distance is not the only problem. Once harm caused becomes the major focus, there can be a tendency to bypass the complexities in the factors contributing to that harm (Aubert, 1952; Moore, 1987). While an armed robbery which results in a teller being shot fulfils most definitions of a crime and a criminal homicide, a death resulting from a rigger falling when he fails to hook up his harness (in a workplace culture which stresses 'getting the job done') is less clear cut. Criminologists such as Cohen (1988), point to the 'amnesia' of some advocating more frequent use of the criminal law, who a few years earlier had highlighted its inadequacies for controlling other contexts.

For a range of reasons then, there has been a shift in regulatory theory away from promoting extensive reliance on criminal law measures to advocating a regulatory mix of punishment and persuasion (Braithwaite, 1985; Stone, 1987; Ayres and Braithwaite, 1992; Braithwaite, 1993). As outlined above, the shift away has emphasized both practical difficulties with a 'prosecution first' policy, and the way such a policy may destroy those qualities within an organization that it would most like to promote—namely an ongoing commitment to the well-being of the diverse stakeholders of the company: workers, consumers and the local community, rather than simply the shareholders or the owners of capital. This latter impetus should not be seen as exclusive to the domain of regulation. It forms part of recent writing in philosophy (for example: the philosophy of communitarianism MacIntyre, 1984; Walzer, 1990), political and economic theory (for example: Selznick, 1992; Cox, 1995; Hutton, 1996), as well as in criminology and regulation. This diverse range of writing emphasizes the need to foster a commitment to community, as opposed to the rights of individuals, and argues for the possibility of this within a mixed, if not a capitalist, economy. As such it seeks to rebut both a New Right emphasis on the rights of individuals and the primacy of competition, and a Marxist critique of capitalism which argues against any meaningful change within any economy based in whole, or part, on the separation of labour from the ownership of the means of production.

Within regulatory theory, the shift to maximize corporate virtue has attempted to provide a rational and practical approach to regulatory enforcement in which moral persuasion forms an integral part. To do so it incorporates insights from game theory,[2] arguing that not only does a 'persuasion first' policy make sense from a 'virtue' perspective, it does also from the perspective of a 'rational actor'. The most prominent of these regulatory models involves the use of a 'regulatory pyramid', relying at the base on persuasive/educational strategies which build up trust and reduce defensiveness, with punitive sanctions being incurred at higher levels only when persuasion has clearly failed (Ayres and Braithwaite, 1992). This is argued to have a number of advantages over the purely punitive strategies. First, it reduces the defensiveness of organizations to regulation, by recognizing the limitations of regulation and policies aimed simply at highlighting the 'bad', rather seeking ways to enhance corporate social responsibility (the 'good'), through manipulation both of individuals and the corporate culture (Stone, 1987). Secondly, rather than always assuming the worst, the model presents a realistic picture of the range of seriousness of harm which results from corporate behaviour. Finally, there is an understanding that use

[2] Proponents of game theory assert that the best outcome for both players, the regulator and the regulated, within a regulatory schema is co-operation and compliance. These assertions are based on mathematical modelling of the 'prisoner's dilemma', a game between a prison officer and two prisoners (housed in separate cells). The aim of the prisoner officer is to get each to implicate the other in the alleged crime. The aim of the prisoners is to gain freedom or at least minimize penalty. There are four possible outcomes to the dilemma: First and second outcome: one implicates the other, and the other remains silent, in which case the prisoner co-operating will be freed and the silent prisoner severely punished (two outcomes, one for each prisoner). Third outcome: both remain silent, in which case both incur minimal penalty. Fourth outcome: both implicate the other and both are severely punished. The choices for the prison officer include punishment or persuasion to gain the compliance of the prisoners, who in turn have the choices of co-operation or non-compliance with the overtures of the prison officer. Game theorists assert, by way of mathematical modelling, that the greatest benefit goes to the player who initially makes a co-operative move, and then follows a 'tit for tat' strategy, which is basically a mimicking of what the opposite player (guard or prisoner) does (Axelrod, 1984:22–73). It is this 'tit for tat' strategy starting from an initially co-operative starting-point based on game theory that Scholtz argues provides an optimal outcome for regulators attempting to maximize compliance opportunities (Scholtz, 1984a and b).

of the criminal law is not necessarily at the pinnacle of punitiveness. This allows creative exploration of other methods of deterrence, for example licence revocations or use of the media (Coffee, 1981; Fisse and Braithwaite, 1983).

In addition to tailoring regulatory strategies to suit the offender, Braithwaite's model includes the notion of tripartism; that is the use of third parties, internal or external to the organization, both to identify corporate harm and to be involved in strategies for its reduction. Inclusion of third parties such as union groups or consumer lobbies in the regulatory process, brings an alternative viewpoint of those most affected by the harm and thus prevents 'regulatory capture' (Ayres and Braithwaite, 1991; Ayres and Braithwaite, 1992, chapter 3). However, despite the inclusion of third parties, or the media to assist in persuading organizations of the benefits of compliance, the key role in preventing organizational harm remains with the regulatory agency. It is the regulator who has the task of ascertaining the trustworthiness (or otherwise) of the target organization, and is then called on to tailor the regulatory measures to fit.

Problems and Possibilities in the Concept of Corporate Virtue

While such a model may be justified, several questions remain. First, how do we recognize virtue? Can we, as Braithwaite (1989) has suggested, adopt Sykes and Matza (1976) and assess 'techniques of neutralization' employed by key corporate individuals in order to identify the non-virtuous organizations? Criminological literature has long identified 'techniques of neutralization' as a mechanism which separates out those which deny responsibility for the harm they cause, from those who either do not harm or take responsibility for what they have done (Sykes and Matza, 1976). Rationalizing and neutralizing the harm of criminal behaviour is seen not only in the area of street crime, but also in the area of white collar crime, for example fraud (Cressey, 1953, 1986).[3] Rationalizations prevent individuals and organizations from accepting responsibility for their behaviour, where accepting

[3] Cressey's work on techniques of neutralization, or in his terminology 'rationalization' precedes that of Sykes and Matza. Sykes and Matza used Cressey's work in the development of their theory concerning the techniques of neutralization.

responsibility for actions is seen as a key to long-term change. Similarly, it may also be possible to identify organizational 'virtue' by the way managers within the organization justify their actions.

Individual managerial behaviour, however, may have a more indirect relationship to the organizational harm which eventually results. Virtue may result from the culture or organizational ethos with which individual managers are imbued. If culture is indeed a factor in virtue, the next problem becomes understanding what gives rise to culture. Is it a product of inherent qualities, or is it a product of the environment or external constraints? Recent theorizing such as that by Shearing (1993) and Gunningham (1993), suggest both the wider context of the environment and the social control between organizations outside the regulatory authority have an important role to play in the actions of organizations. Without clear understanding of the genesis of organizational virtue, regulation becomes a tenuous exercise.

The idea of nurturing virtue also places an onus on the relationship between regulatory and regulated, backed by recourse to formal legal methods. It suggests that good relationships are able to produce enlightened organizations which accept the benefits of regulatory trust. Within this theoretical framework, fear of loss of trust from regulators and potential escalation of penalties, must play a paramount role in organizational decision making. This raises further issues. Can change be so easily achieved merely through the quality of such a relationship? Further, even where third parties are involved, under what conditions is the input of the interest group likely to be perceived as beneficial to corporate long term goals and thus deemed acceptable?

Finally, we need to ask whether virtue is relatively permanent or characterized by transience. Can changes in elements of an organization's environment change it from virtuous to non-virtuous? Shearing's (1993) notion of constitutive regulation alerts us to the possibility that broader social contexts may impinge on the production and maintenance of virtue. To what extent can factors outside law and law enforcement impinge on or distort the best intentions of the regulator?

The central issue of the book and the crux of its theoretical importance is its exploration of what constitutes organizational virtue: the key concept in the new theorizing on regulation.

The book goes beyond definitions of what virtue actually is and attempts to find ways to compare companies in terms of their 'capacity for virtue'. The aim is to find ways to assess what virtue might look like in terms of actual behaviour and how factors both within and outside the organization, including legal constraints, impinge on that capacity.

In order to understand 'virtue' adequately it may be necessary to take a broad view concerning its possible genesis. Shearing (1993) argues that the context within which organizations act needs to be the focus of concern. Exploring context adequately means taking account of changes both in regulation and the nature of late twentieth-century capitalism. Changes in the area of regulation are proceeding at a rapid pace, encouraged primarily by the push of governments both nationally and internationally towards 'deregulation', i.e. removal of constraints on industry so they can compete better in the international market (INDECS, 1992). Paradoxically, the impetus by government to simplify the constraints on business has come at a time when the targets of regulation, the organizations themselves, are increasingly complex (Clinard and Yeager, 1980; Reed, 1992; Rowbotham and Mitter, 1994). Organizations have undergone considerable changes with contracting out non-essential services, and government instrumentalities have been progressively corporatized and privatized (Savas, 1987; Wiltshire, 1991). An increasing part of the regulatory dilemma lies in assessing what constitutes a discrete organization, and identifying the boundaries which separate one organization's responsibility from another's.[4] The changing shape of organizations has not simply resulted from the organizations themselves, but is intricately linked to the government push towards increased competitiveness and level playing fields. Government policy has pursued both macro- and micro-economic reform which have assisted, and in some cases demanded, these sorts of organizational reform. Data used to explore these issues needs to reflect this complexity.

Debate about reduction of harm by organizations is often divorced from economic discussions concerning deregulation

[4] Recent examples of tussles over definitions of what separates one organization's responsibility from another's can be seen in the debate over who is responsible for the conditions of outworkers in the textile industry (Textile, Clothing and Footwear Union of Australia, 1995).

and the need for increased business competitiveness (Brockway, 1993). To some degree this separation of harm from its economic and political context has occurred in recent criminological debates. Arguments about whether to punish or persuade decontextualize organizational behaviour and assume organizations both have perfect choice, and make choices based primarily as a result of the actions of the regulator. This book aims to reconnect the economic and political context of organizational behaviour with the regulatory debate, through an analysis of organizational virtue.

2 Regulation and Context

In order to gain maximum possible benefit from the data, it is necessary to examine theories which may allow greater depth to our final analysis. This is particularly important since the data will be used in a reflexive way, with the initial aim to bring to the fore the 'grounded' theory within it (Blumer, 1978). In this case the grounded theory is that framework which gives greatest insight into the genesis of virtue, or lack of virtue, within the organizations studied.

This book will also attempt to go beyond the analysis at the micro level of the data and attempt to link grounded theory back to formal theory, as advocated by C. Wright Mills (1963). The formal theory concerned here is both regulatory theory as outlined in chapter 1, and that from the wider sociological sphere, which forms the theme of this chapter.

To some extent it appears that much regulatory theory has had a rather restricted focus. In particular it appears willing to analyse the relations between individual regulators and organizations and simply aggregate these experiences in order to arrive at suitable policy directives at the state and national level (Sutherland, 1983; Stone, 1987; Ayres and Braithwaite, 1992; Braithwaite 1993). For Sutherland, Stone or Braithwaite the primary unit of analysis is how one organization, in isolation, responds to regulatory pressure (or in Sutherland's case the lack of it).

This is not to suggest that such theory and research should be rejected out of hand. What is needed is to bring back into view those theoretical traditions which start from a 'macro' level, or a level of structure to see how they may assist us to get a fuller picture of what regulation is about. Centrally then the concern is to understand the micro processes within organizations, some of which are captured by current regulatory theory, and theorize how such processes may be a product of the macro level environment. In this way the context of regulation is brought into sharp focus.

As the previous chapter outlined, regulatory theory, particularly the recent writing of Braithwaite, goes beyond a one dimensional view of organizations as recalcitrant and responsive only to harsh penalties. Organizations are seen as flexible and dynamic, capable of reform under a regulatory scheme which encourages the best they can offer. Such schemes include mandating the involvement of public interest groups in the regulatory process, to improve regulatory accountability (Ayres and Braithwaite, 1992), and making penalties effective through concepts such as enforced self-regulation and corporate probation (Fisse, 1983). Such theory is eminently practical, as seen from the suggestions recently taken up by the (Australian) Industry Commission Report on Occupational Health and Safety (Industry Commission, 1995) and a recent report to the New South Wales regulatory authorities (Gunningham, Johnstone and Rozen, 1996).

Largely silent, however, from this theorizing is an analysis of the social processes involved in the context of regulation. Theories which capture social processes in a way that sheds light on the regulatory debate are centrally concerned with the familiar sociological themes, structure and agency, and the degree to which one or other influence the final shape a society, community or particular economic market takes. For regulatory purposes though agency needs to be expressed in organizational terms (for example organizational culture), rather than purely the will of an individual (such as the top executive of a corporation), and needs to be understood in light of structural demands, rather than assuming an organization has unlimited choice of direction or behaviour.

How social processes impact on regulation and organizational virtue can be seen as critically important within the contemporary economic and political climate. The structure of capitalism is changing from large stable industries to rapidly changing flexible structures based on competitive efficiency, contracting out, and creating 'lean' organizational structures. Central bureaucracies within major companies tend towards flatter management structures, are now much smaller, and communicate via contract to a burgeoning number of satellite companies which service the diminishing core functions of major players within each industry. Regulation can no longer be seen in decontextualized fashion independent from these broader imperatives.

Recent studies of regulation also serve to highlight the importance of the broader context on regulation and corporate virtue.

As mentioned in the previous chapter, work by Grabosky (1994a and b), Gunningham (1991, 1993) and Shearing (1993) all focus on the way the 'market' or broader context influences the behaviour of individual firms. While this research is very valuable, what appears to be lacking at this point is a comprehensive theoretical grounding which can link the disparate findings of this recent research (see, for example, the range of possible market mechanisms which may be used to maximize virtue (Grabosky, 1994b:426–42), or the range of contexts which influence corporate behaviour (Gunningham, 1993:110–12)). How can we understand, for example, *which* market mechanisms are likely to be economically and politically acceptable, or what theoretical framework can help us understand the contexts within which virtue may be more, rather than less, possible?

The Changing Nature of Contemporary Capitalism

David Harvey (1989), in his analysis of the nature of 'postmodern' capitalism provides a base from which a theory of regulation within contemporary capitalism might begin. Working from a historical materialist perspective, Harvey emphasizes the dynamic nature of capitalism; its innate tendency towards constant change in what Schumpeter termed the 'creative destructive' climate of capitalism. This creative destructive nature constantly creates new forms of industry and organization, engendering the enthusiasm of some, while destroying previously existing structures, causing suffering and dislocation.

Harvey argues that in most western societies contemporary capitalism is undergoing a critical phase of change. The relative stability of the postwar years of Fordist production, dominated by large-scale enterprises, is being replaced by more flexible and dynamic forms of capital and labour. In contemporary capitalism, the system is characterized by complex interactions between organizations aimed at adapting to new economic stringency, with production rarely taking place under a single organizational unit (Harvey, 1989; Gill and Law, 1988; Rowbothom and Mitter, 1994).

With the changing structure of capitalism, from old to new, organized to disorganized capitalism, Fordist to 'Just in Time' methods of production, new challenges abound. For example,

Harvey argues that the role of the union in the new capitalist structure with the emphasis on small organizational units is altogether more tenuous. The structural 'space' which allowed the formation and growth of unions has broken down, with the new structure altogether less amenable to the growth of worker solidarity (Harvey, 1989: chapters 8 & 9). Rather, the current situation is characterized by a fragmented labour force divided into a shrinking sector of core employees who are flexibly functional, and a burgeoning secondary labour market which is comprised of such divergent groups as professional and service contractors, subcontractors, casual employees and the self employed. These changes, which can be conceptualized as the growth of a dual economy comprised of core and periphery, have profound implications for regulation and the production of virtue.

Much of the recent change is reflected in changes to the financial markets. The predictability afforded by pegged exchange rate levels has been removed, as have many tariffs, opening the way for the currency to be the target of large amounts of speculative capital (Anderson, 1993). It is perhaps too easy though, to point to these changes as the root cause of current problems. To some, such changes were inevitable. As Harvey (1989) points out:

> The tension between the fixity (and hence stability) that state regulation imposes, and the fluid motion of capital flow, remains a crucial problem for the social and political organization of capitalism. This difficulty . . . is modified by the way in which the state stands itself to be disciplined by internal forces (upon which it relies for its power) and external relations . . . State power can, in the end be neither more nor less stable than the political economy of capitalist modernity will allow. [page 109]

What is undeniable, however, is that the opening up of financial markets has been associated with the need for organizations and states to attract investment by pointing to low taxes, pliant workforces and attractive returns on investment (Stilwell, 1993[1]). This increases pressure on companies to maintain investment through consistently paying large share dividends, possible only through

[1] Stilwell argues that this is certainly the case, although he does not see this as determined. The push for high profits to maintain investment also ultimately undercuts demand.

high profit levels. The rise of the influence of the credit rating agency is associated with these changes, as countries compete on an increasingly international scale for investor funds (Hayward and Salvaris, 1994). The capital investors and fund managers, such as insurance companies and those controlling superannuation, look to higher and higher yield in order to maintain their own capital base.

Such macro changes have been accompanied by large-scale industrial restructuring. The aim again here is to open up the respective industries to the competitive forces of the market, and to increase their efficiency so they are better able to compete on the world stage. This pressure on individual organizations is wide-ranging, and includes government services and public utilities. Most areas of government have been subject to restructuring, some areas being privatized, while others simply corporatized in order to bring the logic more into line with private business (Savas, 1987; Davis and Harper, 1993).

Ultimately Harvey argues, however, that while the particular forms of the current capitalist structure may be new, the logic which propels such structures into existence are not. These current forms were predicted by Marx, who saw capitalism as inherently crisis prone and contradictory (Harvey, 1989:179–80). What lends particular urgency to current crises is the way in which neoclassicism is seen as **the** solution by individuals in positions of power, both within and outside government (Pusey, 1991), at state and national levels (Jamrozik, 1991; Horne, 1992; Eaton and Stilwell, 1993) and international level through forums such as GATT (Atkinson, 1994). Further, while in some countries neoclassical reforms have been pushed on unwilling governments by such agencies as the IMF and World Bank (Maitra, 1993), Australia has been a willing party to the process in many cases exceeding changes made in competitor nations (Eaton and Stilwell, 1993).

The Domination of Virtue by the Dictates of Capital

Harvey's analysis above would indicate that it is the dictates of capital which ultimately create virtue, or non-virtue within organizations. How this might occur, and the way virtue may be created or destroyed by the relations of capital needs closer scrutiny. The roots of this analysis, and indeed of Harvey's own analysis, is Marx. For Marx, not just business activities but most forms of behaviour were determined by the demands of capital, and the need within a capitalist system for profit and growth broadly determines behaviour. Marx argued there is an inevitable concentration of wealth under capitalism. According to this hypothesis, progressively more of the wealth is concentrated in fewer and fewer sites, which correspondingly grow in power (Lukes, 1974). With this economic power major capitalists crucially also hold sway over smaller more marginalized organizations. Large-scale owners progressively squeeze out smaller enterprises which in turn subject their labour to the worst wages and most pitiable conditions. Overt regulation, such as specific legislation, was unable to assist such workers. If small businesses were forced to comply with even the most basic health requirements of legislation, Marx argued, they would simply cease to exist:

> Now just as the Factory Acts, owing to their compulsory provisions, indirectly hasten the conversion of small workshops into factories, thus indirectly attacking the property rights of the smaller capitalists, and assuring the monopoly to the big ones too, in the same way thousands of small employers would be expropriated directly, at a single stroke, if it were made obligatory to provide the proper space for each worker in each workshop. [Marx, 1976:612]

Of critical importance within the current climate is the relationship between small and large business. Within the dual economy the core is characterized by large relatively stable business structures, and the secondary market by flexible mainly smaller businesses. A Marxist analysis would suggest that conditions would be worse in the secondary labour market. Further than this, virtuous behaviour by firms which inhabit this space may not be an option. The conditions of the secondary market are framed in such a way that virtue, or compliance with regulations, may not be a viable choice. Such conditions may also attract opportunistic business which may exploit the rules of the secondary market.

Empirical literature in the area of white collar crime lends support to the above theoretical framework, which highlights the comparative frequency of offences by small business (Leonard and Weber, 1977; Braithwaite, 1978; Clinard and Yeager, 1980;[2] Sutton and Wild, 1988; Tombs, 1988; Croall, 1989; Barlow, 1993), suggesting they may indeed be 'less virtuous'. Further studies in the area of health and safety point to the lower safety standards of smaller organizations, (Tombs, 1988; Nichols, 1989; Carson and Hennenberg, 1990; cf. Hopkins and Palsar, 1987; Hopkins, 1988). A Marxist perspective on such studies would want to stress the marginal position of such small businesses which drives them into immoral behaviour including violations of law, including law such as occupational health and safety legislation, as a means of survival.

Importantly, a Marxist analysis does not oversimplify regulation by confining analysis to a two-way relationship between the state and capital. Marx was keenly concerned with interorganizational formations under capitalism and the effect this had on work conditions. One of the interorganizational forms he subjected to scrutiny was the system of contracting out specific business functions, which has re-emerged as central to much contemporary debate (see for example Harvey, 1989; Battin, 1991; Drucker, 1992; Rowbothom and Mitter, 1994). Marx argued that subcontracting was ultimately in the interest of major capital. Nonetheless, some apparent advantages were had by workers who opted to labour under a contracting system as opposed to more direct wage relationships. His illustration here was the formation of 'gangs' of agricultural workers whose leader 'subcontracted' their labour to various farmers. The gang leaders (subcontractors) acted as small time entrepreneurs, roaming the countryside hiring out the labour within the gang (page 852). Marx was at pains to point out how these arrangements were in the ultimate interest of the landowner, i.e. the owner of capital, who was able to avoid any responsibility for the labourers who work on his property, while at the same time continuing to accumulate wealth (Marx, 1976:850–3). However, he also showed that both the gang leader and the gang workers gained some, albeit temporary, advantages. Wages for the labourers under this system were more consistent, since they were not dependent on the productivity of

[2] Clinard and Yeager do argue, however, that this is an artefact of official statistics rather than a factual situation; see also Yeager (1989).

any one enterprise. The gang leader gained some advantage also, both in terms of wealth, status and perceived independence. Conditions for the individual gangs depended to some extent on the nature of the gang leader, and could be better than their conditions obtained if tied to one farmer. However, Marx argued that ultimately the fate of such workers was determined by structural forces beyond their control.

As well as providing reasons why small businesses may be more likely to violate regulations, Marxism raises questions about the state's role in regulation. For many Marxists, the state's ultimate function is to create laws which facilitate and assist capital accumulation. Laws are primarily structured, not to improve conditions for workers, but to improve conditions for capital. This position has been fleshed out by Poulantzas (1978) in particular, and by writers such as Kolko (1963, 1965[3]) and Marvel (1977). From historical analyses these writers argue that regulations often emerge to advance the interests of dominant business groups. Large business has the resources to comply with legislation, while smaller weaker players working off a very slim capital base are further squeezed and often cannot comply. Reviewing regulation and compliance then, Marxists put emphasis on ways law helps consolidate the positions of some organizations, while marginalizing others.

In a Marxist analysis the demands of dominant fractions of capital form the bedrock to understanding organizational behaviour. Different organizational cultures; relative 'virtue' on behalf of some owners of capital; or the good character of a particular subcontractor tend to be portrayed as epiphenomena, totally dependent on the demands of capital which allow their existence. In contrast to much of the discussion in chapter 1 then, which assumed a fair degree of control organizations have over their actions, a Marxist analysis highlights the **lack** of control many organizations in fact experience. In particular it argues the smaller weaker organizations and those who exist in the 'nether world' between wage labour and ownership, for example the subcontractors, are characterized by marked lack of control. It is the change and development of the relationships within capitalism

[3] It should be noted that Kolko is not coming from a Marxist position but a conflict analysis which argues that the bias in law is the intent of a select few in positions of power, rather than any inherent logic within capitalism.

which predetermine the course of such phenomena as culture and virtue. Within the capitalist system at least some segments of business are doomed to 'lose virtue' due to the inexorable logic and inherent contradictions of that structure.

The Complexity of Organizations and Organizational Agency

Not all theorists concerned about the ways societal structures can influence organizational behaviour are convinced that structure is sufficient explanation for the diverse behaviour organizations display. Other theoretical traditions take account of structure, but argue that cultures of organizations, and the behaviour of the individuals within them, can nonetheless exhibit considerable autonomy (Ackroyd and Crowdy, 1990; Calori and Sarnin, 1991). They argue that culture and other forms of agency should not simply be dismissed as purely dependent on structure.

One such tradition takes as a starting-point Berle and Means's (1967) thesis that, under contemporary capitalism, there has been a progressive separation of ownership from control within large corporations. This, it is argued, has allowed for the development of a 'managerialist culture', a culture which is to some extent removed and isolated from imperatives of the market. Economic constraints remain, of course, but are more distant than pure Marxist theory suggests, making relationships between economic and organizational action complex.

Galbraith (1973) develops a related but slightly different analysis. His views on agency rest on the understanding that capitalism by its structure allows certain sectors to exert power and control, while denying others. Those denied power by their structural position, for example small business and other vulnerable business sectors, such as the arts and aspects of the hospitality industry, are unable to control uncertainties of the market. Any power they do have, which he labels 'protective power', has to be used for purposes of survival. Large organizations on the other hand can use power in more discretionary ways. In particular Galbraith sees them as motivated to secure increases in company size and market share. He labels such uses 'affirmative power'. Affirmative power can allow space for reallocation of resources within the company so that profit may be pursued in different ways at different times.

Perspectives developed by Berle and Means and by Galbraith allow culture, or organizational agency, to have a greater effect than is generally allowed in Marxist analyses. The separation of ownership from control, or the ability to wield affirmative power, is seen to allow corporations space for action and various theories have developed to account for how this space might be filled (for overviews see Reed, 1992 or Perrow, 1986). In our context, the need for regulators to 'nurture virtue', the question becomes how appropriate qualities might be encouraged within the regulatory space allowed by the broader structure. To begin to answer this question we need to understand how organizations, as opposed to individuals, act.

In trying to understand how organizations act, criminological theories of regulation have tended to rely fairly heavily on the 'command and control' model of organizations. The tendency is to suggest that leadership ultimately exerts a hegemonic control over subordinates (Coffee, 1981; Pearce and Tombs, 1990; Fisse and Braithwaite, 1993), and that regulatory problems will be solved by a regulator acting in creative ways to convert the élites of an organization to virtue, whether through punishment or persuasion (Clinard and Yeager, 1980; Pearce and Tombs, 1990; Hopkins, 1994b).

Mainstream schools of organizational behaviour challenge this position. Coming as many do from the perspective of management, or more recently postmodernism (Cooper, 1990), they emphasize the partial nature of the actual control managers, including top management, have over subordinates (Pettigrew, 1985; Perrow, 1986; Morgan, 1986; Young, 1989). Literature on organizational behaviour challenges both the assumption of organizational control independent of context (for example Donaldson, 1985[4]), and of hegemonic management control within the organization itself (for example Pettigrew, 1985).

For organizational behaviourists, analysis within the organization is central to understanding how such entities behave. Much of this theorizing highlights the way organizations can resist and distort the intentions of management (Smirchich, 1983;

[4] There is an interesting parallel here with the Marxist position. Both are keen to emphasize the predominance of external constraints, or structure. To a certain extent also both see that what occurs within the organization is primarily adaptive, rather than formative in its own right.

Pettigrew, 1985; Turner, 1992a). The concept of organizational culture has emerged as of critical importance in explaining this phenomenon. Organizational culture forms the 'touchstone' by which individuals behave and act. It is independent of individual intent, yet may be amenable to change over time. However, it is a great source of strength, both in terms of its normative influence, and the resistance felt when leaders attempt to initiate change. Pettigrew provides a rich description of organizational culture as:

> . . . a continuing sense of what reality is all about in order to be acted upon. Culture is the system of such publicly and collectively accepted meanings operating for a given group at a given time. This system of terms, forms, categories and images interprets a people's situation to themselves . . . [Pettigrew, 1985:44]

Among those who emphasize the notion of business culture, the **organizational symbolists**, are concerned with two interrelated themes (Reed, 1992). The first is such culture can act as a normative device to shape the ways individuals reflect and act within the organization (Schein, 1986; Calori and Sarnin, 1991). The second stresses ways culture can be used as a political device to legitimate particular projects and enable particular political agendas to be made organizational policy (Pettigrew, 1985).

Following on from the first theme, culture can be seen as critical to the conduct of organizations because it can shape the parameters within which decisions are made. In the specific context of regulation, for example, one hypothesis is that virtue or organizational compliance with regulations may depend on the existence of a culture which emphasizes the importance of compliance.

Work of March and Simon (1958) is pertinent here. They argue that managerial decisions are shaped by the underlying premises from which managers work. Such premises are not purely 'objective' but involve a 'bounded rationality'. Boundaries to rationality can emanate from who the decision maker is, their background, and assumptions they hold about the organization. March and Simon argue that certain decisions may not be considered relevant or may not even be countenanced because they violate underlying premises (Perrow, 1986). From this work it can be argued that culture is the receptacle of such premises and assumptions which provides the characteristic normative influence to sway corporate decisions, and direct behaviour.

If organizational symbolists are correct, the focus of management and regulators should be on manipulating organizational culture, rather than resorting to direct authoritarian control. Manipulation of ideology and culture of an organization may be more efficient in altering behaviour than direct power of regulatory or management fiat which engenders greater resistance (Foucault, 1980). The advantages of indirect forms of power are not lost on management which often seeks to harness programmes which promise cultural change. Recent management programmes such as 'quality assurance' and 'total quality management' are specifically aimed at changing culture, to align culture with 'quality', and to place a priority on customer needs while also fulfilling obligations such as compliance with regulations (Berman, 1992; McLaughlin, 1993). Influencing culture provides some promise for the production of ongoing virtue, since it promises some change to fundamental attitudes, rather than producing only superficial change.

Making a further theoretical link between organizational culture, or organizational agency and individual agency is a complex task. As Pettigrew (1985) demonstrated, attempts by individuals to shift corporate culture and practice in a desired direction demonstrate the difficulty faced by individual actors wishing to create long lasting cultural change (see also Sinclair, 1992, 1993). It is necessary to be wary of assuming a simple theoretical link between the agency of any one individual (at whatever level of the organization, or position within the regulatory authority) and organizational agency in the form of corporate culture. This is particularly true with respect to linking *individual virtue* with *organizational virtue*. For many virtue is, quintessentially, an attribute of the individual, with the virtuous actions of the individual showing the potential opposition of organizational imperatives and individual integrity (MacIntyre, 1995). In drawing lessons for regulation we need to retain some scepticism towards seeing written rules as indicators of an ethical corporate ethos, or bureaucratic mechanisms as some sort of corporate conscience (Stone, 1975; Bucy, 1991). Weber's analysis of bureaucracy shows how legal rationality, with the emphasis on adherence to rules and written accountability, can distort the best intention of those individuals who instigate or write procedures for the purposes of improving the ethical behaviour of the organization as a whole.

The perspective on organizational culture as a normative touchstone presented here does not require a direct link between individual agency, or individual virtue and organizational virtue. It leaves open, to a certain extent, how organizational agency arises, but does argue that account needs to be taken of organizational culture as an independent influence on organizational behaviour, and by extension corporate virtue.

The theoretical analysis above provides a complex and ambitious framework for regulation. Such an understanding would focus on the ways in which structure interacts with culture and decision making to produce virtuous or non-virtuous behaviour. This goes beyond analyses of regulation where regulators are those in control of business relations virtually in isolation and which depend on 'command and control' models of behaviour. In order to nurture virtue then, there needs to be concern both with cultural norms which shape the premises underlying decisions, and with ways culture, in particular a virtuous culture, may be constrained by demands of capital.

The Relationship between Structure and Culture

To undertake this analysis adequately the relationship between structure and culture as it applies to regulation must first be addressed. An important part of this discussion concerns whether culture is dependent on structure to the degree Marxist analyses would claim. Berle and Means and Galbraith point to the possibility of culture having influence which is independent of economic constraints. However, the major theorist who traditionally is seen as most prepared to allow ideas to exert independent causative influence is Max Weber. The best known of Weber's theses on the independent influence of ideas on history is, of course, his arguments concerning the Protestant ethic and its influence on the development of capitalism. Weber argued that the Protestant ethic was a formative influence on, rather than an adaptation to, the capitalistic structure. It was this specific religious ethos, with its emphasis on discipline and duty, which acted as a catalyst to the economy upon introduction of the capitalistic structure:

> Labour must . . . be performed as if it were an absolute end in itself, a calling. But such an attitude is by no means a product of nature. It cannot be evoked by low wages or high ones alone, but can only be the product of a long and arduous process of education . . . [and] by far the best chances of economic education are found amongst this [Pietistic] group. [Weber, 1974:62]

Assessing ways structure and culture can combine to produce specific social outcomes is a critical and repeated theme in Weber's work. It should be emphasized, however, he did not see culture as being transmitted purely through broad religious and other 'ethics'. For Weber, culture also could be an important vehicle for exerting and legitimating power. In this context, his discussions of notions of social closure and the formation of exclusive 'status groups' is of critical significance. Weber defined closure as the inherent tendency for individuals and organizations to form exclusive relationships with others (Weber, 1991:186–94). Status results from membership of a group of like-minded people, the membership of which is seen as desirable. For Weber, neither capacity to effect social closure nor status are determined purely by economics:

> If mere economic acquisition and naked economic power still bearing the stigma of its extra-status origin could bestow upon anyone who has won it the same honour as those who are interested in status by virtue of a style of life claim for themselves, the status order would be threatened at its very root . . . Therefore all groups having interests in the status order react with special sharpness precisely against the pretensions of purely economic acquisition. [Weber, 1991:192]

It follows then that those with high social status in a given society may not necessarily command the greatest wealth, or economic resources. They have power which derives from sources independent from economics. The status order, however, may have a distinct impact on the economic order:

> As to the general *effect* of the status order, only one consequence can be stated, but it is a very important one: the hindrance of the free development of the market occurs first for those goods which status groups directly withheld from free exchange by monopolization. This monopolization may be effected either legally or conventionally. [Weber, 1991:193. Emphasis in original]

Status groups thus monopolize certain markets, and dictate conditions under which exchange will occur. Nonetheless, over time economic status and social status will tend to converge. This convergence may, however, have as much to do with a particular individual or group's capacity to exert power through status systems and social closure as it does through economic power.

The influence of status groups on specific market contexts was highlighted in research conducted early in Weber's career, which concerned the ethical standards of various stock exchanges. With one or two exceptions (Sutton and Wild, 1980), contemporary theorists of business regulation seem unaware of this work. In some important respects, however, it anticipates current research analysis and recommendations (see for example Gunningham, 1991). Weber's study on the stock exchanges of Europe pointed to the importance of closure in allowing ethical standards to be maintained. Closure was achieved in the case of the London Exchange through restricting entry to the exchange by admitting only certain people, a process of entry which was akin to membership of an exclusive club. This allowed a situation where self-regulation could flourish in a direction which supported ethical (virtuous) behaviour, by supporting sound business practice and frowning on pure speculation. Since relationships between members of the exchange were important, such autonomous associations could be far more flexible in their choice of sanctions for non-compliance with rules, as well as apply rules in a far more effective and discretionary manner. In contrast, the intense competition of equals which characterized the more 'open' exchange of Berlin led to questionable practices which were ultimately subject to public inquiry. Despite many attempts at formulating formal rules, regulation of this market was ineffectual, floundering in part from an inability to define in law the difference between speculation and sound business practice. Formal law provides little defence against unscrupulous business behaviour, particularly when such behaviour is not subject to controls by peers. In a free market, where opportunities for closure and status formation could not occur, Weber argued the self-regulation of the market was absent and unethical practices could take root (Bendix, 1977:23–30).

Status groups are not, however, an unmitigated good. Status groups may, of course, form around unprincipled behaviour and with malevolent intent. More likely the effect of such status groups will be mixed, as Weber's analysis of the Junkers[5] shows:

> The Junkers of the east are frequently (and often unjustly) vilified; they are just as frequently (and as often unjustly) idolized. Anyone who knows them personally will certainly enjoy their company at the hunt, over a good glass, or at cards; and in their hospitable homes everything is genuine . . . [yet] their minutes in their circle shows one that they are plebeians. Their very virtues are of a thoroughly robust and plebeian nature. [Weber, 1991:386–7]

Such influence, however, cannot be ignored. Concerning the influence of the Junkers, Weber wrote: 'Their social and economic struggle is just as ruthless as that of any manufacturer' (page 387). Further, influence of such status groups may in certain instances extend long after the demise of any economic base. When dealing with business behaviour, Weber argued understanding the influence of status groups in maintaining standards of behaviour (whether good or bad) is critical (Bendix, 1977:43–8).

The influence of status groups on the economy is also affected by broader culture. Weber's studies on China, for example, show how the broader Confucian culture allowed for the emergence of influence of some status groups, while disallowing others (Weber, 1951:107–41). Weber's early work on the independence influence of culture on business has been recently worked into a contemporary context by Francis Fukuyama (1995). Fukuyama's emphasis is on the effect that broad cultural values can have on business behaviour and economic growth. The structure of business, and the way business acts, he argues is closely aligned with the degree to which the broader society is predicated on familistic values. Familistic values, such as those found in China and southern Italy, trust only kin. Businesses flourish only along kinship lines, which preclude the growth of very large enterprises which require extensive influence by managers brought in from the outside. Thus the markets are characterized by small, heavily competitive groups. The degree to which any one company can exert influence on the market is small and their influence limited and transient. Broader cultural influences may then affect the success or otherwise of status groups gaining influence.

[5] German aristocratic landowners.

Agency, whether expressed through status group, culture or individual action, may well require as a precondition for its influence some control of external economic constraints and market structure. This may be provided for by the separation of management from ownership, as proposed by Berle and Means, but may also require some form of closure as suggested by Weber so that competition may be controlled by ethical rules of conduct. Some independence from economic constraints as well as closure and the formation of status groups could be a precondition of virtue. This is not to suggest, however, that this is causative of virtue, merely a precondition.

From preceding pages it is clear that a range of theoretical and empirically-based studies can provide grounds for contesting Marx's view that ultimately market forces will determine any corporation or business entity's 'capacity for virtue' or ethical behaviour. Many of those alternative perspectives have emerged since the 1950s, with the growth in the sub-discipline of management studies. However, more long-standing sociological traditions, for example those associated with Max Weber, also have contested historical materialism, with Weber's work on social closure and the key roles that exclusive status groups played in the regulation of some European stock exchanges particularly significant.

Reviewing the various counter arguments to Marx, it should be noted, of course, that none try to suggest that business values and behaviours can endure in ways that are completely independent of economic forces. To a greater or lesser extent, all take the view that, in principle, while cultural influences may be capable of arising independently, in fact they tend to have effect only if economic circumstances have generated 'breathing space' within which they can work. Weber for example points out that status groups were most likely to have influence during times of economic stability, while their influence wanes during rapid economic flux:

> Epochs and countries in which the naked class situation is of predominant significance are regularly the periods of technical and economic transformations. And every slowing down of the shifting of economic stratifications leads, in due course, to the growth of status structures and makes for a resuscitation of the important role of social honour. [Weber, 1991:194]

The emergence of the dual economy and the rapid changes within contemporary capitalism would suggest then that ours is a time where economic constraints may be dictating behaviour to a greater extent than at times of greater economic stability.

Long-term changes to the 'virtue' of business organizations may then depend upon the influence of various status groups which emerge. Which status groups are able to gain power depends upon the philosophy and culture associated with the current bout of economic transformations. This may be described as the economic rationalist philosophy. A Weberian analysis may want to emphasize, as some contemporary writers have, the degree to which this philosophy extends beyond and contributes to the economic reality (for example Battin, 1991, 1992).

The specifics of the economic rationalist philosophy are thus of interest to us, as it may allow us to explore through the data to some extent its independence of philosophy to economic reality. Central to economic rationalist philosophy is an unswerving faith in the mechanisms of the free market and competition as the solution to world ills. A prescriptive model then ensues regarding how this is to be achieved, namely a reduction of state intervention and a pre-eminent emphasis on individual achievement, individuals motivated by the need to compete. Michael Pusey in his work on economic rationalism in the Australian government points to how this philosophy held by top executives of the public service bureaucracy influences their attitude on the 'proper' direction of government, namely arguing for less reward for collective effort, and more emphasis on the initiative of individuals. Pusey argues the fundamental beliefs of government, due to the influence of these executives, are that: GNP is biased towards wage and salary earners; there should be more individual initiative and less state involvement in the economic and social spheres; there should be little or no state controls on the national economy; doubts and fears expressed about the growing intervention of the state in economic and social spheres are fully justified; deregulation of the labour market is to be encouraged; and (currently) trade unions have equal or more power than government (Pusey, 1991:57–8).

This philosophy is mirrored by key business commentators, and is seen played out through the policies of numerous public and private organizations. Such individuals and their organizations accept the inherent value in pursuing economic growth through free market competition as ultimately in their own interest. They see this as compatible with increased profitability only for companies which reduce the size of core organizations ('downsizing') and contract out or casualize large sectors of labour. The purpose is to increase the intensity of competition both within and between organizations, thus increasing efficiency which in turn increases competitiveness (Friedman, 1962, 1988; Drucker, 1992). The following statement of Drucker (1992) encapsulates this sentiment well in his argument for contracting out:

> In house service and support activities are *de facto* monopolies. They have little incentive to improve their productivity. In fact they have considerable disincentive to improve their productivity. In the typical organization, business, or government, the standard and prestige of an activity is judged by the size and budget—particularly in the case of activities that, like clerical, maintenance, and support work, do not make a direct and measurable contribution to the bottom line . . . An outside contractor knows that he [*sic*] will be tossed out and replaced by a better-performing competitor unless he improves quality and cuts costs. The people running in house services are also unlikely to do the hard, innovative and often costly work that is required to make service work profitable. [page 221]

The joint philosophy of competition and efficiency fuels specific policies and management styles. For example, recent management theories reflect both the structure of economic rationalism, and the philosophical orientation towards flexibility. Contemporary managers, it is argued, should be about creating a clover leaf structure of their organization. This structure comprises of three intersecting but separate groups; core staff, specialist staff, and temporary staff. It is this structure which, its protagonists argue, can best meet the challenges of contemporary markets (Thomas, 1995).

Changes in the Regulatory Arena

On a structural level, if Harvey is correct about changes within capitalism, then there is likely to be a decline in space where virtuous companies can thrive. There are, however, complications to the story. With the burgeoning discussion of economic rationalism, what is less discussed are the changes occurring in regulation. The received wisdom is that the major thrust in the area of regulation is one of deregulation. However, it may be more accurate to view regulation in a state of flux (Braithwaite, 1991), with some areas experiencing re-regulation, while others deregulate. Certainly in the area of social regulation in general more and more is being expected of organizations in terms of their social responsibilities to the environment and their workforce (Head, 1991; Ayres and Braithwaite, 1992; Bradmore, 1993).

Occupational health and safety serves as an example where the trend in recent times is towards an increase in regulatory standards, rather than a decrease. A recent Industry Commission report on Workers Compensation for example points to the increasing standard of safety expected within organizations. Failure to meet such standards leaves considerable legal liabilities (Industry Commission, 1994). Further, most states in Australia have reformed and expanded the reach of their health and safety laws as outlined above to include general duty provisions (Quinlan and Bohle, 1991: chapter 7). Penalties have undergone an increase, which has been partly reflected in a rise in numbers of prosecutions and fine levels in the courts (*Review of Occupational Health and Safety in Australia*, 1990; Perrone, 1993; Hopkins, 1994a; Johnstone, 1994). In terms of ensuring improvement in safety standards reaches the shop floor, there has been a shift to legislate for greater involvement of the workforce, through health and safety representatives and committees.

In addition to state legislation there has been considerable growth in the area of standard setting both on a national and international level, through Australian Standard and International Standard systems (*Review of Occupational Health and Safety in Australia*, 1990; Dawson and Lewelling, 1991). These increased standards place considerable pressure on organizations which attempt to comply, whether through some attempt at 'best practice', or simply in their normal activities which include compliance with standards. This standards market cannot, however, be defined purely as national since national standards in part reflect international trends. Further, where exporting and importing of goods is involved compliance with international standards, as well as the standards of the importing country, may be expected.

National legislation cannot be divorced from the growing internationalization of standard setting (Gill and Law, 1988).

What this suggests is that the role of the state may be more complex than the picture afforded by the Marxist analysis above. As others have commented (Offe, 1984; O'Connor, 1973) the state can be conceptualized as torn by conflicting imperatives. One of these is indeed the imperative to support the needs of capital. However, there are others; legitimation needs for example, to secure mass loyalty, which require governments to be seen to be answering the demands of the populace (Habermas, 1976). Among these demands are the demands to curb environmental damage, and perhaps a poor second, death and injury at work. Hence the increased mass of regulation, discussed above.

One should not be simplistic concerning how demands are expressed. Status interests, such as the demands of lobby groups of professionals, may combine with commercial interest of the safety industry to push through reform. Unions at both national and international level may also play an important role. The standard setting process is itself both a pragmatic and political one. For example Standards Australia publishes standards which result from a committee process. Representation on the committee spans both public and private interests concerned with the particular hazard. Commercial and status interests may thus prevail in the standard setting process. While standards are not enforceable until picked up by regulations, they serve to push the bounds of what is, and what is not, acceptable practice. Heightened public awareness of a particular hazard may see an increase in the number of standards picked up in legislation.

The fundamental dilemma for capitalist democracies remains however, the need to do more with less. This may well explain the phenomenon that while the actual standards to be adhered to in the area of social regulation (such as the environment and occupational health and safety) are increasing, the method of regulation may look more to models encouraging ethical practice through self-regulation. Prosecutions may still be seen as necessary to punish certain cases. However, traditional workplace inspections may give way to self-regulation on application of Quality Assurance principles, for example through 'enterprise safety management systems' (Industry Commission, 1995). Such systems are heavily dependent upon the 'virtue' of an organization to comply.

Ultimately though the ability of recent shifts in regulation to increase ethical standards of business have to be seen in light of changes to contemporary capitalism. As stated, these changes aim to increase flexibility and competitiveness of organizations at the workplace level. How organizational virtue is influenced by the interaction between the structural changes to the economy (felt through increased competition at the worksite level), and the increased demands of regulation forms a central theme to this book.

Conclusion and Structure of the Book

Pulling together the material from these first two chapters it becomes clear that there are a number of implications for 'maximizing virtue' within organizations. A strong theme in this second chapter has been that organizational behaviour does not occur in a vacuum. Constraints on virtue may arise due to the demands of capital, where behaviour is restricted depending on the capital base an organization has, and the degree to which it has control over its environment. Further, behaviour of organizations, where capital and control permit, may primarily result from normative influence of organizational culture, rather than the beliefs and actions of individuals. Understanding the interaction between structure and culture therefore, may be central to understanding how to regulate in order to prevent harm.

Chapters 3 and 4 introduce material which allows exploration of how organizational virtue may be produced. The data used includes both coronial and interview material concerning deaths which occurred in multiple employer worksites in 1987. Chapter 3 highlights the range of contexts which gives rise to such events, and the sequence of events which preceded the death. Chapter 4 highlights how the organizations involved responded to the death, and suggests that the quality of such responses is a useful way of measuring organizational virtue. The investigation of these responses is the primary vehicle for exploration of organizational virtue, and how it is produced.

One of the first questions that needs exploration is whether it is possible to use 'techniques of neutralization' used by key managers about the response the organization made, as an indication of organizational virtue, as suggested by the discussion in chapter 1. However, if the analysis of this chapter is correct, that organizational behaviour is best explained by a combination of the demands of capital and normative influence of organizational culture; individual rationalizations on responsibility for the death may reveal little about the virtue of the whole organization. Rather, such neutralizations may simply be a way to cope with the trauma of the death (Fenichel, 1946; Kroeber, 1969). To explore the possibility of identifying organizational virtue by using the rationalizations of individuals, the data needs to be analysed in order to identify the degree to which the rationalizations of individual managers correspond to the virtuous or non-virtuous behaviour of organizations. This issue forms the basis of analysis in chapter 5.

Analysis of how structure and culture may produce virtue, following the theoretical theme of this chapter, is the driving force behind the analysis of the data. It is this theoretical perspective which holds the greatest challenge to the future of regulation. The influence of both structure and culture on 'virtuous' organizational behaviour threatens to undermine traditional approaches to regulation, where obtaining compliance through punitive or persuasive methods is the central theme. A broad view may be required in order to understand the formative influences on organizational behaviour.

Culture, as asserted by the organizational symbolists, is the framework which provides the touchstone for behaviour. Such a framework acts behind the scenes to affect decision making through determining the premises by which decisions are made. This begs the question regarding the existence and characteristics of such a culture in the data. Are there normative assumptions behind decisions that might indicate the presence and influence of an organizational culture? Does virtue play a central concern in the premises of such a culture, or are virtuous concerns such as safety premised by their impact on success and profit goals? Is it possible to identify distinct cultural 'ideal types' within organizations? Do these ideal types discriminate between virtue, and non-virtue? To explore these issues, normative assumptions behind decisions made by organizations in the data require analysis in order to uncover the nature of such a culture, if it exists. Further, we need to trace the relationship between culture and behaviour. Do distinct cultural types correlate to distinct differences in behaviour? These questions form the basis of chapter 6.

The chapter above has argued though that the influence of the demands of capital on behaviour needs careful analysis. Both the analysis of the dual economy and the Marxist analysis discussed above would suggest that smaller weaker organizations may be pushed into non-virtuous behaviour simply as a means of survival. The data needs to allow us to explore this possibility. Can differences in behaviour largely be explained by the different sizes of organizations and the different positions in the contracting hierarchy? To answer this question the difference in behaviour between those with a large capital base, namely large organizations, and smaller concerns with little capital are examined. Control over the worksite, in terms of position in the contracting hierarchy, is also analysed here, both in isolation to and in combination with size, in order to ascertain the effect it may have over behaviour. The constraints on virtue in terms of size and position in the contracting hierarchy form the initial analysis in chapter 7.

A Marxist analysis does not give scope for differentiation of the larger concern, beyond looking to the ultimate dictate of capital over behaviour. Added insight into the behaviour of large organizations is provided by the argument of Berle and Means (1967) that the progressive separation of ownership and control in larger organizations allows for the existence of a managerialist culture, one which is less constrained by short-term capital return. Large organizations are not only freed from the need to use power in a protective manner (Galbraith, 1973), their relative autonomy allows choice. It needs to be explored whether, given freedom from capital constraints on virtue, a normative culture which supports virtue can hold the key to improving organizational behaviour. Further, if virtuous culture can wield influence at the level of the individual firm, is there any indication that this can influence the worksite as a whole? Are there any examples of closure, where large firms in positions of power seek to isolate the worksite from competition which would undermine virtue? These themes form the basis for discussion in the second half of chapter 7.

Once the effect of the relationship between structure and culture on behaviour has been explored the limitations and the possibilities of use of law to control organizational behaviour is brought back into sharp relief. If the relationship between structure and culture is central to organizational behaviour what effect can law have? This question necessitates looking at the issue of regulatory law broadly, to include not only that stipulating standards and procedures, but also the area of compensation and the use of the common law. Are any areas of law able to influence either the capital constraints of organizations or their culture? Clearly law is not able to influence capital constraints by altering size of an organization, or the position in the contracting hierarchy. Certain regulations may, however, be able to alter the premises by which decisions are made, and in this way alter culture. Law then may affect different organizations in different ways depending on their gross capital constraints, or structural position.

However, discussion in chapter one highlights a further issue that needs to be addressed when looking to law to effect change. That is the way law may have formal effects, such as changing a process or a written requirement, without substantive change. Unless law can effect cultural change, its effectiveness may be short-lived or non-existent. Further, formal law may hinder the production of virtue, with substantive change in an entirely unanticipated direction. With a broad focus on regulation, and a focus on the influence of structure and culture on regulation, it may be possible to understand the logic behind the unintended consequences born of legislative change. These issues will be explored in chapter 8.

With a broad focus on the genesis of virtue, the changing nature of the economy in terms of the growth of the secondary labour market; the increased use of contracting out; and the growth of the small business sector all hold potential threats to virtue. This is accompanied by the rise in expectations of virtue of the firm by the public at large, and by the increase in the number of regulations concerning manufacturing standards, safety and environmental controls. What needs to be explored is the way the shifts in contemporary capitalism affect the industrial contexts which give rise to virtue. For those organizations with a commitment to virtue we need to explore how they respond to the current challenges. Are the current business programmes aimed at producing quality production a useful step in the right direction here, for example? The current preoccupation of the contemporary era on the inherent value of competition needs to be analysed in terms of the effect this may have on virtue and virtuous organizations. Chapter 9 looks at the challenges contemporary capitalism holds for organizations and the possibility of nurturing virtue.

The major concern of this book, following the theoretical analysis outlined in these first two chapters, is that regulatory models may have to take account of complexities of structure and culture if they are to stand the test of time. A comprehensive understanding of how organizations act within a given context, following the work of Shearing (1993), Grabosky (1994a and b) and Gunningham (1993), may also be required in order to provide practical suggestions for policy which will not be undermined by the political process. It is the **context** of regulation or the *regulatory space*, as well as the **virtue** of the organization, which may need to be the focus of scrutiny, as it is in the analysis of the data to follow.

3 Exploring Death at Work

THE task of this book is to analyse current trends in regulatory theory, namely nurturing virtue, by exploring concrete examples of organizational behaviour. The idea here is to use data to develop theory, rather than theorizing in a vacuum or severing empirical research from its theoretical underpinning. The first task then was to find data which reflected adequately the complexities in the current debate on regulatory theory. The data chosen to reflect such complexities was an exploration of deaths which occurred as part of a paid occupation. Further, each of the worksites where the deaths occurred involved more than one company; such sites are defined here as 'multiple employer' worksites.

This data had a number of strengths which enable it to be used to explore the current state of regulatory theory. The area of health and safety is to some degree archetypical with regards to the issues involved in organizational regulation. First, there is a consensus that injury and death at work is a social ill which should be minimized if not eliminated (Polk, Haines and Perrone, 1993; Polk and Stone, 1994). Great physical harm occurs through death and injury at work, which causes considerable emotional and financial trauma, both for the worker and their families who experience the trauma, and the state through workers' compensation schemes and the extra burden on public services such as hospitals, occupational therapists, counsellors and the like.

Secondly, by exploring deaths where more than one organization was involved, the data is able to capture the complexity of contemporary capitalism and the dual economy reflected in the various contracting and subcontracting relationships. The actions of organizations, including those actions which result in harm, arise from the influence of many factors (Shearing, 1993). Important among those factors are the relationships between organizations involved in the production process.

Finally, the occupational health and safety arena adequately reflects regulatory complexity. Modern organizations are subject to a multiplicity of laws which attempt to control their propensity for social harm. Health and safety is the subject of rules and regulations including the criminal law, occupational health and safety law and ancillary regulations, compensation law and common law as well as multiple standards (both Australian and international) and codes of practice. In addition much of the group of theorists which forms the central concern of the book, namely Braithwaite, Ayres, Gunningham and Grabosky, have done considerable research in this area. Their theories of regulation should, at least in some part, reflect this research interest.

A one year period was chosen, 1987, for exploration of all work related deaths which occurred in multiple employer worksites within the State of Victoria, which totalled fifteen deaths. The data collection involved a two stage process. The first step involved gathering sufficient background information to form a comprehensive understanding of the context surrounding the deaths which occurred. This information is presented in this chapter in the form of short case-studies; the bulk of the information presented here was obtained from coronial records. The second step required gaining information about the organizational responses to the deaths. Written sources, including government and company documents, and direct interviewing of the organizations concerned were involved in this stage of the data collection process.[1] The analysis of the responses to the death is outlined in chapter 4 and various aspects elaborated on in chapters 5–9.

The types of environment where the deaths took place varied widely. Common, however, was the fact that the constant organizations within each worksite were bound by contract, either verbal or written, to the tenderor.[2] The tenderors themselves were also involved in the particular industrial process. Such industrial structures are common in many industries; for example construction and logging, as well as various maintenance processes in manufacturing and mining. More widely, capital works in most businesses involve the use of contractors. Table 3.1 indicates the industries and range of deaths involved in this particular study.

[1] For a detailed discussion of the methodology, please see the Appendix.

[2] The term tenderor here is used to indicate the ultimate organization in the contracting hierarchy. It is recognized that their involvement in the production process may vary. Small involvement is given by the example of the owner of land which is logged, large involvement is illustrated by the factory owner where repairs were taking place. Both owners are considered tenderors.

TABLE 3.1. Deaths by Organization Involved

Organization	Industry	Nature of Fatality
*†Gremtrench	Plumbing Contractor	Trench collapse
†Leafytown Council Nagel Constructions *Daytons Service Cranes	Local Council Builders Rigging Crane Hire	Rigger electrocuted when crane hit overhead power lines
†Young Constructions *Better Demolitions	Builders Demolitions	Demolition worker fell down lift well
†Wirral Cement	Quarrying/Cement	Owner driver killed by reversing vehicle
†Mightysteel Arcade *Alltime Rigging	Steelmakers Capital Works/Steel Rigging	Rigger fell from roof
†Harbourtown Council *Roadtech	Local Council Roadwoks	Roadworker crushed during road resurfacing
*†BBM Materials Bristol Forklifts Trent Hire	Building Materials Forklift Hire Forklift Hire	Forklift crushed driver
†Aidans Reid Plumbing *Quicklag	Heavy Engineering Plumbing Lagging	Lagger fell from Ladder
*†Postens Nettles Builders Destruction Inc.	Service Industry Building Contractors Demolition Contractors	Maintenance worker fell down stairwell during renovations.
†International Paper *Adams Logging	Paper Mill Logging Contractor	Crushed by rolling logs when a winch collapsed
†Chemref *Fine Rigging Rowlands	Chemicals Rigging	Rigger fell from roof
†Hoefschtede Mines	Quarrying	Truck driven by owner driver fell into quarry

TABLE 3.1. (Cont'd)

Organization	Industry	Nature of Fatality
*†Bigmill	Sawmill	Log yard man struck by log during unloading
*†Gipp Mills Bigland	Sawmill Landowner	Logger hit by falling branch
*†Resource Mining Stutganst Haddons Lynden Hydraulics Constructotech Sergensons	Mining Heavy Engineering Engineering Hydraulics Hydraulics Electrics/Electronics	Collapse of mining dredger during commissioning

* Indicates employer of deceased worker
† indicates major tenderor

The theoretical themes outlined in the first two chapters, of the interrelationship between structure, culture and organizational behaviour, allow the formation of some possible link between the causes leading to the deaths. From this it is hypothetically possible that indications of relative virtue may arise. However, the initial feature in the case-studies, summarized below from the coroner's records, is the diversity of circumstances where such deaths occur. It is necessary for the reader to have some familiarity with this context in order to begin understanding the complexity of the concept of organizational virtue, or lack of virtue, as a goal of regulation, within the complexity and diversity of the work environment. As Gunningham (1993:110–12) has commented, it is very difficult to divorce regulation from context.

The purpose of the case-studies summarized below is to provide context to the analyses that follow. They show the diversity of contexts within which death occurs, but also give some hints regarding antecedents to the lack of organizational virtue. At this stage however, the comments below on possible effects of structure, and the nature of the worksite cultures, on organizational virtue must be considered tentative. In particular coronial records have limitations when it comes to ascertaining work culture. Nonetheless, where appropriate, comments on culture are made in light of comments of regulators from the coronial files, and the utterances of witnesses which indicate *ongoing* and entrenched practices which were antithetical to a safe working environment. Safe workplaces spawn cultures which emphasize joint responsibility for safety, open communication, top management commitment to safety and safety integrated into the core concerns of the organization (Quinlan, 1996).

In light of the complex range of contexts in which death occurs, the case summaries presented below raise as many questions about the diverse nature of organizational (lack of) virtue, as they do about the possible influence of structure and culture. Nonetheless, in some cases in the study the events and factors surrounding the deaths appeared clear, as did the nature of contractual relations, which in these clear-cut cases typically involved only two companies. Issues of contribution and prevention also appeared clear cut. One example of this type of case involved the death of a plumber's apprentice while laying some pipework:

> Terry worked as a plumber's apprentice for Gemtrench, in a small country Victorian town. His boss, Dan, had considerable plumbing experience, but finding work was not always easy. Further, soils were notably unstable in the area. Dan had developed a method for shoring trenches to cope with local conditions, which he considered adequate. He had used the system with no problems for the past fifteen years. However, the method involved the apprentice standing in an unshored portion of the trench during the shoring process; a procedure described by the Department of Labour at inquest as 'patently unsafe'. It was during shoring operations at a local building site that the trench collapsed burying the apprentice.

Here the cause of death was clear, the unsafe procedure of shoring employed by the company. The influence of other companies appears minimal; this was a business simply fulfilling their contractual obligation of laying some pipework. However, in light of the theoretical themes concerning small business the question of the marginalization of the company as a whole, and its tenuous location in the economy needs to be raised. The relevance of this is indicated by the owner who admitted finding work was not always easy.

The events leading to the second death appeared similarly clear cut. Similar to the case above also is the issue of marginalization of the companies involved. However, in this case cultural themes appear to play an equal role. The demolition worker who died played an active role in supporting a worksite culture which was antithetical to safety. Further, in the case of Better Demolitions below there were a greater number of companies present on the site which complicated the overall picture:

Hazardous conditions characterized the refurbishment of the inner city office building where the death occurred. Both demolition and construction work was occurring in the building at the same time; the floors were cluttered, and holes left unguarded. At the time of the fatality demolition was confined mainly to the fifth floor. The building contractor, Young Constructions, had subcontracted the demolition work to Better Demolitions and basically 'left them to their own devices'.

Stan, a demolition labourer, was working close to his boss on the fifth floor. He had done a number of jobs with Better Demolitions and was a friend of the boss. At the time of his death he was demolishing a lift well by 'working off the wall', that is standing on the wall and knocking bricks down the lift shaft. There was no guard in the shaft. Georgio, an employee of Young's came up to the fifth floor where he spoke to Stan, and according to Georgio the following conversation ensued:
Georgio: 'What are you doing?'
Stan: 'What the fuck is it to you?'
Georgio: 'Just asking.'
Stan: 'Just got to knock down this brick wall.'
(Later in the same conversation)
Georgio: 'You are silly working up there when there is no scaffolding in the lift shaft, or eight by fours running through the lift shaft, you could fall.'
Stan: 'We don't need it.'

At three in the afternoon Stan fell the five floors down the lift well while performing the same task. He died three hours later in hospital.

Here Stan was an active participant in an unsafe work practice which eventually lead to his death. The worksite had an entrenched culture antithetical to considerations of safety, with the major building contractor showing little interest in the welfare of those on site. File documents reveal that this case involved a considerable amount of conflict, in particularly between two unions which were fighting for membership on the site. The company who employed him was small, as was the major contractor. From a theoretical perspective then the marginal nature of the operation may have underpinned both the culture and Stan's cavalier attitude.

The following case similarly reflects cultural elements influencing the death, but illustrates a different worksite structure:

The Wirral Cement yard belonged to a large multinational corporation. It was extremely busy with high noise levels due to the number of trucks entering and leaving the premises: some bringing in materials, others being loaded with cement mixture to fulfil customers' orders. The cement loading operations were co-ordinated via the hand signals of a worker, the loader, to ensure the correct cement mix. The general plant manager noted '. . . the safety of the plant relies heavily on the workers being aware of the trucks and their movements around the site . . . you have to be very alert.'

Tony, a subcontracted truck driver, was walking back to his vehicle from the main office. While crossing one of the loading bays he stopped to attract the attention of the loader in order to indicate how much aggregate he wanted to unload from the truck. Just at that moment a truck reversed into the loading bay crushing him.

In this case the structure of the worksite was very different from the construction site of the previous case, in terms of the size difference between the various organizations on site. Primarily there were two types of organizations: first, the site was controlled by the multinational company, which subcontracted much of the transporting of materials to a large number of contractors, in this case owner drivers. Similar to the construction site though was a situation where unsafe practices could flourish, supported by a management philosophy of everyone looking out for themselves. A different worksite structure, in terms of the size of the major player, may support a similar culture emphasizing 'each to their own'.

The next case involved a similar worksite structure to the loading yard in that large high-profile organizations were involved. Here again the major player considered the safety of subcontractors on their site not to be their primary responsibility. This lead to a situation where a momentary lack of concentration was fatal:

Arcade, a major steel manufacturer, was in the process of constructing a new warehouse. It had recently purchased the steelworks from another company, Mightysteel.[3] Arcade employed a project manager, Geoff, to

[3] From the coroner's documents it was unclear who actually had legal possession of the site at the time, Mightysteel or Arcade.

direct the construction work. Geoff subcontracted Alltime Rigging to do the rigging work. Petro was an experienced rigger, employed by Alltime, who was used to working at the heights required on this particular site. Although Arcade had provided cherrypickers to enable the riggers to use a line to hook up their harnesses, for the riggers the work went more smoothly without bothering to hook them up. Petro was wearing the harness when he died, yet it was not attached to anything.

The day of the death was a Saturday. After checking the progress of the work Geoff, the project manager at Arcade, left to go to the football. Geoff noticed that the lines were not being used but considered that the riggers' business. While erecting the purlins (roof steel), Petro found one length too short to reach the necessary bolts, so as a temporary measure he tied it up with string and continued working on a different section. When Petro returned to the section with the short steel he forgot that it was only tied with string. He stepped on the short steel which broke away from the string. Petro fell nine metres landing on his head.

The culture of this site was focused on getting the job done. The files reveal that despite the presence of the tenderor on site, responsibility for safety was fragmented between the various groups of contractors and subcontractors. Safety was a secondary consideration evidenced in the summary above by the site manager seeing unsafe work practices yet saying nothing. He ignored the implications of not tying up a harness in an inherently unsafe environment. The riggers focused on erecting steel, at the expense of their safety, since work flowed more smoothly without the restrictions of a tied harness. Without safety being seen as central to 'the job', in this case erecting steel, a culture flourished where safety hazards could be ignored.

The next case again involved a number of organizations on site, with a culture similar to that on the Arcade site, where each organization was to take care of their own workers. The difference here is that one of the organizations was a local government council illustrating the way themes, such as culture and structure of the site, may extend beyond private industry into the government sector:

Jesus worked as a freelance construction worker and a rigger, working for a rigging subcontractor, Daytons. Daytons in turn was subcontracted to the main contractor, Nagel Constructions. Nagel Constructions was contracted to build a sports stadium for a local football club on a reserve owned by Leafytown Council. The building was being constructed under an electrical subtransmission line. Permission for work under live power lines had been granted to Leafytown Council by the Electricity Commission. The Commission sent clear instructions to the Council concerning the hazards of the site. It is unclear whether the council ensured that all on the site were aware of the dangers.

Work on the day of the accident involved the use of a crane to help erect steel columns. A crane and crane driver were subcontracted from a sixth organization, a local crane hire firm, Service Cranes. The crane was large for the job and it was discussed between Daytons and the crane driver whether it should be sent back for a smaller one. No action was taken. The Leafytown Council architect inspecting the site also commented on the size of the crane and requested it be changed. She was ignored.

Initially four workers were involved in erecting the steel; the crane driver, two riggers from Daytons along with their boss, Frank. After erecting two columns Frank left. While the third column was being erected the crane boom hit the overhead wires, killing Jesus and seriously wounding the other rigger.

The chain of events leading to the fatality above involved known hazards and so the direct cause of death is clear. Issues of responsibility are more obscure, complicated by the number of firms present on the site. The relationship between organizations appeared haphazard with no one organization taking overall responsibility for the site. The culture on site reflected a 'mind your own business and keep to your own job' mentality, as evidenced by the response to the architect's concerns.

In all of the above cases it is possible to identify immediate pragmatic causes of the deaths, which leads to obvious responses, such as ensuring harnesses are used, using correct procedure in demolition and so on. However, in each of the cases there are also other contributory elements present; namely the presence of unsafe cultures, underpinned by worksite structures which emphasized individual company responsibility for safety and getting the job done. These worksite structures involved both large and small organizations.

In some cases the immediate causal factor was more obscure, which clouded issues of responsiveness and responsibility, albeit while issues of unsafe culture may have remained. Two factors contributed to the ambiguity in the cases below; first, deaths which resulted from a coalition of events, rather than a single event; and secondly, lack of witnesses who saw the death occur. In these cases a large part of the official investigation centres on trying to dispel this ambiguity. With this focus the investigation may sidestep issues of culture, worksite structure and marginalization, although these may still be evident.

The next case illustrated involves the unfortunate coalition of two events; reversing of one truck, while another was moving forward. There was ambiguity regarding responsibility for the death, since it was not clear where the orders for the shifting of one of the trucks originated. Subsequent investigation did not resolve the issue:

Roadtech had been contracted by Harbourtown Council to resurface some local roads. Roadtech in turn subcontracted some owner drivers to cart the asphalt to the road work site. Once the asphalt was laid it was sprayed with emulsion from a tank and hose mounted on the back of one of Roadtech's trucks. The worker responsible for spraying either held the hose while walking behind the truck, or sat on the back of the truck while the truck moved. While it was usual practice to spray while the truck was going forward, the crew often reversed over spots which had been missed. The driver of the emulsion truck was unable to see the worker holding the hose while reversing.

On the day of Grant's death, one lane had been resurfaced without incident. The spray truck had driven to the far end of the road works and planned to reverse back over the tarmac to finalize the spraying process. For reasons that are unknown, Diasano, one of the tip truck drivers drove onto the freshly laid road surface. Grant, a leading hand, was sitting on the back of the truck spraying as the spray truck reversed. Jake, the driver, was concentrating on the traffic in the completed lane and was unaware that the tip truck had moved up closer to him. The spray truck reversed into the tipper crushing Grant between the two.

The elements of the death here are: an ongoing unsafe work practice, spraying when the truck was reversing; a lack of overall supervision; compounded by confusion which lead Diasano to move his truck. This confusion obscured the presence of an unsafe culture, and allows the incident to be rationalized as an 'unfortunate coincidence'. In such a case it is easy to overlook the possible underlying factors behind the death, such as issues of contract and relationships between companies, as attention becomes focused on tracing the exact sequence of events which led to the death.

In the next case confusion arose from a lack of witnesses, rather than the combination of factors evident above. The lack of witnesses obscured the actual cause of the death, which involved a forklift. In this case again the sheer number of companies involved complicates the overall picture, where one of the key issues was the roadworthiness of the forklift:

BBM Materials hired forklifts for use in transporting building materials around its warehouse and factory floor. The forklift involved in the death was requested from Bristol Forklifts, a traditional supplier to BBM. However, Bristol had been short of the required style of forklifts in this instance, and so had hired one from another hiring company, Trent Hire, in order to fulfil its obligations to BBM.

Danny Trang had been rostered to use this particular forklift, and was known to be unhappy with the machine. It had a tendency to creep forward when in gear, without use of the accelerator, which Danny was not used to. He was carrying a load down one of the bays when the load on the forklift became caught on a rack to one side of the bay. Another worker Tiet signalled for Danny to move back and then turned away to avoid the exhaust from the forklift. A few seconds later he heard a bang and saw Danny trapped between the forklift and the rack. He died later in hospital.

An independent mechanic from the Department of Labour found a number of faults which could have exacerbated the problem. However, the existence of these faults was challenged at inquest by the hire companies. It became evident during the hearing that the independent mechanic had limited experience with forklifts, and so the evidence from the hire companies was accepted. Danny was found to have contributed to his own death.

Here, although questions were raised about the machinery, ultimately the deceased was considered to have contributed to his own death. Since the exact reasons for Danny being trapped were unclear, the evidence of expert witnesses at the inquest was central. There was some debate about the forklift, with one expert claiming roadworthiness, the other noting the poor condition of the forklift. The final result of the Inquest emphasized the role of the worker in bringing about the death.

The exact circumstances of the following fatality also contained unresolved issues. Reflecting the issues of the previous case the lack of witnesses added to the confusion regarding cause of death; and the final resolution raised questions regarding the behaviour of the deceased:

George ran a lagging business, Quicklag, with one other partner, Jim. Lagging involves insulation of pipes, for example steam pipes. George had been in the trade thirty-five years and was experienced with all types of lagging work. Quicklag had been subcontracted by Reid Plumbing, who had recently replaced steam pipes in the factory owned by a heavy engineering firm, Aidans. The lagging involved covering these narrow diameter steam pipes, which were located about five metres above the ground. When they arrived at the job they found the trestles they had brought with them were too short to access the pipes, so they hired some extension ladders.

While lagging a piece of pipe obscured by a roofing cross member, George and the ladder fell to the ground, killing George instantly. It is not clear why the ladder fell, as no one directly witnessed the fall, although it was known the ladder was not 'tied off' to a secure place to prevent it slipping. An initial theory of a heart attack was discounted at autopsy. Scuff marks were found at the scene, consistent with George having 'walked' the ladder like a pair of stilts, a dangerous practice, now banned but common twenty years ago. However, some live electrical wires were also found hanging from the roof about one metre from where George was working.

Again in this case the exact circumstances surrounding the death are unclear. An unsafe work practice, walking the ladder, was a possibility in terms of a cause. Also plausible was the involvement of the wires, with the fall resulting from electric shock. If the death did result from walking the ladder, as many concluded, the practice was undertaken by the owner of the company, not an employee, and the owner paid with his own life.

This case may illustrate the point raised by Galbraith (1973) that small firms need to exploit themselves in order to survive. This exploitation involves owners and family members of such businesses as well as employees. The pressures on the subcontractor as a whole in continuing to use such dangerous practices need to be examined. Those involved in small business may take an active role in maintaining the status quo,[4] since their existence may depend upon their willingness to cut corners.

[4] This active role includes exploiting themselves and others to maintain a particular competitive edge. Regulations may be resisted as they may be seen to undermine the competitive edge of small business. Small business may, in fact, become fairly wealthy due to their ability to exploit the spaces left by larger less flexible business.

The confusion in Peter's death below resulted from the coalition of disparate events; the lack of witness; as well as considerable worksite complexity. Several omissions by all companies present at the site combined to produce the fatal outcome:

Peter was a fitter and turner who worked in the maintenance department at Postens. Because of the nature of his work he was entrusted with a master key which gave him access to all parts of the building. Previous to capital works taking place in the basement, a routine part of Peter's work was to check compressors located there. The compressors had been shifted earlier, and it was assumed Peter had no further cause to go to the basement. All keys to the basement had been recalled and given to the builders and demolition contractors. For some reason the master keys given to maintenance staff had not been included in the recall.

The Demolition workers, Destruction Inc., had removed the stairs leading to the basement from an external door, under instruction from the builders, Nettles. They had also changed the cylinders in the door locks. There was however no warning sign to indicate the danger that lay behind the door, a fact that was noted by the coroner as contributing to the death. On the day of his death Peter had completed some repair work in the main building and was seen to leave. Some time later the external door to the basement was found open and Peter had fallen to his death below. Keys on his body were found to open the door.

The death in this case occurred in a 'worksite within a worksite' renovations at an ongoing place of work. The lack of attention to safety of both worksites is implicated here, yet the existence of the two raises the possibility of neither seeing the need to respond. This case also highlights the number of unanswered questions that can arise at the time of the death, which can result in an opportunity for all to evade responding adequately. It is this confusion which investigations into the death and subsequent Inquest attempt to answer. However, after a death has occurred the information arising can become tainted by defensiveness and considerations of liability. Despite all attempts at inquest, the reason for Peter to enter the basement was not uncovered.

There are cases though where lack of witnesses does not preclude a piecing together which reveals a full picture of events leading to the death:

In areas of bush impenetrable to bulldozers it is common to use a 'skyline' winch to haul logs to the logging track. It works like a ski tow and depends for its stability at the logging coop on the strength of an unfelled tree, the 'tail spar', to which the line is attached. A further line from the tail spar to another tree acts as a brace.

International Paper contracted a number of loggers to supply the top half of the trees they felled. These contracts were valuable, as loggers with such contracts got more money for timber they felled. They sold both the lower trunk for mill timber, and the top half of the tree for use as pulp in paper.

Adams had one of these contracts from International Paper and was logging a steep slope using a skyline. Ben Adams, the owner of the company, had hired three timberworkers to work the skyline. One of the workers Jedd, was working at the bottom end of the skyline on his own when he radioed to his mates on the logging track that the tail spar had fallen over. There was no brace tree used. When Ted, another worker, went down to help he found Jedd crushed between some felled delimbed timber. From the investigation it became clear that Jedd had climbed on to the felled delimbed timber to disentangle the line. The felled timber had rolled, with the tailspar acting as a fulcrum, and crushed Jedd.

Here the circumstances leading to the death in terms of physical causes are clear. The wider implications in terms of the lack of a brace tree and the steepness of the slope remain contentious. At the time of the death the practice of using the skyline was rare in most states of Australia, excluding Tasmania. Most of the industry relied on experienced crews coming over from New Zealand.

The impact of changing technology in an industry aimed at increasing efficiency and accessibility to steep slopes, in this case the increased use of the skyline, needs consideration. Here profitable contracts were controlled by a single large organization which could encourage the use of potentially unsafe equipment.

Yet other cases illustrate the involvement of issues outside the influence of those present on the worksite. In the following case involvement of an independent third party complicated the implications of the death for the parties specifically involved in the productive process:

Mack worked as a rigger for Fine Rigging. On the job where he died, Fine Rigging had been contracted by a small chemical company to erect steel for a warehouse extension. The factories in the area were close together and it was possible for the workers to step from one roof to the roof of the factory next door. This Mack had done, possibly to prepare some extra nuts and bolts. He was walking on the next door roof when he fell through a skylight hitting the ground head first. The skylight was made from perspex, discoloured from age, and virtually indistinguishable from the surrounding galvanized steel. There was no safety netting under the skylight. Another rigger, Julio, who went to his rescue also fell though a different skylight. Luckily in his case there was a roof beam directly below him which prevented him following Mack's fate.

Here the unsafe roof belonged to a factory unrelated to the contract process. Their involvement in the death clouds the issues involved, since Chemref's knowledge of the unsafe roof of their neighbour is unlikely, as is their likelihood of warning the builder of its existence. General standards are at issue here with regulations regarding safety wire being compulsory under skylights only extending to buildings erected after 1981. The building in question was erected before that date.

The involvement of a third factor outside the direct work environment can similarly complicate the issues involved and so reduce the pressure to respond. The next case illustrates this, not by intrusion of an outside organization as above, but through the onset of sudden illness:

The Hoefschtede family owned and operated a small limestone quarry. They subcontracted an owner driver, Ted, to do some of their deliveries. It was during one of those deliveries to the quarry that it appears Ted suffered a heart attack and drove over the bund wall into the quarry.

Similarly, freak or unusual work circumstances can have the same effect of limiting the involvement of the major contractor:

Frank worked as a Log Yard man with Bigmill. He had done a number of safety courses, and was a safety representative for his workmates. His job involved assisting logging transporters (who were subcontracted to the mill) unload timber to be milled. During one of these unloading operations an abnormally short log catapulted into the air at a time Frank had failed to step back to his normal unloading position. The log struck Frank on the head killing him instantly.

Further complicating issues are involved where the level of inherent dangerousness in the industry is very high, but the predictability of the specific causal factor occurring at any particular time impossible to pinpoint. Such is the case with logging. Deaths in the industry, while not common, occur regularly. A proportion of these deaths involve branches falling with no prior warning onto loggers below. There is a term for these branches in the industry, they are known as 'widowmakers':

John had only been in the country for two weeks. He had experience in logging in his native New Zealand, and found a job with a team subcontracted to the local Gipp Mills. On the day he died he was working out of sight of other members of the team. Tony, the bulldozer driver, heard John's chainsaw idling for an unusually long period. When he went to investigate he found John lying dead killed by a falling branch. John's hard hat proved no protection as it shattered under the impact of the branch.

The cases above illustrate the diverse range of contexts within which death occurs. It may not be possible for regulatory theory to take account of all contexts where such harm occurs. However, there are some common themes which deserve further investigation. These include the issue of a culture which allows unsafe behaviour to go unchecked. In some cases such culture may result from particular worksite structures. For example, marginalization and the need to cut corners may give rise to a culture and behaviour cavalier of risk, as in the case of Gemtrench and Better Demolitions. Further, unsafe cultures may be sustained by the oppressive role of large organizations ignoring the safety needs of smaller operators by restrictive contracts.

Also illustrated are the complexity of the relationships between organizations and confusion of responsibilities. Such complexities allow the focus on the deceased as causing his own death, and possible 'buck passing' between the various organizations. This avoidance of responsibilities, and focus on the role of the deceased in their own death, may also be exacerbated if the specific chain of events leading to the death were ambiguous. This concentrated attention on the disparate nature of events that led to the deaths, bypassing the similarities with other deaths that may hold the key to prevention. Finally, the influence of factors outside the organizations' control, such as the role of poor regulations, is implicated in the case of Chemref.

The last case-study brings together many of the themes highlighted above. It is notable for its considerable complexity, due to the diverse range and size of organizations on site, which in turn complicated issues of liability in the aftermath of the event:

Resource Mining, the owners and operators of a large open cut mine, had contracted Stutganst, a multinational, to construct an open cut mining dredger. There was considerable communication between Resource Mining and Stutganst since the soils in the area were particularly heavy, and previous dredgers from Stutganst had a problem with clay sticking to vital parts. Nonetheless Stutganst were considered the expert in design of the dredger. Being a large project, the engineering firm Haddons were contracted to manage the labour, with Sergensons responsible for the electrical wiring and electronics.

The dredger was being constructed on site, as it was too large to move any distance. It consisted of two major sections: a crawler mounted digging unit and a crawler mounted loading unit; with a connecting bridge in between the two. Each unit had attendants' cabins attached. The loading unit attendants' cabin was mounted on a single beam. It was equipped with a levelling mechanism, a hydraulic arm which kept the cabin level despite changes in ground angles. The hydraulic arm was obtained from Lynden Hydraulics, who contracted Constructotech to manufacture the arm to Stutganst's specifications.

The project was complex and behind schedule, due both to industrial disputes and earlier mismanagement by an initial project management team from Means engineering. Their contract had been terminated and they had been replaced by Haddons some twelve months earlier. In light of the tight schedule it was decided to commission the attendants' cabin while construction was continuing on the digging unit.

Commissioning on the day of the collapse involved the placing of limit switches on the levelling mechanism of the attendants' cabin. During this process it was found there was some fouling on the steel when the cabin was tilted. The limit switches were removed to allow the steel to be reshaped. During this process the hydraulic arm was extended beyond the position where it could pull the cabin back to the horizontal. Stutganst's (the designer of the arm) representative was not present when the arm was fully extended and so did not alert the others as to the dangers of their actions. Late in the afternoon when an attempt was made to pull the cabin back the hydraulic arm failed. This caused the attendants' cabin to fall from approximately 11 degrees from the horizontal, to a vertical position. Nine people were on and in the cabin at the time of its collapse. Three were thrown to the ground. One of them, a dredger driver, was killed, and another permanently injured. Several others were saved only by being able to cling to the structure when it collapsed.

Investigation into the incident revealed a number of factors which led to the collapse. The design of the levelling mechanism was not fail-safe; and the stroke in the sleeve of the hydraulic arm was longer than necessary, leading to it being placed in a position with the limit switches removed, from which it could not recover. The hydraulics were badly constructed, with a number of screws in the sleeve of the arm 'bottomed out' weakening its strength. There was non-compliance with formal procedures for the commissioning, and an unnecessary number of people on the structure during commissioning. There was no formal hierarchy during commissioning, and at the time of the collapse Stutganst's representative was not present. Changes were made during commissioning without concern for the broader consequences of the actions undertaken. Finally, the hydraulic arm was not classified as a structural component which meant it was not subject to the scrutiny that it should have been. In summary no one involved in the design, manufacture or commissioning of the hydraulic arm was exempt from blame.

Here the combination of multiple factors, many with a separate genesis, combined to produce a tragic outcome. The investigation revealed many errors, yet it was the combination which proved fatal, over and above any one element. There are issues of the structure of the workplace which require analysis, and the poor relationships and communication between the various players which contributed to the eventual collapse. The context of this case was rich in complexity, and the behaviour by each of the organizations in this case could not be viewed in isolation to the relationships they held with each other.

Conclusion

The case-studies presented here highlight the complexity of the issues involved in deaths which result in sites controlled by more than one organization. As well as complexity there is considerable diversity, with some involving apparently clear-cut issues, and a clear chain of events leading up to the death. Others contain considerable ambiguity regarding the exact chain of events, although underlying issues concerning contribution may still be apparent. Yet others illustrate the way contribution is scattered between a number of companies, where the errors of each combine to produce the fatal outcome.

From the perspective of the implications of the cases for regulatory theory, also illustrated are some the themes arising out of the discussion of the literature, namely the possible interaction between worksite structure and culture which may influence the construction of virtue. One striking issue in a number of the cases above was the influence of the on-site culture, where safety was pushed to the background in an environment where the focus was on the smooth passage of work. In some cases those who died played an active role in maintaining that culture, either actively as in the case of Stan, the demolition worker, or passively, as in the case of Petro, the rigger who failed to hook his harness up to a secure point when working at a great height.

However, many of the studies could also be analysed usefully from a Marxist perspective, which would explain the maginalization of smaller companies on site as an illustration of the consequences of capital accumulation, where work conditions of subcontractors are inevitably dictated by larger more powerful players. The case of Wirral Cement, a large powerful organization, is illustrative here, where the owner drivers, one of whom died, were left to do their job as best they could within a clearly unsafe site. The combination of issues of marginalization and cultural factors could also be gleaned from some of the cases, such as in the death of the rigger Petro, cited above. What is not clear is the way the two may interact, and the degree of independence, or interdependence, between the two.

The complexity illustrated by the cases also obscures what should be the target of regulation, and complicates the legal issues. They illustrate well how regulatory theory has to be able to cope with the relationship between organizations as well as the virtue or otherwise of a single corporate entity. Problems in use of law enforcement techniques for the purposes of prevention are also highlighted by the presence of more than one organization on site. As the confusion surrounding the particular death increases, it increases the possibility for legal liability issues to influence ongoing behaviour. Organizations may be persuaded that it may be in their best interest not to respond to the issues raised by the death, lest their response indicate their responsibility for the event. The question then arises regarding the degree to which formal legal measures, such as an inquest process, can lead to substantive justice in terms of understanding the real contribution to the death.

The brief case-studies described above would seem to show that such data are well suited to allow critical engagement with the debate concerning the possibility of maximizing corporate virtue as a regulatory strategy. The themes tentatively alluded to in the cases—of the influence of marginalization, workplace structure and culture—highlight the need to focus attention on the regulatory space within which organizations act for clues concerning the genesis of corporate virtue, rather than restricting the focus to the relationship between the regulator and the regulated. What is needed at this point is a way to operationalize the concept of organizational virtue, using data on death which occurs in multiple employer worksites, in a way that captures the breadth of possible reasons for its absence or presence within a given workplace. This is the focus of the next chapter.

4 Operationalizing Virtue: The Responses to Death

In this chapter, what virtue **is** in a regulatory context is examined, and how it may be operationalized for the purposes of furthering debates on regulation. It explores organizational responses to the deaths at work outlined in the previous chapter, as a method of making the rather abstract concept of organizational virtue visible.

Reading Braithwaite (1993) it is not always clear what he understands by the term virtue, or how it might be identified. In some respects his work, and the work of other theorists, such as Stone, who argue for recognition of the 'good character' of some organizations, contain inherent assumptions that virtue is a common sense 'given' open to recognition by all (Stone, 1975; Braithwaite, 1993). However, the situation is clearly more complex, since ethics may indeed be relative, and the problem of definition may not simply be resolved by suggesting that there exists 'non-virtue' as well as virtue. In order to resolve this difficulty, Braithwaite speaks of organizations and individuals having 'multiple selves', with all organizations having aspects of both virtue and non-virtue (Braithwaite, 1985; Ayres and Braithwaite, 1992). Simply put, Braithwaite argues that all organizations have the capacity within them for both non-virtue, or virtue. Ultimately the solution for Braithwaite it to see virtue in simply behavioural terms. Virtuous organizations are those which do the right thing.

Support for an analysis of virtue in light of action can also be found from the philosophical literature, particularly that literature which emphasizes pragmatic ethics, ethical reactions that are tied to specific contexts and specific times and in specific action, rather than predefined in a Platonic sense as abstract form. A good example is Alisdair MacIntyre who defines virtue in terms of individual acts which occur as part of a set of 'practices'. These practices MacIntyre defines as:

[A]ny coherent and complex form of socially established cooperative human activity through which goods internal to that form of activity are realized in the course of trying to achieve those standards of excellence which are appropriate to, and partially definitive of, that form of activity, with the result that human powers to achieve excellence, and human conceptions of the ends and goods involved, are systematically extended. [MacIntyre, 1995:191]

For MacIntyre there are key qualities for achieving excellence within any sphere or practice, namely justice, courage and honesty (MacIntyre, 1995:193). Adherence to these principles leads to excellence in practice, and constitutes virtue. For our purposes here, safety management could be defined as a 'practice', since it has goals which are internal to the endeavour, namely the promotion of health and well-being within an organization. For safety management the virtue lies with the honesty, courage and justice with which safety issues are dealt with as part of the overall organizational life.

For regulation we need an overtly organizational concept of virtue. Stone (1975; 1987) and Braithwaite both seek virtue at the level of the organization (in Stone's case through the notion of corporate social responsibility). Stone (1987:17) elaborates on the link between individual virtue and organizational virtue. For Stone, the relationship between the responsible individual and the moral organization is that for the firm the bureaucratic structures mimic the decision process of the responsible individual.

Following the discussion in chapter 2 though, we need to be wary of attributing to organizations qualities, such as virtue, that might only be pertinent to individuals. Indeed there is a problem with the concept of virtue at an organizational level. For MacIntyre virtue is predominantly a quality of the individual. The virtue of individual practice is in tension with the institution which both sustains such practices, yet has the potential to distort individuals from their pursuit of internal good. For safety then, the possible organizational distortion is away from the value of safety as an end in itself, towards safety seen in light of the additional profit or status it may accord the organization. Organizations are primarily concerned with external goods (money, power, status) while virtue arises from the pursuit of internal good (MacIntyre, 1995:194).

Other theorists highlight problems with seeing bureaucratic structures as evidence of the institutionalization of virtue at the level of the organization. Bureaucratic structures bear an imperfect relationship to corporate behaviour, most easily evidenced by the work of Weber (1991:220–1, 331) on formal and substantive rationality; work which shows the way the substantive reasons behind the setting up of bureaucratic structures become sidelined by adherence to the rules themselves. More recent work also illustrates problems, for example Pettigrew's (1985) work highlighted in chapter 2, on the influence of culture on bureaucratic directives. This suggests we should be wary of seeing bureaucratic structures as being *the* repository for virtue; it may be better to take a broader view on the processes of institutionalization as a whole as a better candidate for the genuine example of virtue which is not tied to any one individual. Institutionalism has the potential to show the enculturation of values in organizational norms (see Di Maggio and Powell, 1991:12–19).

However, even here there are pitfalls as the 'new' institutionalists would point out (Di Maggio and Powell, 1991: 1–37). Individual values (including ethical values) may have less influence on the process of institutionalization than the groping in the dark by individuals for shared norms, and unreflective repetition of action which cements such norms of the organization in place. The analysis of organizational virtue should be broad enough to encompass both possibilities, namely that good outcomes may result from serendipity, coincidence and irrationality, as much as from single-minded intent and moral action of the individual. The approach taken here is one which uses culture as a means to achieve such breadth, but views culture in a specific way, namely that outlined in chapter 2. As was outlined in that chapter, culture is seen as a normative device which shapes the way individuals reflect and act within their organization (Schein, 1986; Calori and Sarnin, 1991). The genesis of such norms may result from either values or some means inherent in the interaction between individuals sharing the same organizational space.

The first step though is to review overt behaviour. The primary method of 'operationalizing' virtue in this book, i.e. making it concrete and visible for the purpose of exploration and analysis, follows the suggestion of Braithwaite and others, that is, that behaviour of organizations should be examined to ascertain their relative virtue. As Selznick (1992:236) argues: 'We must infer operational goals from actual practice'. Once made visible in this way, the next task is to ascertain whether identification of virtuous behaviour, and the response of the regulator to it, is sufficient to 'nurture virtue'. This may be undertaken by uncovering the correlates to virtuous behaviour to ascertain whether such correlates are amenable to change simply through the actions of regulators.

One possible means of identifying virtue through organizational behaviour is to analyse further events leading to the death to identify those who acted 'virtuously', and those who did not. This would be consistent with the general trend of criminological and sociological research which has tended to focus on the causes of industrial harm, and the possibility of ameliorative measures, through analysing the antecedents to a catastrophic event (Turner, 1976; Perrow, 1984; Hopkins, 1989b and c). However, as the case-studies indicate, these events could be complicated by a certain amount of unresolvable confusion concerning course of events which lead to the death. Secondly, the 'wisdom of hindsight' may cloud judgement regarding what the organization should have done. In analysing contributing factors to the death it may be too easy to both condemn actions of an individual organization, and see it as an independent actor in control of its own destiny. Thirdly, analysing contributing factors to the death, where organizations were seen to contribute to the death,[1] makes the possibility of finding virtue, as opposed to lack of virtue, difficult. Finally, the discussion in the first chapter highlighted the difference between formal and substantive justice. The documents used for analysis were formal court documents and subject to the problem outlined by Van Maanen and Pentland (1994), that is they were targeted at a court rationality, rather than uncovering the real virtue or otherwise of the parties to the death. For these reasons a different approach was followed.

The approach chosen in operationalizing virtue in this book was to investigate organizational **responses** to the harm they cause, in this case the responses to the deaths outlined in chapter 3. Analysis of response also allows some insight into the likelihood of future repetition of tragic events. A virtuous response would be the one where repetition was the least likely. Further, understanding how organizations respond to human tragedy can be seen as central to understanding how organizations deal with ethical dilemmas in light of their social and economic demands. This study aimed to enter the mind-set of the organizations

[1] The definition of contribution is discussed later in this chapter and in detail in the appendix, pages 250–1.

involved in the above cases to understand both the responses they made, and the way organizational norms and expectations were replayed through those responses. This gave the analysis of virtue presented here an advantage over previous surveys on organizational ethics (see for example Burke, Maddock and Rose, 1993), since it was able to analyse what was actually done when an event occurred, rather than posing the question 'what would you do if . . . ?'.

There is also some support in the literature for using responsiveness as an indicator of virtue. For example, a view which equates responsiveness with virtue is consistent with those who advocate viewing the quality of organizational response to harm as an indication of criminal culpability, the opposite of virtue (Bucy, 1991; Fisse, 1991; Fisse, 1993). Responsiveness by organizations, or lack of responsiveness, is also seen by some as an indicator of ongoing compliance or non-compliance with the law (Clinard and Yeager, 1980). Analysing responses to the death, then, provided a novel way of exploring organizational virtue.

In reviewing responses reference was made to the principles which underlie excellence in safety management. These are well laid out in a number of occupational health and safety texts (see Mathews, 1985; Quinlan and Bohle, 1991; Quinlan, 1996), and were covered briefly in chapter 3. To recap, these principles involve a demonstrated senior management commitment to health and safety; a programme of safety integrated into core activities; a focus on the safety systems which exist within a company, as opposed to the actions of individuals; a management system that addresses change; and finally a system that values worker input (Quinlan, 1996:22–3). Good safety management understands occupational health and safety incidents as symptoms of an underlying cause. That cause is to be found in the safety management system that allowed the machine to be unguarded, the harness not to be worn, the apprentice to work in the unshored trench, and so on (Rees, 1988).

Responses to Workplace Death

Ascertaining the nature of responses to the deaths experienced by the various organizations was gained primarily through interviews, supplemented by coroner's documents and a limited number of company documents made available at interview. Table 4.1

TABLE 4.1. List of Comparies and Members Interviewed

Organization	Industry	Who Interviewed
Gemtrench	Plumbing Contractor	Owner and Director
Leafytown Council	Local Council	Council Architect
Nagel Constructions	Builders	Out of business
Daytons	Rigging	Owner and Director
Service Cranes	Crane Hire	Owner and Director
Young Constructions	Builders	Owner
Better Demolitions	Demolitions	Part Owner
Wirral Cement	Quarrying/Cement	Interview refused
Mightysteel	Steelmakers	Safety Officer
Arcade	Capital Works/Steel	Construction Manager
Alltime Rigging	Rigging	Previous owner
Harbourtown Council	Local Council	Safety Officer
Roadtech	Roadworks	Safety Officer/ Manager (2)
BBM Materials	Building Materials	Interview refused
Bristol Forklifts	Forklift Hire	Interview refused
Trent Hire	Forklift Hire	Interview refused
Aidans	Heavy Engineering	Safety Executive
Reid Plumbing	Plumbing	Owner and Director
Quicklag	Lagging	Interview refused
Postens	Service Industry	Interview refused
Nettles Builders	Building Contractors	Directors (2)
Destruction Inc.	Demolition Contractors	Manager
International Paper	Paper Mill	Safety Officer
Adams Logging	Logging Contractor	Owner and Director
Chemref	Chemicals	Manager
Fine Rigging	Rigging	Out of business
Rowlands		Unable to be traced
Hoefschtede Mines	Quarrying	Previous owner
Bigmill	Sawmill	Sawmill Manager
Gipp Mills	Sawmill	Manager
Bigland	Landowner	Safety Officer/ Regional Officer (2)
Resource Mining	Mining	Project Manager
Stutganst	Heavy Engineering	Manager (Australian Division)
Haddons	Engineering	Project Manager
Lynden Hydraulics	Hydraulics	General Manager
Constructotech	Hydraulics	Manager (unclear)
Sergensons	Electrics/Electronics	Safety Officer

Note: (2) Number in brackets indicates where more than one person interviewed outlines the organizations who took part in this part of the study, and who was interviewed. In all twenty-eight of the possible thirty-seven organizations in this part of the study, to varying degrees of access.

In reviewing responses to the death the first concern was to ascertain the range of responses. Responses could include changes to equipment, personnel or changes to procedure and management orientation with respect to safety. The next concern was to establish whether the range exhibited different qualities, that is, whether one type of response was superior to another, which could be used to indicate varying levels of organizational virtue. As the case-studies illustrated, organizations needed to go beyond immediate causes in order to influence safety in the long term. The case-studies pointed to issues of culture and safety focus which would need to be addressed if safety were to improve comprehensively. In terms of quality of response then a key issue was to identify those companies which went beyond immediate causes in identifying what changes needed to be made in light of the safety system as a whole. This requires going beyond obvious causes, tied to the individual, to systemic causes which required attention.

In order to achieve the above an initial task was to ascertain the number of companies which in some way contributed to the death, as this affects both the willingness and ability of the organization to respond. Without contributing to the death, it was considered that changes could not as directly be tied to virtue. Contribution is also important since all deaths took place on multiple employer worksites, and it was possible that not all those on site contributed to the death. With this in mind, if a company made no changes, yet did not contribute to the death, it was considered that lack of action in this case held a very tenuous relationship to lack of virtue.

Category 1: No Contribution and No Change

With contribution being a necessary precondition to responsiveness, in cases where there was no contribution, responsiveness, or lack of responsiveness could not be seen as an indicator of virtue. There was one company which did not contribute, either by its action or inaction, to the fatality, and therefore its response cannot be seen to symbolize virtue or lack of virtue of the company.

This company saw itself as not responsible and no changes were made as a result of the fatality. Although only one, this organization demonstrates that companies can be involved in fatalities, at least in multiple employer workplaces, yet not contribute to injuries or fatalities in that workplace. This company, Sergensons, was a subcontractor on the construction of the mining dredger where the fatality occurred when the dredger collapsed. This company's responsibilities in the construction (electrical wiring) did not contribute to the collapse, neither were they in a position in the workplace hierarchy to influence the organizational issues that led to the collapse. Any positive or negative changes in this company were independent of the fatalities, and it perceived no threat in terms of its legal liabilities.

Contribution and Change

In all the other cases there was some contribution by the organizations in the sample to the death, and so their response can be understood as indicating, to some extent at least, their level of virtue. The case-studies illustrated two styles of response which could be anticipated, depending on the breadth of vision of the organization. In many of the cases a narrow focus would have perceived the need for some changes, such as changes to machinery and equipment. However, the case-studies in chapter 3 also pointed to the need for broad cultural changes. Perceiving the need for changes on this level may emanate from a wider perspective by organizations regarding their safety responsibilities. Changes to the safety level of the organization could therefore vary from the dramatic, that is the death could be a turning-point for the organization, the point which stimulated a total overhaul of safety in the organization, through to a response which involved no changes at all. In between these lie possibilities for substantial changes in terms of creating a new safety programme or re-emphasis of an existing programme, as long as that programme is well constructed. At the other end of the scale exists *ad hoc* change to a specific machine involved in the death, where little else in the organization is affected, in particular the overall safety orientation of the company which although deficient, is left untouched.

This range of possible responses can be distilled into two basic groups, labelled here a 'virtuous' or a 'blinkered' response. The virtuous response re-evaluates the organization's safety levels, altering workplaces or work practices where necessary, as well as re-emphasizing current safety policy. This type of response can be seen to hold out considerable hope for ongoing high levels of safety, when compared to the blinkered responses. The policies instated or re-emphasized in response to the fatalities in this category should incorporate many features which research has shown to correlate with high safety levels, such as good channels of communication, a high priority on safety with key safety personnel having direct access to higher level management, and an emphasis on line management responsibility for health and safety (Braithwaite, 1985; Mathews, 1985; Grabosky and Sutton, 1989; Quinlan and Bohle, 1991).

In contrast the blinkered response is far more muted. The aim of these responses could be described as being targeted to isolating those visible and specific factors which had to be dealt with and changed, often the immediate precursors to the death. The response here is limited to altering only those specific factors. It can be argued that these responses are less likely to produce lasting positive changes in safety levels, as organizational issues are unlikely to be addressed. Similar or related hazards in other parts of the organization similarly may not be changed by such a response.

However, the case-studies also indicated the possible need for organizations to respond to their legal liabilities. Changes also needed to be identified which were designed to reduce or remove the legal liability of the organization.

Category 2: Companies which went Out of Business

The two organizations in this category did contribute to the death on the particular site, however there were no changes to the companies as such as they went out of business. One of the first findings of the analysis of the data in terms of response, therefore, was that the experience of a fatality could lead to a demise of the company. An example here is the case of Better Demolitions working on the site controlled by Young Constructions. The fatality here was that of Stan, a demolition worker falling down a lift shaft which he was demolishing. As the case-study above showed he was 'working off the wall', i.e. removing bricks from under his feet while standing on the wall of the lift shaft. He was under the direct eye of his boss, the owner of the demolition company. Both companies involved in this fatality, Young Constructions and Better Demolitions, went out of business **directly as a result of the fatality**. The director of the defunct Young Constructions was bitter about the experience:

> 'That incident was when the shit hit the fan. Well the impact if you want to know, is that I lost a hell of a lot of money and I went out of business. Is that good enough for you? It is an incident I would rather forget . . . it was pretty traumatic for me . . . The fatality was the prime factor behind me winding the company down; but as well I could see the boom coming to an end, so I am glad I am not in the business any more.'

Both Young Constructions and Better Demolitions were investigated by the Director of Public Prosecutions with a view to bringing manslaughter charges against them. Both companies were marginal in that they were small and did not have a good reputation in the industry. However, charges were never laid because of poor investigation of the fatality at the time it occurred (1987), and the time lapse between the fatality and the time manslaughter charges were actively being considered in 1989.

The remaining twenty-five organizations were still in business at the time of the interviews, and so the quality of their response in terms of the ongoing safety of their workers remained pertinent.

Category 3: 'Virtuous' Response

A virtuous response was one where the actions taken addressed both immediate causes and the wider issues of culture and safety focus highlighted by the death. There was a demonstrated commitment to safety expressed by the organizations in this category, which was evidenced by worker participation in the health and safety issues arising out of the death, either through safety committees, or direct representation. There were seven organizations which responded in a virtuous manner to the death they experienced. A good example of the company wide nature of the virtuous response was Mightysteel's actions after the fatality, which occurred on a building site at a steel mill they were in the process of selling to Arcade. It will be remembered from above that this case involved the death of Jesus, a rigger employed by Alltime

Rigging, who slipped on some roof steel and fell to the ground. In response to the fatality the steel mill at Mightysteel addressed both the issues raised for their own employees and the contractors. With their own employees they ran a campaign highlighting the need for all workers to wear harnesses when working at heights. In addition the organization brought in new safety procedures concerning subcontractors. As the safety officer expressed it:

'Since the accident we put in some fairly strict procedures that they (subcontractors) must follow, sign contracts that they must abide by our safety rules on site.'

These new measures were followed up by action of management and workers. Worker health and safety representatives, as well as the safety officer, had the power, and did send non-complying contractors off site. Independent of the safety officer, the worker health representative stated: 'If they don't toe the line here, we will kick them off site.'

For companies responding in a virtuous manner, constant vigilance on safety issues was seen as essential. Emphasis was placed on the responsibility of both management and workers towards safety, as the manager of a timber mill, Bigmill, stated, 'management has to put it into the worker they must be thinking safety all the time'. Safe work practices were emphasized by management in this category, with ideas for methods of improving safety by workers welcome: 'We love to hear any ideas the workers can come up with because they are on the ground . . . they are actually operating the stuff'.

In one company, Haddons, the major effect of the fatality was highlighting the need to re-emphasize existing rigorous safety procedures; the project manager stated:

'What is embedded in my mind, it has really made me push much harder to ensure that these measures are taking place . . . They recognize that (because of) the dealings I went through if I say something I mean it.'

Importantly then, rather than the fatality being the stimulus for a virtuous response, the elements for such a response existed before the fatality occurred. The responses in this category must therefore be seen in light of the generally proactive attitude to safety exhibited by the companies before the fatality occurred and in all cases safety was seen as integral to the organization. As the project manager of Haddons stated: 'I am just stating from the managing director down we all have a commitment to safety'. In addition to the statements of commitment to safety that were made in this category, the proactive stance was backed up by organizational structures which promoted safety. The large organizations had safety personnel who had direct access to high-level management where significant budgetary decisions were made. This was particularly true of Aidans, a heavy engineering firm, where the personnel manager (responsible for both health and safety and industrial relations) made access to top-level management on safety issues a condition of his employment:

> '... I would not accept the job unless I reported to the board on a monthly basis (concerning) where we stood and what we needed to do. Safety had to be top end driven, the same as any other need in the organization.'

This was backed up by a safety committee structure throughout the organization, and although this was required by the relevant legislation, the Victorian *Occupational Health and Safety Act* 1985, many of the companies had such structures in place before it was legally required. The nature of safety in these organizations had the capability to address the common organizational problems associated with safety incidents such as poor communication and lack of training. In this case re-emphasis of existing policies became an important part of the response.

An interesting finding was that the response of these companies was not dependent on whether it was their own employee who died; in only two of the seven organizations in this category did the fatality involve an employee of the company. This finding indicates the willingness of organizations in this category to view their responsibilities broadly. To some extent also it indicates these organizations' awareness of their power within the worksite, and their willingness to use that power to influence for safety's sake.

There was one organization in this group, a small crane subcontractor Service Cranes, who believed their ability to influence others on site was limited. The response of this company differed because of this belief. The comprehensive nature of the response was directed more at the company itself rather than an attempt to influence worksites as a whole, the ultimate aim being to protect their own workers from harm. The outward nature of the response was demonstrated in the policy of refusing dangerous jobs. The owner of the company would personally inspect sites where his men may have been put at risk. If the risk was considered too great the owner would refuse the work. Similarly, if the contractor requesting the crane work was not willing to provide the necessary safe working environment through proper equipment, adequately trained personnel (for example riggers and dogmen), and procedures, the work would be refused.

However, similar to the six large organizations, responsibility for safety was seen as shared between the owner and the workers, in this case the crane drivers. The owner of the company explained:

> 'To ask the clients about the risk initially is my responsibility. If they say there is, I go and inspect the site. If they say no, then I rely on the drivers (when they arrive) not to do it if it is too dangerous. The drivers know that, there has to be a level of trust between us.'

Category 4: 'Blinkered' Response

With a blinkered response the focus by the companies here was narrow, considering only those changes which would only prevent a repetition of the *exact* same event, that is the immediate precursors to that event which were clearly identifiable in the case-studies. This meant either a review of the exact piece of equipment involved in the fatality, or the actions of the specific worker who died. If there were no apparent changes considered necessary, no direct action to improve safety would be made.

It is important to recognize that these two different conclusions to the narrow focus, some safety change as opposed to no safety change, arose from similar mind-sets about appropriate safety levels, and degrees of necessary risk, within organizations. For the sake of clarity however these two types of changes are discussed below separately. Thus this category is further subdivided according to whether the blinkered focus led to some limited safety changes, subcategory a, or to subcategory b where the company considered no need for safety changes could be found, the only changes being those designed to limit legal liability.

Subcategory a: Limited Safety Changes

Limited safety changes involved changes to the exact piece of equipment involved in the fatality, or changes to worker behaviour in the absence of addressing any broader issues. Six companies made blinkered safety changes as a result of the fatality. The case of Roadtech illustrates changes to equipment involved in the fatality. In response to the death of one of their workers Roadtech placed a new bar at the rear of the truck which prevented workers sitting with their legs over the back of the truck. It was by sitting this way that the worker, Grant, was crushed to death when the driver reversed into another truck behind. No other changes, including changes to supervision practices, also integral to the chain of events, occurred.

With the organizations in this subcategory, if changes to the equipment were considered unnecessary or impractical, changes were made to the immediate personnel involved in the use of a particular machine, with a response such as 'we look at who we employ and who we don't employ more carefully', a response employed by Adams Logging. Alternatively in some cases the response was of a limited organizational nature, such as a temporary slow-down in construction work:

> '[When the fatality happened] the momentum of the building slowed down. It took certain effects on the building, everyone was more conscious . . .'

Major contractors or tenderors on the same site could, and did, influence how these companies worked, but only as long as the contractor or subcontractor worked for them. For example, Aidans, a large manufacturer, who exhibited a virtuous response, regularly employed a plumber, Reid Plumbing, involved in the same fatality who exhibited a blinkered response. As the case-study showed, this fatality involved work at Aidans who required some plumbing and lagging work. The plumber in turn subcontracted the lagging work, which involved insulating the pipe work installed by the plumber, to Quicklag. The lagger fell from his ladder (possibly as a result of trying to 'walk' the ladder like a pair of stilts) and was killed. As a result Aidans required that all ladder work be undertaken with two people, one holding the bottom of the ladder. Reid Plumbing complied when on Aidans' site, but had different practices on different sites:

'[W]e still only have one man on a ladder, because that is the way we have always done it and it's accepted as a safe way of doing it. But we make sure our ladders are tied off, or our men are supposed to make sure they are tied off.'

Here the underlying causes of the fatality are left untouched. The practice of having one man on the ladder remained as their company policy, leaving open the possibility of 'walking' the ladder under constraints of time and tight contract conditions. It is interesting to compare this to the position of Service Cranes, the virtuous respondent above, who actively sought out safety conscious contractors, and refused other more dangerous work.

Another example of a large organization which fell into this category was Arcade which was constructing a new warehouse at a site it was purchasing from Mightysteel. Mightysteel exhibited a virtuous response, outlined previously. The effect on the construction project however, which was controlled by the construction manager at Arcade, was a temporary slow-down of work. The construction manager stated that the top priority was getting the job done:

'People tend to put it to the back of their mind and get on with the job. They are not conscious about it until something occurs. The number one priority is getting the job done . . . as far as health and safety it is something secondary, nobody pays attention till something happens.'

For one company in this category, Adams Logging, the priority was to limit the damage of civil action, the death involving a logger working on a winch system. One aspect of the company's response was to bring in a team experienced in using the winch from overseas. However, an important part of the response was to limit legal liability, particularly as the fatality involved their own employee, and thus the link between the death and the company's responsibility was more direct. The owner of the company chose to change the status of the firm from a partnership to a limited liability company in response to the fatality, reducing his personal liability for the practices which led to the death. The company had a lawsuit pending arising out of the incident:

Interviewer: 'So it was some of the lessons you learnt by going through the whole thing?'
Owner: 'Yes that's right, yes to get away from the liability part.'

Subcategory b: Legal Changes Only

A blinkered response comprising of legal changes only involved changing the legal status of the company, altering insurance conditions or changing company name. The twelve organizations in this category considered themselves as not contributing to the fatality and thereby absolved themselves of the need to make health and safety changes. However, their action or inaction influenced causal factors which led to the fatality and thus was categorized as having contributed to the fatality.

The organizations here highlight a number of reasons why organizations chose to make only legal changes without changing the overall safety of the working environment. Primary among these was the nature of the multiple workplace which, in these cases, lacked an adequate definition of responsibility between the parties. Loose definitions of who was in charge or responsible for certain events made distancing from the need to make safety changes an easy option.

This distancing is illustrated by the reaction to responsibility for a subcontractor's employee on site. If a company was high in the workplace hierarchy, such as a major contractor, they would emphasize the responsibility of the subcontractor because 'He is the one who employs them', or shift the responsibility onto 'site management' as separate and distinct from the company itself.

Loose definitions of responsibility meant companies low in the hierarchy were ignorant of the major player's intentions and denied the need to inform themselves. The supplier of hydraulic equipment in the dredger collapse, Lynden Hydraulics, stated: 'We acted like a parts supplier'. Yet the part supplied by this company was pivotal to the safety of workers driving a mining dredger; a fatality and two serious injuries resulted when it failed.

The confusion of responsibilities also made it difficult for those in an overseeing role to exercise their authority. Leafytown council architect visiting the building project on council land where a crane hit overhead wires, killing a rigger, said:

> 'I believed that when the builder was told to remove the crane he should have moved it and not argued. I felt a responsibility towards that situation which I was not able to enforce. They simply said "we know what we are doing, don't muck around with us lady, who are you . . ."'

In all but one case the organizations in this category were responding to the death of someone else's employee. The general manager of Lynden Hydraulics admitted: 'If it had been one of our own employees it would have been a totally different experience'.

Various other factors were also cited as reasons why only legal and not safety changes were made. Inherent dangerousness of the job was stated as a reason. This view was coupled with an understanding that deaths caused minimal disruption to the work, since the worker or subcontractor was easily replaced. In response to a logging fatality the accounts officer of Gipp Mills, a timber company, stated: 'There were plenty of others willing to take his place, [the fatality] caused a minimum of disruption to the organization' and later 'The response was it was tragic, but it has happened before and it will happen again'. This was confirmed by a manager in a central organizational office of the landowner, Bigland:

> 'There was no effect centrally, it is unlikely that we would hear about that sort of thing. [We would] possibly [only hear] if it was a valued contractor and couldn't be replaced, but that is not likely.'

The pervasive feeling within these workplaces was that accidents were not unusual, and further, they were accepted as part of the job.

For others the 'unique situation' of the fatality precluded the need for changes other than to minimize legal liability. Both the inevitability and the 'one off circumstance' arguments could be used to explain events in the same fatality. The manager of Lynden Hydraulics saw the fatality as a 'one off': 'The accident was like a space shuttle thing, it was a one off scenario that no one could have foreseen'. However, an engineer of major contractor, Stutganst, speaking of the same fatality: 'Gave the impression that with heavy engineering and commissioning accidents were not surprising' (author's notes).

The involvement of lawyers in these cases was not unusual, for although the companies had absolved themselves of the need to make safety changes, many were concerned about the insurance and legal liability ramifications of the fatalities. Many were experiencing, or feared, civil action. Lawyers altered the emotional intensity for some managers. An engineer explained: 'There is a terrible feeling when a serious accident occurs, engineers like building things, they hate seeing people get hurt in the process. Lawyers take this emotionality out, they are cool and calm.'

There was one spin off for occupational health and safety arising out of a legal focus. Two of the companies placed an increased emphasis on formalizing responsibilities. Significantly one of these, the hydraulics manufacturer, Constructotech, now asks what the final purpose is for the part they are manufacturing. If they see some problem with its use, they will refuse to do the work.

Conclusion

The aim of the chapter was to find data which could be used as a vehicle to explore regulatory theory, and the notion of organizational virtue. Occupational deaths which occur in multiple employer worksites appeared to fulfil the requirements of such a vehicle. The case-studies illustrated that such data does indeed capture the complexity of capitalism in terms of both organizational and regulatory complexity. Themes of economic and workplace structure and the effect on safety, as well as issues of worksite culture, were also evident showing that the concept of virtue, and its contributory factors, could be explored using such data.

Rather than look at events leading up to the deaths as indicators of virtue, this chapter argued that organizational responses to harm may give a clearer picture of virtue within an organizational setting. In the latter half of the chapter a more concerted attempt was made to explore issues of organizational virtue by looking at organizational responses to the deaths which occurred. There was, as might be anticipated, a range of responses to the deaths made by the organizations in the sample. Discounting where contribution to death did not occur, and where companies went out of business due to the fatality, the responses were able to give some sense of organizational virtue. It was found some companies responded in a 'virtuous' manner, ensuring that as much thought as possible went into the changes that were made and that the response was far-reaching. Others on the other hand pulled away from such extensive measures, choosing

TABLE 4.2. Allocations of Organizations by Response Categories

Response Category	**Number of Organizations**
1. No contribution/No changes	1
2. Out of business	2
3. Virtuous	7
4. Blinkered Responses: Total	**18**
(a) Limited safety changes	6
(b) Legal changes only	12

instead to focus on changes that were obvious, and where these did not arise simply focusing on limiting legal liability. The final allocation of the organizations by response category is shown in Table 4.2.

The responses to death outlined in this Table have allowed a differentiation between virtue versus absence of virtue in behavioural terms. The task now is to ascertain the correlates to virtue in order to understand how to promote such virtuous behaviour in an ongoing sense. Is regulatory response, through punishment or persuasion, sufficient to nurturing an organizational climate which is supportive to ongoing virtuous action? Braithwaite and Ayres argue that this is indeed the case. Since they postulate all organizations have the capacity for virtue, always resorting to persuasion as a first response to non-compliance is ultimately the precondition maximizing virtue within a given context (Ayres and Braithwaite, 1992; Braithwaite, 1991, 1993). Following 'tit for tat' rules, which begin with the least intrusive techniques, it is argued virtue will be enhanced. If this is the case, the correlates to virtue need to be amenable to change through regulatory action. By inference then the emphasis is on organizational free will, organizations have ultimate power to decide whether they will or will not comply with regulations.

However, it can be argued that selection of effective techniques by regulators necessarily extends beyond behavioural criteria. Response to organizational behaviour after an event has occurred may simply be too little too late. Regulation is ultimately as much about **risk** of non-compliance, as it is about non-compliance itself. As Keith Hawkins points out:

> A great deal of social regulation, however, is concerned with risks, rather than acts, and as a result is pre-emptive, preventative, and proactive in character, rather than responsive and reactive. [Hawkins, 1990:457]

What this means is that regulation is as much about assessing future risk of disaster, as it is about responding when disaster has occurred. Regulation is thus a dynamic, proactive role. Nurturing corporate virtue has to work in the predictive and proactive sense, in order to capture this dimension of regulation, as much as in the instruction of how to respond once disaster (non-compliance) has struck. To do this it is important to be able to identify factors which are associated with virtue, or which determine the capacity for virtue. Unless one identifies the preconditions of virtue, it is very difficult to envisage a regulatory strategy which could engender virtue in the long term.

The following chapters will then systematically explore factors associated with virtue, following discussions in chapters 1 and 2 regarding possible candidates. Following the debates outlined in chapter 1 the first task will be to explore the possibility of correlating virtuous behaviour, measured here by response to the deaths, with 'techniques of neutralization' as suggested by Braithwaite (1989) and Cressey (1953, 1986). Next, chapter 6 will explore the influence of culture on virtue in light of the discussion of Weber (Bendix, 1977), Pettigrew (1985) and March and Simon (Perrow, 1986). The influence of structure is the subject of chapter 7, which assesses the influence of size and position in the contracting hierarchy on virtue, highlighting the possible contribution of a Marxist analysis to regulation, as well as those who argue for a strong role of structure in determining organizational behaviour (Berle and Means, 1967; Galbraith, 1973; Bendix, 1977; Weber, 1991). The role the law played in moulding response and virtue will then be addressed in chapter 8, with particular attention paid to the possible separation between the intention of law and law enforcement by the regulators, and the actual effect on the actions of the organizations (Macaulay, 1969; Weber, 1991: 216–21). Finally, since the evaluation of response took place five years after the deaths, chapter 9 will explore how organizations cope with the changing nature of capitalism and regulation.

5 Preliminary Responses: Coping or Denial

THIS chapter begins the task of identifying correlates to virtue in order to identify useful targets for the purposes of regulation. The subject here is to ascertain whether the rationalizations of key individuals within organizations are associated with the presence or absence of virtuous behaviour. In this way the chapter attempts to relate individual ethos to organizational behaviour through an examination of the techniques of neutralization, or rationalizations, employed by individual managers whose organizations were involved in the death. In particular the question concerns whether techniques of neutralization, that is the verbal means by which individuals attempt to deny or minimize their involvement in criminal activity (in this case their organizations' involvement in the death), are centrally involved in the absence of virtuous behaviour by organizations. This question is a pivotal one since it centres on the issue of whether virtue is primarily an individual, or organizational, construct. Is a virtuous organization simply an aggregate of virtuous individual actors? If this is so then a lack of virtue in terms of organizational behaviour should be reflected in the behaviour and rationalizations of individuals within the organization.

It has long been argued that techniques of neutralization are principally implicated in the behaviour of individuals engaged in criminal activity, in that they allow those individuals to distance themselves from taking responsibility for their actions. Sykes and Matza's (1976)[1] analysis, extending on from earlier work by Cressey (1953), asserted that rationalizations concerning responsibility for an event held the key to understanding how individuals could engage in harmful or criminal behaviour, while still identifying with the core value system in society:

> Social controls that serve to check or inhibit deviant motivational patterns are rendered inoperative [by internal rationalizations] . . . the delinquent both has his cake and eats it too, for he remains committed

[1] This work was first published in 1957.

to the dominant normative system and yet so qualifies its imperatives that violations are 'acceptable' if not 'right'. [Sykes and Matza, 1976:160]

This ability to engage in harmful behaviour while holding to the value norms of society would seem crucial in the area of white collar crime and organizational deviance. One of the defining characteristics of white collar criminals is their conflicting characteristics both on the one hand of upstanding citizen, in terms of their contribution to voluntary civic activities for example, and on the other criminal, displayed through the harm they caused through their illegal activities (Benson, 1984). Studies, both preceding and subsequent to Sykes and Matza, have explored the way rationalizations play a key role in white collar offending, for example in cases of embezzlement and fraud (Cressey, 1953, 1986; Geis, 1967; Benson, 1985).

The association of techniques of neutralization with behaviour present and future is also echoed in Braithwaite's (1989) work. He argues that non-virtuous actions by individuals within organizations occur where such individuals, and by extension their companies, have formed subcultures of resistance to norms society holds. These norms are expressed by rationalizations or 'techniques of neutralization' which allow key individuals within those organizations to distance themselves from what has occurred, while indicating no intention to alter such behaviour in the future (Braithwaite, 1989:127–8). The way key individuals within organizations rationalize about the harm they cause may then be a way to discriminate between those organizations which are virtuous, and those which are not.

The problem of identification of virtue in this chapter can be explored by using the data to ascertain if the rationalizations by managers and other key individuals involved in the death correlated to the actual responses undertaken by their organizations. The question is whether there were corporate personalities which could be used to identify corporate virtue or the opposite, corporate malevolence. This would mean that the nature of their rationalizations concerning the death, and the contribution of the company, could discriminate between a 'virtuous' and 'non-virtuous' response. In particular identification of non-virtue, or malevolence, is important since the consequences of failing to identify such organizations, which have a high probability of causing future harm, would be seen as regulatory failure.

The tentative proposal here concerning the identification of virtue is that the virtuous respondents in the data accepted responsibility for what happened which spurred them to their characteristic response, while the others denied responsibility, which justified to them their blinkered stance. If this was the case individual rationalizations about the harm which results from organizational activity may then help the identification of corporate virtue, or ethos, and hold the key to an ongoing reduction in corporate harm. In order to do this though the rationalizations about the harm need to help distinguish between categories of responses. Rationalizations must relate to actual behaviour.

Techniques of Neutralization

Turning to the data it can be shown that the individuals interviewed did attempt to distance themselves from events surrounding the deaths. Initial review of the responses revealed rationalizations about individual involvement which closely resembled some of the 'techniques of neutralization' outlined by Sykes and Matza. In particular two features of Sykes and Matza's descriptions of those techniques were reflected in the data, namely the denial of responsibility and the denial of the victim.

In their description of the denial of responsibility, Sykes and Matza talk about the delinquent as seeing the event as outside their control, as an 'accident' which negates their personal involvement, 'in effect the delinquent approaches a "billiard ball" conception of himself in which he sees himself as hopelessly propelled into new situations' (1976:161). This description of the billiard ball is very apt to the present data. A common conceptualization of the death was that it was somehow preordained, a result of forces beyond individual control. The architect of Leafytown Council illustrates the rationalization (or neutralization) of denial of responsibility due to the inevitability of the event well:

'It seems to me that this accident was almost bound to happen because of the number of things that were happening, which people were assuming it wouldn't happen. The builder wasn't on site all the time because he had gone off to get the dumpie level; the crane which had arrived on site was oversized and they talked of sending it away; but they said no, this one's on site so we'll use it, and it had the extra long boom. You know it just sort of seemed ordained [that] it was going to happen because it seemed to have a lot of additive themes. I don't know if this is true of many accidents but I suspect it is'.

Such rationalizations in this case lead to the death taking on an unreal quality and limiting the effect it had on the building project. When asked about the effect of the death on morale on the site the architect replied: '[there was] not a lot, I hate to say there should have been some, but I don't think there was a lot . . . the subbies changed and the building went on'.

The second example of a technique of neutralization in the data is the analysis of the role of the victim. Sykes and Matza point to the denial of the victim as being a technique which allows the delinquent to excuse his or her behaviour. By the denial of the victim they mean either denial that there is harm to the victim (for example tax evasion, where the government is not seen to 'hurt') or that the victim somehow asked for it (i.e. they were unreasonably provoked). Here the technique is not so much denial of harm to the victim, as this directly threatens the normative value of preventing future harm, but another familiar theme of **blaming** the victim for what occurred. This technique of blaming the victim should not surprise us, since it is a common theme found in health and safety literature (Reasons, Ross and Patterson, 1981; Tombs, 1991; Nichols, 1994; Quinlan and Bohle, 1991). If the death can be attributed, at least in part, to the deceased it reduces the emotional pressure on others in the company to accept responsibility. The following is a quote from the manager of Bigmill which shows the shifting of blame onto the worker who died:

'I feel for that job he might not have been the right person, [or] had the right attitude. . . . There are certain people who can do certain jobs and they react quicker to other people. He sort of didn't react as quick as a normal person, fine worker and that, but his reactions were just a little bit slower than the average person. Well that's my interpretation.'

This explanation for the cause of the death lying with the dead worker provided for easy solution in terms of preventing future harm. Once the problem was identified with the individual worker, the logical response becomes one of picking a more suitable worker. The owner of Adams Logging saw his worker who died as contributing to his own death and so looked to more careful selection of workers as the solution: 'We look at who we employ and who we don't employ more carefully . . . The guy in my opinion wasn't as experienced as what he was supposed to be and he tended to rush'.

A more graphic illustration of the process of neutralization and projecting blame onto the individual comes from a discussion with a safety officer of Bigland over the death of a bulldozer driver. Although occurring outside of 1987 this case illustrates the potential consequences of such neutralizations. Neutralization and projecting blame can lie behind the organization's lack of commitment to change, a classic blinkered (non-virtuous) response:

'. . . some time ago one of our plant drivers was killed. It was a few years ago, and there tends to be a lot of hiding that goes on. He had been around a long time and was very popular. It was a great shock to everyone that he was killed. He was known by a lot of people. But I'd have to say nothing has really changed. There is a hiding factor, someone made a mistake and they feel guilty, they don't say anything. There was a report that pointed out a lot of errors but it was just swept under the desk, nothing really changed. The inquest didn't make any difference, nothing came out of it. He jumped out of a grader, he was not wearing a seat-belt and got crushed by the ROPS [roll over protection].

Everyone latched onto the fact that he was not wearing a seat-belt, but everyone knew there were so many other factors; such as the operator training of the machinery. He had been driving a long time but only on the one machine. One week before he was killed he was swapped to a new machine. He was given no training on this machine. He followed procedures that were quite safe on the machine he was used to driving but made this one overbalance. No one wore seat-belts. It was just a culture that had built up, and the managers knew, but they did nothing about it. The seat-belts were just muddy in the back of the seat. It was easy to blame that because the only one you could blame then was the victim. So the only improvement that was made was an increased awareness and campaign about the use of seat-belts, so now they are used a lot more. The issue was one of using seat-belts.'

The data reveals then, that there are indeed identifiable techniques of neutralization operating which allow individuals to deny or minimize their own (or their organizations') contribution to the death. Twenty out of the twenty-seven individuals made 'neutralizing' statements. These rationalizations served the same purpose as Sykes and Matza's techniques of neutralization in that they allowed the individuals to deny responsibility, either on behalf of themselves or their organizations. Through seeing the deaths as inevitable and projecting blame on the victim individuals distanced themselves from the event, which as the last quote illustrates, appears to bode ill for organizational virtue.

Reviewing the Link between Techniques of Neutralization and Response: The Need for Broader Explanations

Reviewing responses, though, it is clear that the need to 'explain away' the death as somehow inevitable was widespread and associated with **both** blinkered and virtuous respondents. Indeed six of the seven 'virtuous' respondents employed neutralizing statements at some time during the interview. What this shows then is that some other explanation for such statements is necessary, since they are not directly associated with the virtue or otherwise of the response. To do this we need to look to the emotional issues surrounding the deaths.

The emotional impact the deaths had on individuals who were closely involved holds a possible key to an alternative explanation for the rationalizations above. At the most extreme the trauma on those involved in the death could itself be life threatening. The crane driver from Service Cranes, who swung the boom which hit overhead power lines killing a rigger, experienced considerable ongoing trauma from his involvement in the death. The director of the company explained the severity of the psychological impact on his employee: 'The driver took it pretty hard and we spent most of our time trying to pep him up, he wanted to kill himself and all sorts of things . . . '.

The deaths stirred considerable emotion and the overwhelming motivation for the changes made in response to the death, whether virtuous or blinkered, was stated in terms of the desire to prevent further harm, and to protect the safety of the workers. This was exemplified by comments such as, 'we don't want it to happen again', 'we like to look after the safety of our workers', and 'you don't like people getting killed or hurt'. The prevention of future loss of life by the changes made was paramount. The site manager at Arcade shows the centrality and finality of death in the response: 'I think my main reason [for the changes] was the thing just not happening again. Loss of life is loss of life'. The emotional impact of the death lingered. For some the actual site of the tragedy reawakened sentiments associated with the event, a plumber stating 'It's very sad to go into that particular area of the factory'.

There was a general feeling of repulsion at another death, particularly if the manager or owner saw themselves as part of the cause of future deaths. Feeling responsible for the death would have meant considerable personal anguish. The owner of Reids Plumbing illustrates the connection between causing the death and repugnance at the consequences this could bring:

'. . . Nobody wants anyone to get killed, not even injured. Because if someone gets really badly injured on a job, I mean, it could ruin your company, it could ruin your business and ruin other people's lives. It's something you have to live with if you caused it . . .'

While there are clear indications then of individuals construing the death as inevitable or the victim's fault, the emotions involved in the deaths point to complicating features associated with labelling these rationalizations as simply 'techniques of neutralization' whose primary aim is to enable a denial of responsibility and a need to change. The emotional trauma for those involved in the deaths held considerable psychological threat to the well-being of the individual. The threat was particularly acute if the individual perceived themselves as somehow responsible. The crane driver who contemplated suicide above had been one of a number not willing to move the crane which hit overhead power lines, and as a consequence of feeling responsible had to shoulder much of the pain and guilt himself. It is not surprising then that many sought to avoid such feelings of pain and guilt. The techniques of neutralization allows this avoidance, and so may be central to enabling the individual to cope with the death.

Techniques of Neutralization or Individual Coping Strategies?

In light of this a possibility arises that perhaps the rationalizations outlined above are not entirely explained by construing them as 'techniques of neutralization'. Rather, they may instead reflect coping strategies. This is supported by the psychological literature which points to the common tendency to externalize responsibility for catastrophic events. Rather than viewing this in a negative light as a rationalization or neutralization, this literature sees the tendency to distance oneself from blame as a healthy response, involving transformation of an event of high anxiety and threat, into one more harmless where the stress of the event is able to dissipate (Fenichel, 1946; Kroeber, 1969).

A good illustration of interpreting such rationalizations as coping mechanisms is shown by the project manager of Resource Mining, a virtuous respondent. Here the manager uses the metaphor of a Greek tragedy to illustrate the apparent destined inevitability of the death, a classic neutralization technique:

'It's like a Greek tragedy when you read it. The number of screws that were in there, the number that had just got by chance the wrong side of the Australian design equivalent and some of them had bottomed and actually weren't in . . . Its a bit like a sort of poker machine—99 times out of 100 you don't get the four apples in a row, and on this occasion up they come and you keep going on down the track.'

This manager, however, was also at pains to point out the human trauma associated with the dredger collapse:

'The result here of the accident was the cost of a life . . . The deceased had family obligations—a couple of kids, family obligations. . . . One of the supervisors has effectively left the workforce with very serious back injuries (due to the collapse). I think he was in his upper 20s, early 30s, and he has been taken right out of the workforce due to the severity of the back injury . . . he desperately wanted to work.'

Here then there was certainly no denial of the impact the accident had on those involved. Acceptance of harm stimulates the need for soul-searching, and leads to explanations which extend beyond human agency. Such explanations can absolve the individual actor from guilt, a guilt which is highly threatening to an individual's well-being (Raphael, 1993). One way, as illustrated by the first quote, is to point to the inevitability of the death which occurred.

There were other ways in which emotions were central to the aftermath of the deaths. The emotional consequences of the death did not only lead to the need for individuals to distance themselves from responsibility for the death. The emotional stress of such a traumatic common experience could bring people closer together. In some cases those who died were friends, as was the case in the death of the rigger at the Nagel construction site. The owner of Daytons (rigging) explained the emotional pull of common experience at the time of the death:

'It brought people together actually that day because he was not just working for us, he was a good friend of ours . . . We knew him personally not just at work. I've known him for a very long time.'

Even where there were no friendships, the common experience coupled with mutual respect between those on site could break down traditional worksite loyalties, as the project manager at Haddons explained:

'At the time of this particular incident I had one [union] organizer who came to my house personally and said "Are you alright? Can we help you?" I said "No I'm OK." He said "OK fine, I will see you tomorrow in a different vein." That was the [personal] level which I had with the organizer.'

The heightened emotions surrounding the event also had the potential to flare into considerable conflict between management and workers in the longer term. Conflict could stem, for example, from the traditional one-day stoppage after all fatalities which unions called. Unless management accepted the need for this stoppage, which workers saw as a way to show solidarity with their dead comrade, the trust between management and workers could be lost. Management acceptance of the need for unions to show solidarity (although not actual support) was necessary for management to retain trust with the workers.

In addition, the anxiety surrounding the death could spill over into other work processes, also requiring an empathetic response. The project manager of Haddons indicated the importance of taking account of emotional issues when recovering from such incidents:

'Under normal circumstances we would have said no [to the workers' request to recheck a piece of equipment soon after the fatality]. But when you consider the human emotion involved at the time and how people would have felt; to gain people's confidence back in those type of activities, it is far wiser to show them, yes you are open and receptive to what they are saying . . .'

While both virtuous and blinkered respondents engaged in techniques of neutralization, the rebuilding of both trust and credibility by empathy with workers appeared to be a distinctive feature of the virtuous response. Credibility could be gained by managers involved in a virtuous response through their involvement in the death, particularly if they took an active role in the aftermath:

'[T]here was a lot of emotional shock associated with it [the death] because of the way the fatality occurred. I think I gained a bit of credibility because I had to clear up the mess, this happened right in the middle of the workplace.'

This increased credibility of the manager could be used to encourage support for a virtuous response and lend weight to these particular managers' subsequent directives, 'they [the workers] recognize because of the dealings I went through at the time that if I say something I mean it, and very rarely that it doesn't occur'. This was particularly important in cases where what was necessary was re-emphasizing existing safety procedures which had over time become bypassed or ignored.

There were positive side-effects to this empathetic response by management. Individual managers involved in the death who used their experiences to work through the trauma could be used as a resource by others in the company. In the case of Haddons, the manager involved in the dredger collapse was in a position to use his experience of the death to assist others, a role the company allowed him to fulfil:

'Just because I have been through it people use me as a reference, so I don't like digging it up all the time, but that is the way it happens. You learn from experience unfortunately. It has been traumatic, but at the same time it was a personal growth period for me; and then that the company has allowed me to be available for other people, if they wish to phone up they do.'

It is important, however, not to overstate this positive outcome. Such positive features need to be contrasted with the devastation of others, also responding in a virtuous manner. The trauma could be overwhelming for some and the long term holding little relief, particularly if they had been seen to directly contribute to the death, as exemplified by the suicidal feelings of the crane driver of Service Cranes shown above.

Cognizance of emotion is central to understanding individual behaviour and reaction to harm arising out of organizational activity. In light of this, the overall impression from the emotional issues surrounding the deaths, and the consequent rationalizations, is that the explanation of coping fits the data better than the attempt to trace particular rationalizations or techniques of neutralization with particular responses. In light of the devastation possible from experiencing a death at close hand it is essential people find a way to cope with the trauma to be able to continue living. Inability to cope with such trauma leads to a plethora of long-term consequences (Raphael, 1993), suicide being one of those possibilities. The various ways all individuals, from both virtuous and blinkered respondents, sought to limit their control over the events that occurred could indicate that while such rationalizations did indeed bear the hallmarks of techniques of neutralization, they may also be part of a coping response of both management and workers.

Distancing and Denial: Preliminary Conclusions

What the data have illustrated is that rationalizations which allowed individuals to distance themselves from the death extended beyond 'techniques of neutralization' where the sole outcome is denial of the need to respond. The ubiquitousness of the use of techniques of neutralization by respondents, coupled with the obvious trauma some underwent as a result of the fatality, leads the techniques at this level to be seen rather as a coping mechanism rather than simply a rationalization in order to deny responsibility. For regulatory theory, then, the task of identification of virtue is possibly going to be more complex than simply viewing the rationalizations of key individuals in the organization.

However, it can be seen that the coping mechanisms expressed by individuals with the subsequent distancing from responsibility for the death which these entail, hold potentially damaging long-term consequences for the organization in terms of ongoing virtue. The rationalizations used appear at times callous, with the possibility that such sentiments could form the basis of the underlying philosophy for the organization. Coping with tragedy in the context of health and safety involving ongoing threats to human life is a two-edged sword, with the possibility of distancing oneself and the company from the death so completely that individual managers are persuaded that either the incident was inevitable and therefore nothing could have prevented it, or the culpability of another organization exonerates them from any need to act. While certain 'techniques of coping' might be beneficial for the individual concerned, they raise thorny issues when applied to organizations which need to prevent future tragedy. In order to respond in a virtuous manner the organization has to combat the distancing 'impulse' present in the coping response, and rebut the 'organizational distancing' which leads to a blinkered response. The question now becomes how did the virtuous respondents avert the organizational distancing process? How did the denial of individual responsibility, albeit to aid coping with the death, present in the individual responses of the managers of these companies translate into acceptance of organizational need to make comprehensive attempts to ensure the ongoing safety of workers? This suggests that it is organizational attributes, rather than those of the individual, which hold the key to virtue.

6 Business Cultures: Consensus and Conflict

THIS chapter examines the possibility that different organizational cultures lay behind the two responses; the virtuous and blinkered. Rather than viewing the responses as arising out of individual attributes, such as techniques of neutralization proposed in the previous chapter, here the focus is on organizational attributes, in particular organizational culture. The proposition explored here is that organizational culture is that element which either combats, or exacerbates, the 'distancing' impulse evident in the coping response or 'techniques of neutralization' analysed in chapter 5.

This chapter draws on relevant literature which assists in outlining possible elements of a virtuous culture, in contrast to a culture which lacks virtue, and then explores evidence for the existence of such cultures through the data. Here virtue is seen primarily as a quality of organizations, not individuals. Organizational level constructs are understood as qualitatively different to individual actions. Organizational behaviour is primarily directed by organizational goals, such as survival, profitability and other measures of success, which build upon, and alter, individual decision making (Weber, 1991:196–8; Vaughan, 1982; Morgan, 1986; Perrow, 1986; Hassard and Pym, 1990; Reed, 1992; Sitkin and Bies, 1994a). Organizations mould individual decision making by providing the bounds of rationality, or normative framework, which form the premises behind individual decision making (Pettigrew, 1985; March and Simon, in Perrow, 1986). In this way the organization, or more specifically the organizational culture, may influence individual action in an unobtrusive and indirect manner by manipulating premises and providing normative frameworks, rather than any direct authoritarian control from above.

It is important to recognize that the analyses of ethical organizations conflict in some respects with analyses of virtue. In particular, chapter 4 pointed to the possible conflict between individual virtue, and organizational or institutional imperatives.

While taking seriously the possibility of virtue existing at an organizational level, it is necessary to be alert to the possibility of conflict between virtuous individuals such as safety managers, and organizational culture. The stresses caused by conflict between individual and organization though, do not preclude the possibility that organizational level constructs mould the actions and beliefs of individuals in directions that are more, or less, harmful.

At an organizational level then, how might a virtuous culture differ from one lacking in virtue? Some clues to the characteristics of a virtuous culture may be gained through the ethics literature. Discussions within this literature point to the need for reflectiveness within an organization, where long-term concerns drive short-term action rather than the other way around (Cartwright, 1990). Secondly, ethical organizations are seen as transparent and accountable, willing and able to share problems and decisions with key others, such as interested third parties (for example unions and regulators) (Gray, 1990). Perhaps crucially the business literature on ethics (as opposed to the academic literature) looks at the ethical or virtuous organization as one which can blend business and social goals, i.e. 'harmonize' their two aims (Cartwright, 1990; Leroy, 1992). In light of this a virtuous culture would be one which seeks to harmonize and 'blend' the various demands it faces, rather than one which dichotomizes and forces choice. The harmonizing principle may then be the one which forms a major premise behind decision making.

To a certain extent such a 'harmonizing' culture fits certain parameters which have been central to a strong safety focus, and to the professional ideology of safety management. In particular those commenting in the area of safety highlight the need for adequate communication (which would also increase accountability) (Braithwaite, 1985; Grabosky and Sutton, 1989). Secondly, safety focused cultures can be seen to be advanced by inclusion of worker representatives (Biggins, Phillips and O'Sullivan, 1991), which would in turn increase transparency and accountability of management. Further, safe cultures are seen as those which steer away from 'blaming the victim' approaches to safety, that is where the individual injured shoulders the predominant responsibility for his or her own injuries (Tombs, 1991; Nichols, 1994). Safety is encouraged by a 'systems' approach which integrates safety into the whole enterprise, not as a marginalized and isolated element located within a single department (Braithwaite, 1985:65–71; Mathews, 1985; Coulton, McCulloch and Noble, 1990). Under the strong safety focus illustrated by adherence to the above principles, safety professionals argue, success is enhanced (Rees, 1988:93).

How then might these various elements be explored through the data? The way chosen was to explore the rationalizations which surrounded the death and its aftermath. The premises which underpinned the rationalizations were assumed to reflect the cultural values of the organization, values which influenced the decisions made concerning response to the death. Further, it was hypothesized that such rationalizations could be ordered according to a harmonizing or dichotomizing principle, reflecting either a virtuous culture, or one lacking in virtue. Key attitudes within the work context were analysed (such as attitude to the role of the manager, attitude of the manager to the worker) as well as rationalization on relationships within the organizations, and between the organization and other agencies (for example, relationship between the organization and the union, or between the organization and the regulator), in the data. The key element differentiating the two cultures was that the virtuous culture would see safety as integral to organizational activity, while the culture lacking in virtue would tend to push safety into the background in order to focus on short-term demands. A virtuous culture would then see the role of the manager as one of harmonizing and integrating demands and would view workers as a positive resource in maintaining safety. The emphasis would be away from the workers as totally responsible for their own safety to a primary focus on the company's responsibility, with the workers' responsibility ancillary to that primary responsibility. Further, close co-operation with bodies inside and outside the organizational structure would be essential to maintaining safety, so relationships with worker representatives, such as unions, would be good. Regulatory bodies would be seen as a resource rather than a threat. Finally, since all the deaths took place within multiple employer worksites, it would be anticipated that a virtuous culture would emphasize the responsibility of a contractor for the subcontractor's employees.

A culture lacking in virtue would in contrast dichotomize choice and focus on short-term demands of the organization which would marginalize issues such as safety. Managers would be keenly aware that short-term goals and 'getting the job done' were paramount considerations. Workers would be seen to be the major cause of injury and death, with carelessness and forgetfulness seen as the predominant reason for incidents occurring. There would tend to be an 'us and them attitude' which would breed suspicion of those outside the workplace; unions would be seen as interfering and self-interested, and regulators would be kept at bay. Finally, with the emphasis on individual responsibility within such a culture each organization and each employee would be seen to be responsible for themselves. The primary responsibility for the subcontractor's employees would lie with the subcontractor and the employees, not extend to any other party on the site. The essence of the two cultures is shown in Table 6.1.

It was hypothesized that there would be two distinct 'sets' of rationalizations or assumptions which were internally consistent (i.e. the way x 'culture' perceived the role of the union and its relationship to it was the same for all categories of all those who adhered to x 'culture'). It was also important to establish that the sets were mutually exclusive (i.e. the way x 'culture' viewed the role of the union and its relationship to it was separate from y 'culture').[1]

Cultural Differences and Organizational 'Success'

By looking at these attitudes and relationships in the data it was possible tentatively to develop two different cultures: the virtuous and the blinkered, which did indeed reflect the attributes in a fashion similar to that outlined in Table 6.1. This section explores in detail these characteristics. A secondary purpose in doing so is to reveal the robustness of such cultures when the organization

[1] It is important to remember at this point that the data is concerned with the rationalizations that underscored actual responses. This was crucial in the interviews, as without reference to any specific event, the interviews could largely have revolved around a decontextualized reconstruction of the principles of safety management, since the correlation between these principles and the virtuous culture was very close. The research might have told us little more than what could be gleaned from professional safety association pamphlets. During the interview process I was aware of the need to keep the discussion grounded in concrete examples, which included the death under discussion, but ranged beyond this to other illustrative examples in the interviewees' workplace.

TABLE 6.1. Cultural Attributes Concerning Managers' Attitudes, Roles and Relationships

	'Harmonizing'	**'Dichotomizing'**
Attitude to success	*Focused on bringing all aspects of business together*	*Focused on placing priorities on certain aspects of business*
Role of a good manager	*A good manager makes a success of all aspects of business including safety*	*A good manager is the one who gets the job done, which involves setting priorities which may conflict with safety*
View of workers' attitude to safety	*Worker Participation in safety is central*	*Workers push safety to the background so accidents will always happen*
Attitude to and relationship with unions	*Unions have a legitimate role in representing workers, the relationship is a good one*	*Unions are an unwarranted intrusion on business, there is conflict in the relationship*
Attitude to relationship with regulator	*A close relationship with the regulator is a good thing*	*It is best to keep a distance from regulators*
Attitude to safety of subcontractors' employees	*Primary responsibility for the safety of subcontractors' employees lies with the major contractor*	*Primary responsibility lies with the subcontractor and the individual concerned*

is challenged with circumstances which do not accord with the overall ethos.

There were then fundamental differences in attitude in all areas which constituted the two different cultures. The different aspects of the two cultures of the virtuous and blinkered can be conceptualized as various manifestations of an underlying exclusive or inclusive logic. Attitudes of what constitutes a good manager, for example, illustrates this well. Attitudes varied markedly between the two cultures: the virtuous saw all aspects of the manager's concerns coming together, consistent with their inclusive logic, whereas the blinkered culture saw the manager as having to place a priority on 'getting the job done' over all other interests, including that of safety.

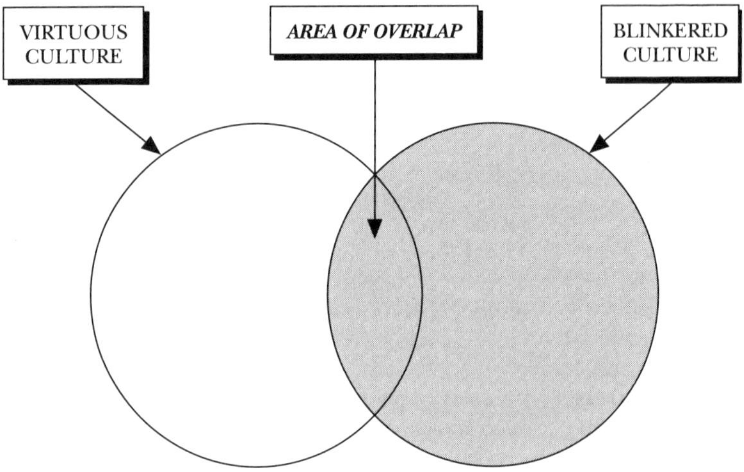

FIG. 6.1. Diagrammatical Representation of Relationship between Cultures

However, while there were clear differences reflected in the data between the two cultures, there was also some overlap. This is conceptualized in Figure 6.1. This overlap was true of all dimensions except attitudes to the role of the manager. An example of such overlap is in the view of the safety attitude of the worker. Both cultures identified a tendency for workers to put safety in the back of their minds as they concentrated on their daily tasks as a problem for safety. This tendency to put safety to one side, however, was viewed by the virtuous culture as a constant challenge which needed constant vigilance and consciousness raising about the need to be aware of safety issues. On the other hand the blinkered culture saw the tendency as inevitable with the resulting notion 'accidents will happen'. The harmonizing imperative as outlined by Leroy (1992) is also shown here with the logic of the virtuous culture inclusive, while the blinkered culture reveals an 'either/or' logic. To maintain inclusiveness, the virtuous culture sought to **combine** safety concerns with other business concerns with a characteristic 'win—win' reasoning (Gray, 1990). The tendency to put safety in the background cannot be seen as 'inevitable' otherwise the whole culture is constantly frustrated by the attempt to achieve the impossible.

Before turning to the detail of each area a final point to note is that all areas in Table 6.1 contained various complexities which also had the potential to undermine the overall coherence of the underlying organizational ideology if they were not addressed. These complexities largely threatened the integrity of the harmonizing logic underpinning the virtuous culture as they introduced conflicts in the workplace which were not consistent with a win—win solution promoted. As such they illustrate the tensions, which are emphasized by MacIntyre and Weber among others, between values, including virtuous ones, and organizational imperatives. These complexities could be brought about by various dynamics internal or external to the organization, such as worksite or organizational structure or the particular context of the work. For example, one organization with a virtuous culture also paid piece-rates to their workers. Key personnel, such as the safety officer, identified piece-rates as setting up a dynamic which ran counter to worker attitude of care towards safety which they were ultimately trying to engender. Piece-rates encouraged workers to take risks by cutting corners in order to save the company time and make more money. In this case the workers **either** made more money, **or** could work safely, hardly a win—win scenario.

The Role of the Managers

Attitudes towards the role of the manager and the concept of effective management provide a clear illustration of the differences between the two cultures; the blinkered culture with its exclusive either/or reasoning, and the virtuous culture with its inclusive logic. While a blinkered approach saw management as a focus on 'getting the job done', those individual respondents who subscribed to a virtuous view of organizational goals often spoke of 'good' and 'poor' managers in terms of their ability or inability to successfully combine all their roles.

The blinkered perspective was clear that the primary aim was 'to get the job done' whatever that was perceived to be. In reality this meant putting a priority on that aspect of the work that produced a profit, or reduced costs. The owner of Reids Plumbing illustrates the way that managers, particularly those with a 'hands on' role, such as site managers and foremen, put a priority on getting the job done, even if this means taking short cuts:

> 'The foreman he's there to make sure the job goes as smoothly, as quickly and as safely as possible. But ultimately his main aim is to make money. The job has to be done on time and up to schedule, the majority will allow people to take short cuts within reason.'

In some cases this meant turning a blind eye to unsafe work practices, which was made easier where there were natural difficulties in supervision, such as in logging. The owner of Adams Logging corrected his loggers when they were working in an unsafe manner, but for much of the time they were left alone to get on with the job:

> 'The men have got a job to do and they set out to do it . . . if I don't think they are doing it the safe way then I will tell them. Very rarely if I say, "do this" will they say, "No it is not safe enough", because it is not a closely supervised occupation. That's how it happens.'

Some managers were more aggressive in terms of the emphasis on getting the job done. The project manager at Arcade was one such manager, illustrated by his following characteristic comment: '[If] we want to do something—let's do it, the market is there today—go for it'. This 'do or die' attitude could then push other issues into the background, as they would not be perceived as pressing, but rather as mundane. The project manager at Arcade again illustrates how safety in such an environment becomes a secondary consideration of the manager's job, both in meetings and in practice:

> 'It [safety] really wasn't on the agenda. It was on the [written] agenda at meetings, but it wasn't a priority . . . I'd leave it up to the people on site to do . . . once the decision was made I left it up to them. I'd look and see if it was done or not, and if it wasn't I would question it. But I wouldn't be involved in it day by day, it wasn't one of my priorities.'

The virtuous culture stands in contrast to this. The situation described above would indicate poor management to this cultural standpoint; here the 'good' manager was one who managed the social goals of the organization (such as safety, environmental issues and a consensus approach to industrial relations) in tandem with 'hard nosed' business concerns of time, money and productivity. These 'good' managers understood that the social goals were good for business. The project manager at Haddons pointed to the accountability each project manager had for each of their projects:

'He is responsible for the whole project and he reports on a monthly basis: on the industrial relations scene, and the safety scene, as well as the commercial scene, and the costing scene. . . . If it is going off the wheels in any area the divisional manager will say, "I want to see you about this and this, we've got a problem here, what can we do about it?" '

The accountability of each area was translated into a monetary bonus for managers in Resource Mining. Managers in this organization were seen as responsible for a number of key areas, failure to come up to standard in any one area meant losing the bonus:

'Each manager is responsible for seven or eight key result areas: one is production, another is cost, another is health and safety, and another would be industrial relations. . . . In more senior areas we have payment by results, someone whose performance in health and safety was not good, would not be able to get a bonus . . . each area is interrelated. It would be hard to see someone with a bad health and safety record not also having a bad industrial relations record, and probably having production problems. They are not mutually exclusive.'

Poor management according to the virtuous view resulted in a splintering of these various aims with a mentality which cut corners (illustrated by the blinkered approach above), which was seen as ultimately counter-productive using the virtuous logic. Proponents of the virtuous logic, such as the safety officer of Mightysteel, asserted that this did not only result in a lack of safety, but a degeneration of other aspects of management such as a conflictual approach to industrial relations and a lax management of contractors. Speaking of a manager with a conflict style he stated: 'We weren't happy with what was going on, before I came here there were a lot of short cuts, a lot of sweetheart deals were being made . . .'. When the manager concerned was interviewed he emphasized the role of the manager being one with a primary focus of 'getting the job done', a blinkered logic, which inherently places a priority on immediate demands rather than an overall view.

From a virtuous view there could be poor managers within a large organization and it was these managers who prevented the good policies of the owners or directors of the organization from being put into practice, by their prioritization of short-term goals. However, it was still the responsibility of the organization to educate those managers, or replace them. The safety officer of Mightysteel acknowledged the existence of poor managers in the factory: 'The family is committed [to safety], some of the managers aren't but the family is very committed'. Aidans concurred with this and was adamant about the need to keep educating to persuade managers about the advantages of safety to success:

> 'I don't see there can be any justification for short-term gain, that is the main argument I have had with engineers for donkey's years. . . . I have got engineering qualifications and I can incorporate safety into the design.'

As with all the concerns which illustrated the divergent cultures there were complexities. In this case complexities arose in conceptions of the role of the manager, when the role and aims of the individual manager were contrasted with organizational aims, stated or unstated. The focus here is on **organizational** culture, not the **individual** character of the managers. Managers are perceptive when it comes to identifying the organization's key priorities (Mintzberg, 1990). For example top management within an organization could espouse a virtuous logic, yet demand such a multiplicity of roles from a manager so that a virtuous approach to their work was untenable. An illustration here is the company Roadtech. Two managers from Roadtech were interviewed, and one clearly espoused the virtuous inclusive philosophy, the other was less sure due to the multiplicity of roles demanded of him by the organization. This manager stated: 'I have two hats, one is safety the other is engineering . . . but I can't do half a job'. In such a situation a common solution is to respond to the most pressing demand and adopt a blinkered logic.

With respect to the attitude towards the role of the manager then, the two cultural perspectives had a fundamentally different logic. For the blinkered culture the role of the manager was to get the job done, for the virtuous culture the role included a harmonization of multiple roles which, when combined, were perceived to enhance the organization's success.

Management Perspective on Workers' 'Attitude' to Safety and the Promotion of a Safety Culture

The cultures illustrated clear differences in their perception of workers' attitude to safety. The blinkered approach saw worker complacency about safety as inevitable, and as a consequence accepted that 'accidents will happen'. It was simply not feasible according to this cultural perspective to avoid all accidents as workers would always forget about safety in their focus on getting the job done. This link between getting the job done, safety being pushed to the background and the inevitability of accidents is well illustrated by the project manager at Arcade:

'They are not conscious about it until something occurs. The number one priority is getting the job done. As far as health and safety [is concerned] it is something secondary, nobody pays attention to it until something happens. Let's say a carpenter is stripping off the formwork of a job, he has taken the timber off and its got nails in it. He rips it off and throws it on the ground, not thinking there are nails sticking out and someone will walk through and step on the nail. If someone steps on it it's, "Oh shit, sorry mate", then he leaves what he is doing and clears it up. Barricading, the machine goes in to excavate a hole. The hole is usually left open till the end of the day before it is barricaded off, instead of barricading it off straight away. It's left without barricades over night although they have been told, "Before you go home that needs to be barricaded off". Its time to go home, "see you later", you know. That's how it goes . . . On everyone's mind is to get the job done. Nobody thinks about the safety factor until something happens . . . something happens and rears its ugly head, then he acts on it.'

In contrast the virtuous culture saw this 'apathy' as something to be fought and overcome; the goal was to raise the consciousness of individual workers concerning safety as part of a constant battle, illustrated here by the manager of Bigmill: 'Management has got to put into the worker that they must be thinking safety all the time.' The virtuous culture saw an individual worker's tendency to push safety to one side as a problem for safety. Despite the existence of safety measures and procedures, the safety officer of Mightysteel lamented about the tendency for workers to take short cuts: 'We've got these terrific procedures, sometimes people take short cuts. My biggest problem is making sure people abide by them [safety rules].'

Also seen as a problem for the organizations with a virtuous approach was the observation by managers of how familiarity could lead to the feeling of invulnerability on the part of the worker with the consequent risk taking and a diminishing awareness of safety. The manager of Bigmill illustrated a virtuous approach in describing the problem of familiarity:

'What I find is that people get too familiar with the job that they are doing. My attitude is when they first start on the machine, say a saw, and they think 3 feet is as close as they should get to that saw, that is where they should stay for ever and a day. But people as they work on constantly think, yes I can get a bit closer . . . People just get too familiar, and just take everything for granted.'

The difference between the two cultures is further illustrated in the attitude towards workers' use or lack of use of safety equipment. Getting workers to use safety equipment was cited as a problem common to both cultures. However, lack of use was seen as inevitable by the blinkered culture, while the virtuous culture saw it as a battle to be won. The following quote from a blinkered culture found at Reids Plumbing illustrates the resignation towards the use of hard hats:

'We enforce that they wear boots and we enforce that they wear protective clothing and so on; but the hats are a hard thing to get people to wear . . . I don't know, I suppose it's like kids, they feel embarrassed if they wear a helmet. On a building site we are supposed to wear helmets . . . we've got people working above us with spanners and hammers. But the majority of people won't wear a hat, it feels out of place, or poor design or something . . . They've all got them in their trucks.'

The following quote from the safety officer of International Paper illustrates a consensus approach on the same problem. In this case the reluctance to wear hats was related to a 'macho' image that workers had, but this was seen as an attitude to be changed rather than an inevitability:

'First complaint is that they [hard hats] were too hot, well they are no hotter than a beanie; or too heavy or all this sort of thing. But deep down its the he-man image, I'm the big tough bushman. I mean its only in the last couple of years that I have had any luck at all getting bush workers to wear industrial gloves, Oh no they have to have big gnarly hands. You will find that is really prevalent outside our own workforce. I had a student who came once. She went up to the pubs and met the guys and saw their hands without fingers and so on, and they were bragging about it, which is crazy. It has taken me years and years, all these years to knock that dumb thinking out of them, and the dumb thinking will continue till someone gets out there and starts knocking it out of them.'

The consciousness raising demanded by a virtuous ideology to combat the tendency for workers to put safety to one side took many forms, with some focusing on behavioural criteria—as the project manager of Resource Mining stated: 'I say [during training] "Listen I can't make you like Collingwood supporters but I can certainly stop you thumping them." ' Others used creative ways in attempts to also capture the minds and imaginations of their employees. For example, Haddons held periodic competitions to promote safety which resulted in safety videos and safety orientated T-shirt logos.

Importantly the virtuous ideology also recognized limitations to an emphasis on changing attitudes and behaviour in improving safety, as disasters could occur from a minor lapse in concentration. While this approach promoted the importance of training and consciousness raising they were not naïve in this endeavour:

'[A]ll it is is a minute of not concentrating—that is all it took. That fellow down there he had his belt on yet he had a roof purlin which wasn't long enough, so he tied it up with a bit of wire . . . He forgot that he tied it up with wire and he stepped on it, leant on it and it came away. He swung on it 40 odd feet down and he landed on his head.' [Safety Officer, Mightysteel]

Those with a virtuous culture recognized that the severity of the consequences of individual inattention was in part determined by the inherent dangerousness of the industries involved and the specific events that take place. Their refusal to allow worker 'apathy' as an excuse for injury and death meant that solutions to safety outside consciousness raising had to be sought. As the safety officer of Mightysteel commented regarding induction into work at the smelter: 'I always tell them its not a flower shop out there'. Such a sentiment concerning the inherent dangerousness of the work was echoed by a safety representative at the plant:

'Most of us are pretty honest about the kind of environment we work in, so we do know the eventuality of something happening is always there.

The danger is always there . . . We do take precautions, we do try to avoid any mishaps and things like that, but OK they do happen; and we seem to be psychologically prepared for that . . .'

In such environments those committed to safety through a virtuous approach saw the need to 'make it [the workplace] idiot proof so that if the person does have a lapse in concentration or whatever [they] can't get into trouble'.

Both cultures, then, recognized that safety was not something that was necessarily uppermost in workers' minds at every moment. Both cultures had an understanding that safety was something the workers primarily had at the back of their minds, rather than being a conscious driving force for action. As the manager of Bigmill stated: 'People get too familiar, and just take everything for granted.' Such a sentiment was echoed by the project manager at Arcade: 'People tend to put it to the back of their mind and get on with the job.' The focus on the 'job' as opposed to safety also combined with a number of other factors which managers saw as emanating out of individual workers' psyche and limiting the safety of the workplace: 'people have got different mentalities, they don't think the same' so 'something is always overseen, something is missed . . .'. Also here was the notion of invulnerability of the self: '. . . it's like a car [accident] you think it will never happen to me . . .'.

Nonetheless, the difference between the two cultures reflected what they did with this common perception. The virtuous culture was constantly aware of the problem and sought to minimize it through engineering out safety problems and raising awareness. The blinkered culture on the other hand was resigned to the problem and so accepted the inevitability of injury as part of the job.

The virtuous culture's emphasis on consciousness raising and eliminating reasons behind cutting corners on the job could, however, highlight structural problems with the organization which undermined the overall harmonizing thrust of success **and** safety. Individual choice to push safety into the background, or decide on a quicker but less safe procedure, could stem from individual workers' monetary reward acting as a disincentive to work safely. This was true where piece-rate wages were the norm, such as in the timber industry, as the safety officer of International Paper commented: 'that's one of my biggest problems, because everyone is on piece-rates, you have to earn in the summer months enough money to last you a year'. International Paper espoused a virtuous culture, yet the aims of that culture could be undermined by the forced choices made under a piece-rate regime of wage payment.

Similarly, the use of overtime could undermine the virtuous culture. This issue arose out of this research and yet is not well documented in the literature, while the use of piece-rates and the effect on safety has been the subject of some studies (for example Crowe, 1986). Considerable monetary rewards could be gained by working overtime, but lapses in concentration become more frequent under such conditions. The safety officer of Mightysteel illustrated the impact of worker fatigue through working overtime and the lapses in concentration that resulted in his reflections on the death of a crane maintenance worker:

'. . . he'd done 60 hours, 72 that week, and 80 hours the week before and 50 the week before that. He was a workaholic, he would take any bit of overtime . . . These operators are earning $60–70,000 per annum. [How much is overtime?] 'Half, we had a mechanic last year who earned $73,000.'

This organization had predominantly expressed a virtuous ideology, one which was challenged and to some extent undermined by the existence of workers gaining significant proportions of their income from overtime. This was recognized by the safety officer, who replied when asked his attitude towards such overtime:

'Wrong, wrong wrong. We have blokes here who will put in a 22 hour day, and a 10 hour break, and come back and do more work.'

In conclusion, then, although safety was seen to be susceptible to be pushed into the background in both cultures, the blinkered culture saw this as inevitable while the virtuous ideology saw it as necessary to constantly counteract that inherent tendency. This difference resulted in the blinkered culture leaving issues of safety at the level of individual attitude and individual difference while the virtuous rationality was constantly on the look out for organizational structures which may have undermined safety and exacerbated the tendency to forget about the safety implications of a particular measure.

Unions

The **difference** between the cultures was the underlying trust or mistrust of the fundamental motives of the union. The blinkered culture doubted the motives of the unions, a feeling which was reciprocated; these organizations where characterized by suspicion and mistrust. The divisions and disruptions caused by the underlying suspicion between unions and managers could permeate the whole worksite. The project manager at Arcade illustrates the suspicion of the blinkered culture towards the motives of the union:

> 'The job will bog down into what becomes a battle of albeit personalities, or whatever, over an alleged safety issue which is probably not [related to safety]. [It] may or may not be a genuine safety risk to anybody, but [the industrial action is] because of some other ulterior motive.'

In contrast those working from a virtuous ideology would try to minimize conflict between unions and management. Problems would be seen to arise from an individual who was 'a bit of a stirrer', rather than an illustration of union motives as a whole. There was a clear recognition that the role of the union was a legitimate one 'to keep us honest'. The virtuous culture emphasized the legitimate role of unions, the blinkered model emphasized the unions' 'ulterior' motives.

The blinkered ideology was quite candid about their dislike of unions: 'I haven't got too much time for the unions . . . I've had lots of arguments. A lot of the boys know me, I'm known in the industry.' This particular project manager at Arcade quoted above illustrated the ramifications of a stand-off between unions and management and the resulting escalation of conflict, which could arise from within this culture, particularly where many unions were involved:

> 'If a union organizer from town was coming in I would never get one off to discuss the issue with; let's say the Electrical Union, the Plumbers Union or BWIU individually. They would all come on site together and say, "let's get Geoff" . . . Each one wanted to be represented on site. There would be a dozen of us walking around the site, we wouldn't achieve any more than if there had been two or three of us walking. Because let's say there would be two or three of us being constructive

taking notes, looking at things. The rest would be walking 20 paces behind us having a smoke and a chat and laugh at what they did last week. So it was an abuse sometimes more than being constructive.'

Here it can be seen that the blinkered ideology divides 'legitimate' and 'illegitimate' along with the various functions. This is consistent with the way the ideology fragments and splinters in order to place priorities. In particular, the interference of unionists 'off site' was seen as illegitimate when compared with unionists on site. External interference was considered politically motivated and unwarranted. The project manager of Arcade explained this political influence at the site of the new steel warehouse they were constructing:

'Instead of resolving the problems with the guys, the guys from the city would come in. The union would come in from town and they would get the rah, rah, you know; the thumping of the fists and the stomping of the foot to get payment. . . . It makes the organizers feel good because the guys have gone home. They didn't have to work for the day and they got paid for it.'

The blinkered culture then resisted the influence of the union. In some cases worksites with such a culture were non-unionized and glad to be so. As one director of a quarry, Hoefschtede Mines, stated: 'We never had a union, thank goodness, it was the one thing I managed to avoid.' In other cases, if union membership was compulsory, businesses could avoid the open conflict at Arcade above due to the perceived apathy of their employees towards the union, illustrated by such comments as, 'They belong to the union because they have to but most of them are anti-unionist.' The director of Reid Plumbing illustrates this well:

'All our people are in the union for the simple reason that we work on lots of union sites. But none of our men are union orientated. . . . All our men are paid over the award and they've all got trucks and whatnot. . . . If it came down to a choice of whether they had to be in the union, or they didn't, they wouldn't be in the union.'

In contrast the virtuous approach saw a legitimate role for unions in terms of their representation of workers on site. In accepting their legitimacy the various managers working from this culture would work at maintaining a positive relationship with unions, and were ultimately quite comfortable working within a unionized structure, as illustrated here by the project manager of Haddons:

'I have never had any problems with the unions. I have always been able to get on reasonably well, because we have always advocated negotiation, and we have always worked closely together with the shop stewards.'

There was within this culture a recognized need to retain the trust with the unions. The project manager of Haddons again explained one way this was achieved:

'After the incident they requested that we have a look at all our slings, because we were doing heavy lifts, 230–240 ton lifts. As a part of our normal procedure we would be briefing, through the designated work group, all employees as to when the lift would take place; and the requirements and the calculations which were there. So they could see what was happening before it occurred, therefore by means of lines of communication we didn't have problems.'

The need for open communication with the unions regarding safety was seen as necessary to maintain a good relationship, which was emphasized at Aidans:

'There was a positive support role in fact offered by the local shop stewards because we got them together the day after the event, and had done a full debriefing with those people straight off the top. They were told, it is an accident that had happened in their area and they will be party to the investigation and the process. It overcame the feeling of any backhanded deals or anything sinister.'

This quote is a good illustration of how the virtuous culture seeks to draw all relationships into the consensus, including historical adversaries such as unions.

This desire to harmonize relationships extended beyond the union representation on site to the central bureaucracy of the union. External union influence was considered of little consequence as all parties were seen to have the same ultimate goal of promoting safety, a view well expressed by the safety executive at Aidans:

'Externally from that you have your state co-ordinators that come in from the union. They were not able to raise any issues of an OHS nature with us, because we already had it covered. So they left us pretty much alone in that regard.'

Despite these differences between the two cultures there was some overlap in perception of the union. Both saw the union as fundamentally political, and so would, as they saw it, confuse safety with industrial relations issues.[2] What was meant by this is that both ideologies felt the union would pick on an insubstantial safety issue, and use it to push other agendas, use it as a bargaining tool to win wage increases, or changes in non-safety related conditions. Part of the problem as they viewed it stemmed from the power of the unions under legislation. Under the *Occupational Health and Safety Act* 1985 (Vic.) the union had a strong formal role to play in the promotion of safety in the workplace.[3] The Act stipulated that employers were bound to pay full wages during stoppages and strikes due to an unsafe or unhealthy workplace. The director of Nettles Builders, a company with a blinkered culture, illustrates the confusion of safety issues with health and safety which he saw as leading to unnecessary strife:

'I would have to go on to say that industrial action by unions over matters of H&S, to some extent cloud[s] the whole position of H&S on the site. I think if anything it distorts the real site safety issues on job sites. So much industrial action does take place over alleged safety matters that you can never tell what is a real safety matter, and what is not a real safety matter. [Can you give an example?] Oh well its such an everyday occurrence. It's probably the strongest industrial weapon that there is in the industry, to claim that something is unsafe.'

The safety officer of Mightysteel (a company with virtuous culture) was able to cite an example of what was considered a 'mixing of issues':

'... they called everybody out one night at 2a.m. because the toilet was dirty, the cubicles were dirty [and] they reckoned it was unhealthy. It was they [*sic*] who did it, they used it at the start of every shift. There was another toilet 60 metres away they could have used, they all sat in the canteen for three hours ...'

The difference, however, arose on how this was dealt with. For the blinkered culture the situation was inevitable, and an instance

[2] For a rebuttal of this perspective see Quinlan, 'The Industrial Relations of Occupational Health and Safety' in Quinlan (ed.)(1993), 140–69.

[3] Much of this role was repealed by the Liberal Government which came to power in 1992.

of the ulterior motives of unions which precluded useful discussion. For the virtuous culture the fundamental belief in the legitimacy of the unions meant that such instances would be seen as personality problems, rather than undermining the union role as a whole.

Nonetheless, the genuine nature of some conflict between the unions and management, and between different unions, could threaten the virtuous culture. These threats came from two sources: first, the existence of different unions with different attitudes to safety; and secondly, the impinging of different roles of the wider union structure on the company. This could complicate the desire of those from the virtuous perspective of bringing all parties to a common position which furthered the interests of the company. An illustration of the first complication is in different unions' attitudes towards the use of harnesses and the acceptability of 'walking the steel'. The Riggers Union saw safety in terms of training and walking the steel as part of their expertise, with a need to protect their skill base, and resist the wholesale use of harnesses as the major focus of safety. In contrast, the Building Workers Industrial Union saw walking the steel purely in terms of safety equipment, namely harnesses and scissor lifts. There was considerable tension between the unions regarding this issue which could complicate the companies' desire to harmonize their views.

Secondly, unions also span a wide range of concerns that extend beyond safety on site including an important concern for the next of kin of the dead worker. They often provided legal representation for the next of kin at inquest, and provided much needed support services. This could be an area where a consensus on site between union and management could break down. The family of the dead worker were in a unique position, not being part of the culture of the worksite. They also stood to bear the brunt of the pain of living with the death of a loved one, exacerbated by the loss of their earnings. This, combined with the family's need to prove negligence, could challenge the virtuous culture particularly where a union became involved in the support of the family and use of civil litigation.

Although not directly involving a union, the following case illustrates how a consensus between parties can become shaken by the involvement of the family and the pursuit of civil action. In the following case a lagging contractor, one of two partners in a small business, fell off a ladder to his death while doing some contract work for a heavy engineering factory. The safety executive at Aidans explained the changes in the perceptions of causal factors of the death that occurred at the inquest:

'Initially they [the contractor] acknowledged that we had done everything right, . . . they were terribly upset of course, . . . so they had nothing but praise for us initially. It was the wife of the deceased who got upset . . . absolutely [the only reason they changed their mind was because they wanted more compensation]. I spoke to the other working partner who was the other guy on the ladder at the time. He met me after the coroner's inquest out the front of the coroner's court and he said he was sorry I had to go through all that, he still felt the same.'

Often it is the union's role to represent the family of the deceased, and this role inevitably puts them in conflict with the organization. The litigation following the death causes conflict which is hard to reconcile with the virtuous culture.

The Regulator

The attitude towards the regulator, in this case the Department of Labour,[4] well reflected the harmonizing and dichotomizing principle behind the two cultures. The blinkered culture with its basic mistrust of 'outsiders' sought to keep the regulator at bay, while the virtuous culture nurtured the relationship between the local inspector and the company.

The blinkered ideology was not openly antagonistic to the regulator, but aimed to keep the relationship at arm's length: 'they sort of follow things a different way, they set the rules and we know if we break them'. The lack of desire for a closer relationship stemmed from an understanding that compliance with all regulations was impossible, as the director of Nettles Builders highlighted: 'I think there is a genuine feeling that if you did comply with everything [regulations] you couldn't get anything done. Productivity would drop to nothing.' With total compliance being impossible disagreements could arise, as the director of Reids Plumbing illustrated:

[4] Now known as the WorkCover.

'We always had disagreements, 'cause often they'll ask for things that might go overboard, just to make sure they get a certain safety. So you'll always have disagreements with DLI[5] inspectors.'

Co-operation with the Department of Labour at the time of the deaths could stem partly from the fear of recriminations, illustrated again by the director of Reids Plumbing:

'We co-operated with them very thoroughly because we didn't want any recriminations back on us as well. . . . There are plenty of times I have found them uncooperative.'

Additionally, if the perceived neutrality of the inspector was in doubt, forming a close relationship could be a threat, thus reinforcing the need to keep a distance from the regulator. During the time of the interviews the involvement of the inspectorate in the timber industry was increasing. However, the new inspectors had a union background. The inherent suspicion of the blinkered culture towards the union movement meant that a close relationship with the inspectorate was a risk not to be taken, if there was a possibility that the inspectors' union background may influence their decisions. When asked about the relationship between his company and the new inspectors the owner of Adams Logging stated his suspicion of the new inspectors' background:

'The new field officer, he was the union representative for the area. I have been notified that the DOL[6] had to put on an extra amount of field officers for the timber industry, and they all had to have a union background. [Do you think that helps safety?] No, not with the union background.'

Regulation and changes in prosecutorial direction often entered into the discussion with those coming from a blinkered culture as a reason to change practices. This is not surprising given their position regarding full compliance with regulations, which they saw as impossible, and their arm's length relationship with the inspectorate. They lived with the apprehension of being 'caught out'. The project manager at Arcade emphasized the effect of the new legislation, in particular the shift to make individuals accountable for the harm their organizations caused, which stimulated awareness about safety in company directors:

[5] Department of Labour and Industry, previous name for the Department of Labour, now known as WorkCover.

[6] Department of Labour.

'I think that with the new laws that have come in where the directors of the companies are becoming responsible and liable, it is putting more emphasis on the company itself to be aware, and that they are responsible at the end of the day.'

Also mentioned by these companies was the effectiveness of advertising campaigns: 'That ad on TV has certainly hit home amongst the trades people. I can tell you that in the workplace that has hit home. That ad works very well.' (Director, Reid Plumbing.)

In contrast the relationship between the Department of Labour and companies with a virtuous culture was close. The relationship between regulator and safety officer, for example, could be used to put weight behind a safety initiative and sidestep budgetary constraints from other departments within the organization. The safety officer at Mightysteel explained his close relationship with the departmental inspector, and how he used this to promote safety:

'I use him [the inspector] from time to time myself to get things done. You've got to use the system to its advantage, and you know there is something that needs to be done, and you can't get the finance to do it you put a bit of weight behind it.... They are all tools to be used aren't they?'

Here the use of the relationship with the inspector was done without higher management knowledge, which indicates a degree of tension certain departments of this particular organization had with a full virtuous ideology. Other organizations, such as Aidans, were more wholehearted in their use of the inspectors to get things done. In the following case senior management were fully supportive of such moves, recognizing the constraints of their own bureaucracy:

'Fortunately our process was that anybody can ring the DOL to seek assistance if they were thwarted [by bureaucracy], to try and get it done. We had two occasions with a plant, not at M [where the death occurred], because of budgetary constraints at these plants we couldn't spend the money. So we, in concert with the manager, myself, the safety rep., and the local DOL inspector we got Prohibition[7] notices written out to breach

[7] A Prohibition notice is a document stipulated under the *Occupational Health and Safety Act* 1985 (Vic.) which prohibits use of a particular piece of equipment until the relevant safety measures have been undertaken. It may be placed on a workplace or piece of machinery which is considered too dangerous to continue working in or using until changes have been made. See *Occupational Health and Safety Act* 1985 (Vic.) section 44.

budget requirements. There was no money available there, no money left in the kitty. We couldn't take money, so we said we need an extra $35,000 to do this project. They [the inspectorate] wrote out a PIN, sent it by Fax, and we had the money approved inside five hours.'

The Department of Labour was seen as a resource by those within virtuous culture, a tool which could assist them to improve safety; as the personnel manager at Aidans stated, 'they have always been there to help, they would rather help than prosecute.'

Any changes in regulatory policy from persuasive to prosecutorial, including the setting up of a central prosecuting body which occurred at the time, had little effect on those coming from a virtuous culture. The setting up by the Labor Government of the Central Investigation Unit, a specialist unit aimed at increasing the number and quality of prosecutions for breaches of health and safety regulations and ultimately criminal prosecutions, was not seen as making much difference to the importance of safety within these organizations. Primarily these changes were seen as a central push, not something arising out of the regional offices, with which they had more contact:

'CIU [Central Investigation Unit] want prosecutions. CIU to me is a political appointment, the whole set up. . . . The regional people have much more influence with what goes on here than some high flier from the city . . .' [Safety officer, Mightysteel]

These organizations were more concerned with their good relationships with their local inspectors. The close relationship meant a two-way flow of information, and the organizations could be used as a 'training ground' for new inspectors. Relationships could be strong between inspectors and particular safety personnel, relationships which could extend beyond the period of employment:

'They used to send their new inspectors in to show them how it was done, it was an interesting relationship. I still talk with a number of the inspectors I used to deal with.' [Safety executive, Aidans]

The close relationship with the investigating body has often appeared as a problem in the health and safety literature, with the assumption being that the close relationship leads to regulatory capture where the inspector is so imbued with the standards and culture of the organization that they 'turn a blind eye' to breaches in legislation and specific regulations (Stone, 1975; Clinard and Yeager, 1980; Grabosky and Braithwaite, 1986). The data illustrates a possible example of regulatory capture, where Aidans refused access to an investigator after the fatality because of his espoused prosecutorial stance. The safety executive instead chose to work with a different inspector, one whom he had worked closely with for a number of years and with whom he had a close relationship:

'BC [the regional inspector] was terrific, I have known him for donkeys years. I overheard what the other person who was with him said, "let's go and see who we can prosecute, who we can screw yes". I spun round and said he is not to go on site. . . . I was deliberately breaking the law in refusing the DOL entry in that regard, and I said I was prepared to stand on that. The two of them were welcome to go on site, we had forklift drivers we had all the witnesses available. We had everyone that was necessary for them to conduct their inquiry fully and completely. But not under threat. BC went out and talked to the other chap, came back and assured me that he would be kept on the mechanical investigation only, and that his views would be vetted before papered.'

Such a response could quite clearly be viewed as regulatory capture, where the 'preferred' investigator, the one with views most closely aligned with the target organization, was in a position to 'vet' the views of the other who was possibly in a more 'neutral' or impartial position. Alternatively though it could be viewed as an example of 'building of trust' between regulator and regulated, mooted by Braithwaite and Ayres, which they suggest may lead to a more productive relationship where improved compliance with regulation is the result (Braithwaite, 1985; Ayres and Braithwaite, 1992). The context of this fatality and the extensive nature of the safety programmes on the site where the incident occurred tend to support the latter explanation. In addition, the investigation which was conducted appeared to be thorough with no indication that the 'preferred' inspector compromised in his investigation. As the safety executive stated later:

'The investigation was pretty exhaustive too, which was great. I think it was really only the other chap pumping himself up to face a circumstance of investigating a fatality. I was already concerned about our people, and I wasn't going to have them threatened, walk into the place and start cracking the whip. No way, I was prepared to be prosecuted for it.'

Here then the human dimension of the tragedy comes through and the positive support of people emotionally at the time of the death by the safety executive has an almost 'heroic' quality about it. Nonetheless, doubts remain when the relationship between inspector and organization becomes close. There are well documented examples of regulatory capture, and so the close nature of the relationship between inspector and organization cannot be viewed as automatically healthy. Rather, such relationships need to be viewed in light of their overall culture, rather than a simple assumption that a close relationship is either necessarily healthy, or an example of regulatory capture.

While there were clear differences in the cultural attitudes towards the investigators both cultures accepted their legitimacy in two areas: mediating in disputes between union and management on issues of safety and the department's need to investigate after a death had occurred. The main regulating body is empowered by the *Occupational Health and Safety Act* 1985 (Vic.) to mediate in disputes regarding health and safety. Most seemed happy with this role, with this sentiment expressed by the project manager of Arcade:

'On a few instances where the unions brought in an issue with regards to health and safety, the DLI would be notified to go on site and act as a mediator. A couple of times we lost, a couple of times we won. But overall I found them co-operative.'

Their role as mediator could take away the pressure from the company and allow business to continue. They were brought in to resolve the 'toilet issue' at Mightysteel cited above, which they did to the satisfaction of the company:

'They brought the DOL in and he gave that safety rep. one hell of a caning and they lost the case. They never got paid, and that fellow made the toilet wall, and when you make the toilet wall believe me that is bad news. He was sent to Coventry shall we say. That particular safety rep., he was a bit of a stirrer, and you'll get them in any organization. You'll get one who'll try the system on but that's all behind us.'

The Inspector then was seen as a legitimate mediator by both cultures when conflicts over health and safety arose. While from the latter quote this may have been due to the company's 'success' with the Department of Labour's decision in their favour, the former quote suggests that the acceptance of the Department's role was not totally dependent on the decision going for the company.

The second area of agreement between the cultures concerned the legitimacy of the Department of Labour's involvement in investigating the death.[8] Both saw this as legitimate. The perceived legitimacy of this essentially reactive role is well explained by the director of Reid's Plumbing:

> 'When it comes to someone dying, then you have to co-operate fully 'cause they're the experts, and they are the ones that have to go to the coroner's court. They're the ones that have to deal with all the procedures . . .'

The relationship between the regulator and the organization, then, has areas of overlap between the two cultures, with both seeing the need for a regulator who is an arbitrator, and a reactive investigator. The clear difference arises in terms of the proactive role of the inspector. The blinkered culture comes from a position where total compliance with regulations is impossible. In light of this an arm's length relationship with the inspector is prudent, and conflict possible when paths do cross. This position makes the culture aware of changes in prosecutorial stance and wary of shifts to hold individuals responsible and regulators' increased use of prosecution. On the other hand, the virtuous culture actively cultivates their relationship with the inspector, encouraging collaboration and a problem solving approach to safety issues. Changes in prosecutorial stance were viewed as 'political stunts' with little effect on relations between them and their local inspectors. However, this close relationship could be brought into question with the possibility of regulatory capture. To assess the desirability of such a close relationship, however, the overall culture of the company needs to be addressed, not just the immediate relationship between inspector and company.

[8] The actual involvement of the Department of Labour in the fatalities was varied. One organization with a virtuous ideology actually complained about the minimal involvement of the Department in the death. The safety officer of International Paper commented, 'I wasn't involved with the Department in that case at all, they didn't even contact me.' This poor investigation by the Department of Labour was commented on by the coroner in various cases, in particular in the case of Young Constructions where the poor investigation was the primary reason this company was not prosecuted for manslaughter.

The Role of the Contractor

Since the relationship between organizations is important to current theorizing about regulation, it is useful to extend the analysis of culture and business ideologies beyond the boundary of the individual organization. In particular what needs to be explored is the nature of the relationship between organizations regarding responsibility for safety. How did organizations view the safety of another's employee? Did this relationship between organizations shed light on the nature and influence of culture at the worksite level?

The difference between the cultures lay in how much emphasis was given to individual and organizational responsibility, over and above the responsibility the contractor has for the subcontractor's employee.[9] The blinkered culture focused on the separate responsibilities of the various organizations on site for the safety of their workers, a sentiment well illustrated by the project manager at Arcade:

> 'I felt the subcontractors were responsible for their people because there are so many different subcontractors, so many people working on site from different companies. I felt they were responsible for their own guys for the job they were going to do, because the job was subcontracted on an individual basis for the particular job.'

The subcontractors interviewed acknowledged that these organizations, identified here as having a blinkered culture, had little interest in their safety with the major view being that they were basically left alone to get on with the job in the best way they saw fit, as explained by the director of Reids Plumbing: 'they [the major contractor] tend to leave it to really sort of leave it up to yourself'.

In some cases the fragmentation of responsibility under the blinkered culture with everyone only concerned about their own safety could lead directly to the fatality. This was illustrated by the case at the Leafytown Council site as the owner of Daytons Rigging explained:

[9] It will be remembered that the *Occupational Health and Safety Act* 1985 (Vic.) stipulates that the contractor is responsible for the subcontractor's employee, in the same way they are responsible for their own workers.

'The only people who were concerned were ourselves; the crane driver, myself, the rigger who was killed. We were all discussing the power lines and we could see it was going to be too dangerous . . .'

In contrast the interviews highlighted that the virtuous ideology saw their obligations to maintain safety extending beyond the limits of the home organization. When those high in the contracting hierarchy were asked about responsibility for their contractors on site these respondents clearly saw it as their own: 'We are, we hire them and maintain that they follow our rules and regulations to maintain good safety standards. If they don't come up to what we believe is the right standard we tell them.'

When asked why they felt the subcontractors' safety was their responsibility the virtuous culture again emphasized the inclusive nature of the workplace, and pointed to how mistakes by subcontractors could affect all employees. Haddons did a lot of work on oil rigs and explained: '. . . if one person makes a mistake the whole place could go up . . .'. The direct employees of the major contractor or tenderor would also reflect this culture and assist in maintaining a high standard of safety on the site as a whole: 'The employees of the company are usually right on the ball as to who is working dangerously, if someone does work dangerously they generally report it back . . .'.

The influences on culture, and the constituent nature of organizational culture, become complicated then when there is more than one organization on site. This is particularly true when organizations with different cultures are working on the same site. Here the power structure of the site becomes important. A major contractor with a virtuous culture can influence the safety of a subcontractor's employee. The safety officer of Mightysteel commented that the subcontractor simply got 'sent off site' if they did not comply with safety rules. It was for this reason that competition between contractors was considered a good thing. With competition, the safest and best contractor could be chosen, increasing the safety of all workers.

The situation was more complex with the roles reversed. A major contractor with a blinkered culture gave subcontractors little choice. If the job was dangerous they had to refuse the work, and forgo the contract; a difficult choice in tight economic times.

Common to both cultures was an understanding that each individual, including the employee of a subcontractor, had some responsibility for their own safety. This responsibility was explained by the owner of Adams Logging in terms of where the ultimate pain for injury would be felt:

> 'The men themselves have got to make sure that it is safe because they are the ones that feel the pain. If they break their leg it hurts them; it hurts my pocket—but it hurts their leg.'

The need for individual responsibility could also be explained by the impossibility of having constant supervision of a subcontractor's employees, particularly in an industry like logging, as explained by the safety officer of Bigmill:

> 'We can't be there. It's different to a factory, where the safety personnel in the factory can be walking around constantly. . . . We are not in the same situation, very different so we can't be there all the time.'

The difference arose with the responsibilities undertaken by the major contractor. Those from a blinkered culture felt that they had little responsibility to enforce safety rules on subcontractors and their employees; those from the virtuous culture felt that this was central to their role. Complications arose when there were divergent cultures on the same site, particularly when subcontractors with a virtuous approach were working under major contractors with a blinkered culture. Ultimately, to maintain safety, they may be forced to refuse work.

Culture and Response

There were, then, two distinct cultures to be found in the data. Crucially, now, it is necessary to ascertain whether these cultures relate to response. Was the 'virtuous' culture correlated to the 'virtuous' response? Reviewing the data, there was support for the idea that the difference between the cultures did correlate in this way with response. That is, a virtuous response was associated with a virtuous culture, and a blinkered response was associated with a blinkered culture (see Figure 6.2).

However, it needs to be highlighted that the response according to culture was a majority response, not a unanimous one.

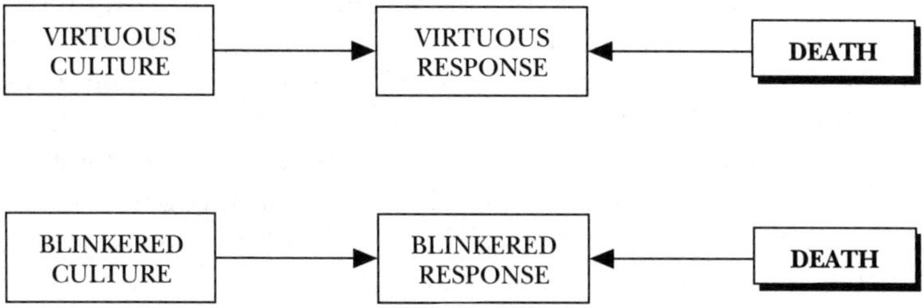

FIG. 6.2. Relationship between Culture and Response

This arose partly due to differences between some of the organizations within their own group with respect to a small number of the criteria in Table 6.1, and also because of the limitation of the data. Thus in the majority of cases the blinkered culture was associated with a blinkered response. Importantly, in no case was a virtuous culture associated with a blinkered response. However, in eight cases of the eighteen exhibiting a blinkered response there was not enough information to give a full account of all the areas of culture, although the actual nature of their response could be ascertained. Nonetheless, of the ten remaining organizations seven exhibited all aspects of the blinkered culture. Two exhibited substantial areas of agreement with the blinkered culture with an anomaly in only one organization, Roadtech. Roadtech had been taken over after the death by a company with a virtuous culture. As far as could be ascertained the culture at the time of the death closely equated to a blinkered culture.

Similarly, the majority of those with a virtuous culture exhibited a virtuous response. Four out of seven organizations exhibited the expansive virtuous ideology in all the areas in Table 6.1. A further two agreed in all but one area, with some confusion between the two cultures in that particular area. The final company, Service Cranes, had a virtuous culture but was in a powerless position as a subcontractor on site. In the area of the role of the unions and the relationship with the regulator this company exhibited some aspects of a blinkered culture.

The matching of culture to response is a less than perfect one, restricted in part by the data, but in part by the presence of anomalies. In light of this it may be helpful to view the cultural distinctions as a pointer to an underlying business ideology or logic rather than a discrete or essential entity of itself. This underlying logic in a full manifestation in organizational culture represents more a Weberian 'ideal type'. The reality may be a far more messy translation of logic or ideology into culture. Organizational ideology as an 'ideal type' of doing business is therefore unlikely to be **directly** represented culturally in any given historical instance in a pure form (Bendix, 1977:271–81). With respect to this data, this means that each organization was unlikely to subscribe solely to one approach to the exclusion of the other. Nevertheless, the logic defined the rationality for that particular organization, and formed the premises behind decision making. Rationality was bounded by the underlying logic (Turner, 1992b), rather than emerging out of a neutral 'objective' assessment of the possible responses to the deaths. This logic then mediated the action or inaction taken in response.

Conclusion and Summary of Culture

The central feature of this chapter has been to show the two distinct ideologies which surround notions of 'good business'. The first of these, the blinkered culture, defined good business in terms of getting the job done, with an individualized and fragmented philosophy which involved a conflict of either safety or production and demanded priorities. The second ideal type was the virtuous culture, which had an expansive philosophy where all roles of the organization could blend into a whole, in a manner which was considered more successful than emphasis of one area over another. A summary of the two ideologies of the organizations is presented in Table 6.2. As the representation of the two organizational cultures in the table shows, with regard to each organizational role there may be areas of agreement between the two cultures as shown, but in all cases there are also distinct differences. The purpose of this chapter has been to emphasize the need to see each row of this table as a larger whole rather than a discrete entity of itself. The various rows influence and construct aspects of the culture of an organization, whose underlying logic or ideology then directs behaviour.

At the core of each culture was the understanding of how to achieve 'success' as an organization. The blinkered culture

TABLE 6.2. Summary of the Cultural Elements of the Virtuous and Blinkered Business Ideologies

Cultural Elements	Virtuous Ideology	Blinkered Ideology
	Success achieved through blending all aspects of business in a win—win scenario	**Success achieved by constantly placing a priority on getting the job done**
Role of a good manager	*All aspects of business, the environment, product safety, worker health, costs and profit ultimately come together *A focus on short-term gain is the Achilles' heel of management	*A good manager is the one who gets the job done
Rationalizations of workers' attitude and the promotion of a safety culture	*Workers tend to push safety to the back of their mind*	
	*This tendency has to be overcome and the organization must actively promote safety as a priority *The organization should 'engineer out' problems wherever possible	*This tendency is inevitable, and so accidents will happen
Unions	*Unions tend to confuse safety with Industrial Relations*	
	*This is usually only a problem with certain 'stirrers' *Unions are the legitimate representatives of the workers *They exist to keep management honest	*Their primary motive is industrial relations, that is to gain increases in wages and disrupt work *Unions are an unwarranted intrusion on business *Unions increase costs
Regulators	*Regulators have a legitimate function as mediators, and to investigate reactively injuries and fatalities*	
	*A close relationship with regulators is a good thing, so they can be consulted to improve safety	*The number of regulations is onerous and total compliance is impossible *There will always be

TABLE 6.2. (Cont'd)

Cultural Elements	**Virtuous Ideology**	**Blinkered Ideology**
	*They are useful to circumvent bureaucracy and gain extra budgets for safety	disagreement with regulators *It is best to keep a distance from regulators
Contractors	*Contractors have a responsibility for their own safety*	
	*The major contractor has the primary responsibility for the safety of the subcontractor's employee *The safety and well-being of the contractors is in the long-term interests of the company *The company should build up mutually beneficial relationships with preferred contractors which understand the philosophy of the company and the commitment to safety	*Contractors should primarily look out for their own safety, and the safety of their employees *How they achieve this is their problem as long as they get the job done

worked from an exclusive logic, which saw the central concern of the organization as 'getting the job done', which was opposed to and had a priority over other demands. One opposition, for example, was between production, or getting the job done, and compliance with legal requirements. The choice was 'getting the job done' **or** 'compliance with everything', but not both. This culture was related to the blinkered response. The virtuous approach in contrast, was underpinned by an inclusive logic which sought to bring all concerns of the organization into a 'win—win' scenario. In this scenario the aims of safety, profitability, limiting legal liability and success, it was argued, could all be achieved simultaneously since they were essentially in harmony with each other. This was associated with the virtuous response.

What is being suggested then is that safety 'culture' cannot be seen as distinct from the overall culture and concerns of the organization regarding success. It is the relationship between 'doing safety' and 'doing business' which is key to understanding culture. Attitudes to safety form one part of the overall cultural milieu, not as a distinct entity separate from other key organizational concerns. Differing concepts of 'good business', then, affected the organization's perspective on safety, and the priority safety had *vis-à-vis* other organizational interests.

The identification of both cultures, the virtuous culture, with its 'win—win' logic, and the blinkered culture, with its 'either/or' logic, was best understood through exploring how the culture impinged on attitudes towards various aspects of organizational activity, rather than in isolation from specific concerns. In identifying concerns other than those directly concerned with production (or the aim the organization saw as 'doing business'), it was possible to identify either an inclusive or exclusive logic when the relationship between that concern and production was explored.

There is some support then for the proposition that response is associated with the organizational culture or ethos of the company. It could be argued that decisions regarding appropriate organizational behaviour are formed using a 'bounded rationality' (Turner, 1992b), that is managers make decisions based on the premises and underlying logic which arise from the organizational context. These premises concern the direction of organizational success, the logic of which guides behaviour. The virtuous culture has an expansive and inclusive philosophy which allowed the freedom to explore creative solutions to the dilemmas posed by the death; the blinkered approach with the focus on getting the job done and placing priorities in an either/or fashion restricted responses to the strictly necessary as illustrated in the blinkered response.

However, there are some important questions remaining before concluding observations concerning culture. The first question concerns the unitary nature of the organizations. It is necessary to ascertain if there are any examples where different departments of the same organization exhibited different cultures. Secondly, the discussion of the attributes of culture above pointed to complications which shed some doubt on the malleability of culture, particularly if the responsibility for cultural change is vested solely in the regulator and their persuasive powers on the target organization. These complications point particularly to apparent weaknesses in the virtuous culture, which in the absence of a power base on the particular worksite (i.e. it was the culture of a subcontractor as opposed to the major contractor) meant that the choice to work safely was severely constrained. Even where that culture was associated with the major contractor it could be undermined by subtle changes in priorities of the organization leading to excessive demands on middle managers, incentives such as piece-rates and overtime payments which increased risks at the worksite, battles over the 'confusion' of industrial relations and safety, and the organization abusing their close relationship with local inspectors. The impact external constraints have on culture will be our major concern in the next chapter.

Different Departments and Different Ideologies

The question relevant to this chapter concerns the possibility of different departments exhibiting different organizational cultures, as would seem to be indicated by the work of Gross (1978). There was in fact in the data one company which had two departments which exhibited different responses, and had different cultures. The company in question was Mightysteel. From the coroner's records it was assumed that the building site at the steel mill was controlled by Arcade and the project manager employed by Arcade. Arcade had at the time purchased the steel operations from Mightysteel. In fact, it emerged during the interviews that the steel warehouse construction site was owned and controlled by Mightysteel, and the project manager employed by Mightysteel, not Arcade. The two sections of Mightysteel, the central organization and the construction site, responded differently and had different underlying ideologies concerning what constituted 'good' business. Here, the conflict between the two ideologies was for each part of the organization to respond in a way considered appropriate to their understanding, resulting in one blinkered response and one virtuous.

The existence of two ideologies within an organization indicates the organization as characterized by flux, rather than a stagnant structure dominated by a single cohesive logic. This is supported by the observation that Mightysteel was one of the two companies which did not exhibit a full adherence to the virtuous ideology. Change of culture and behaviour within an organization may arise through different departments gaining ascendancy within an organization (Dent, 1991).

Such a finding also adds further complications concerning control by law enforcement. The question needs to be asked concerning to what extent the adverse finding on one section of a company can reflect poorly on the rest of the organization. A recent court case (*Pacific Dunlop* v. *Kamburn,* January 1994, Victorian County Court) suggests that the courts can view separate divisions of an organization as separate entities. In the case of Pacific Dunlop, trading as Holding Rubber, an appeal against the severity of a sentence was upheld when this sub-organization held that the prior convictions of separate divisions of a company should not be held against them. They had no prior convictions. The wider organization had twenty-two.

Conclusion

At the beginning of the chapter questions concerning the genesis of virtue were directed towards uncovering organizational attributes. It was suggested that such attributes could be seen to mould behaviour either towards or away from virtue, as shown by response. This chapter has demonstrated that organizational attributes, in particular organizational culture, may be important in the emergence of virtue.

There were indeed two fundamentally different cultures illustrated by the data, the virtuous culture and the blinkered culture which, at least in 'ideal' form, underpinned the two types of response, the virtuous and the blinkered respectively. This was achieved by the culture and its underlying premises providing the 'bounds' or premises behind the rationality of the response. Under the virtuous culture improving safety was perceived as an integral part of success, making a virtuous response possible. In contrast, under the blinkered culture there was the underlying dichotomy where success was not necessarily seen as being achieved through improving safety. In these organizations then, while the immediate cause of the fatality may have been addressed, wider issues were left untouched. This was because to do so would have challenged the cultural perspective as a whole, such as beliefs about the 'apathy' of the worker, or the ulterior motives of the union regarding safety campaigns. From the point of view of the regulators virtuous organizations were indeed the ones to trust, and by implication these organizations could be described as 'virtuous'.

Nonetheless, there were complications to the picture of culture and therefore the issues of trust and virtue. In particular the virtuous culture appeared to be more vulnerable to challenges. Complications were evident within each of the attributes of culture discussed: the possibility of the multiplicity of roles demanded of management, the existence of overtime and piece-rates encouraging workers to cut corners, the existence of multiple unions with different attitudes to management, the possibility of regulatory capture, and finally the invidious position of being a powerless player with a virtuous culture on a worksite where the major players subscribed to a blinkered view. Some of the challenges could be addressed through internal organizational changes, such as the existence of piece-rates and understaffing. Others point to factors outside the control of the organization which may affect their capacity for virtue, such as control, or lack of control, over adverse economic or industrial conditions; control, or lack of control, within a particular worksite.

These challenges point to possible complications with depicting culture as solely formed from 'within', as the idea of organizational virtue would seem to suggest. While the existence of divergent cultures within the same organization would seem to indicate that cultural change is possible, it is not clear whether that culture is controlled in totality by the organization and its top management. Culture may not be independent of the structure of the worksite and the industry as suggested in chapter 2. It is to this question of structure that we now turn.

7 What Constrains Virtue? The Role of Size and Position in the Contracting Hierarchy

ANALYSIS in this chapter concerns the degree to which differences in both organizational response and culture result from constraints to organizational choice. Previous chapters have suggested that it is possible to distinguish relative virtue through how organizations respond to death. Further, it was proposed that this response (and by extension virtue) was related to organizational culture, rather than individual intent (as measured by the techniques of neutralizations individual managers used when discussing the death). Here the question is asked whether the difference between organizations (concerning response and culture) is purely a result of free choice on behalf of the organizations concerned. The chapter explores factors which may constrain virtue, and force choice in a direction antithetical to virtue.

The rationale behind turning attention to constraints on virtue relies to a considerable degree on a Marxist analysis outlined in chapter 2. Such an analysis argues that it is the process of capital accumulation, i.e. the progressive concentration of capital, which creates an environment where the choices of smaller weaker organizations are severely constrained. In order to survive, small organizations in a position of weakness, such as a subcontractor, are forced into making decisions which focus on profitability in the short term. They cut corners in order to survive, and so avoid compliance with onerous regulatory standards. Adherence to such standards, it is argued, would severely reduce the viability of small business.

Such a position is fleshed out by Galbraith who points to the 'protective purposes' of the actions of small business. He argues, similar to the Marxists, that such businesses have severely constrained choices. The choices they do make necessarily have to protect their ongoing viability, which is under constant threat. Galbraith points out that the choices which are available to such businesses involve exploitation of themselves, their families and their employees (Galbraith, 1973:71–7).

By implication then the ability to choose a virtuous path requires some degree of power over the environment within which an organization does business. Large organizations, and those in a high position within the contracting hierarchy, have more choice, and a choice which includes 'virtuous' options. Size brings with it control of greater amounts of capital, and greater power to influence the legislation of government (Kolko, 1963, 1965; Marvel, 1977). Legislation can then be made consistent with organizational success. Further, Berle and Means (1967) point to the separation of ownership from organizational control (i.e. management) in larger organizations, which allows a greater focus to be made on long-term goals rather than short-term returns on investment.

The first task of this chapter then is to ascertain the degree to which size and position in the contracting hierarchy determined response. The impact of size and position in the contracting hierarchy is explored both separately, and in combination. From the analysis above it would be expected that large organizations in a high position in the contracting hierarchy would be the most likely to act in a virtuous manner. That is, to be in the 'virtuous' category of response. Small organizations in a low position in the contracting hierarchy would be expected to respond in a 'blinkered' fashion.

However, it is necessary to go beyond a simple analysis of constraints on virtue, i.e. size and position in the contracting hierarchy, and its relationship to response (as a measure of virtue). There is the intervening variable between such constraints and behaviour, namely the influence of culture outlined in chapter 6. To include the insights of this chapter, namely that behaviour results from cultural assumptions about the direction in which success is to be achieved, it is necessary to explore the relationship between constraints on virtue and culture as well as constraints on virtue and response. Fundamentally arising out of the literature is the concern with the degree of **dependence** of culture on structure. This chapter asks if culture can be totally explained by external constraints as Marxists would have it, or if culture exerts some independent control on the directions and decisions organizations make. To some extent this can be

TABLE 7.1. Responses of Organizations by Size

Response	**Large**	**Small**
Virtuous	6	1
Blinkered	4	14
Total	**10**	**15**

explored using the data, by looking at the connection between constraints on virtue, culture and response. The chapter explores whether there were organizations where response could not be explained by external constraints alone. It is the culture of such organizations which may give some insight into the possible independence of culture, or in sociological terms the independence of agency from structure.

This chapter then proceeds as follows. First the effect of size and position in the contracting hierarchy on response will be reviewed. In the second half of the chapter those cases where size and position in the contracting hierarchy alone could not explain the virtuousness, or lack of virtue of the response, are reviewed. Finally, the relationship between constraint to virtue (as measured by size and position in the contracting hierarchy), culture and response are explored to attempt to shed light on the possible dependence or independence of culture on such constraints.

The Influence of Constraints on Virtue as measured by the Relationship between Size and Response

Here we want to explore whether the responses organizations made to the deaths they experienced were influenced by external constraints measured by their size. Table 7.1 shows the responses of the organizations, blinkered or virtuous, sorted by the size of the respondent.

The distribution of the organizations according to size and response as indicated in the table shows support for the proposition that external constraints as measured by size influence the responses made. The trend illustrated by the table follows that which would be expected from the literature, namely that the small organizations, hypothesized to be influenced more greatly by external constraints, were more likely to respond in a blinkered fashion, while larger organizations, with greater freedom from external constraints, were more likely to respond in a virtuous manner.

It is the interview material, however, that gives the greatest insight into why this was the case and supports the theoretical link between size and the degree of impact of economic constraints. Small firms were essentially reactive, as proactive thinking about long-term risks and costs associated with safety in general become submerged under immediate needs. The following quote from the safety officer of Roadtech[1] illustrates the concern for the immediate, and the reactive nature of safety in a small business, well:

> 'For small companies it is hard enough to keep your head above water. People only do what they have to do when the shit hits the fan; then they do something about safety.'

Safety was an afterthought because of the understanding that ultimately safety and profit were in conflict. The predominant concern of the small businesses interviewed regarding safety was the immediate cost of the safety equipment required for the job at hand, and the extra time involved in safer procedures. The owner of Daytons[2] explained about the time and cost involved in using a mobile lift (known as a scissor lift) in construction:

> '. . . it slows down the work by 50 per cent, maybe 40 per cent, it's slower to put up the building, I'd say by 50 per cent. The size of this building, just the white bit there [indicates] if we were just to put the steel up it'd be say 5–6 weeks we could put it up, finished. This has been here for a year and not finished.'

The project manager at Mightysteel/Arcade[3] explained the juggling act that went on trying to make the job pay:

[1] The safety officer was employed by Roadtech, a small firm, at the time of the death, but the company had subsequently been taken over by a large business. The safety officer had remained and was in a position to compare his experience under the two regimes.

[2] He was currently working for someone else as he could no longer make his own business pay.

[3] The project manager had left Mightysteel and was now running his own small business as a trucking contractor. It was this manager that court documents had indicated was under the instruction of Arcade. As explained in the previous chapter it was during the interview that it became clear he was working for Mightysteel and the site itself was controlled by Mightysteel.

'Let's face it safety does cost money, OK? Like I mentioned before the bigger companies—they have got more funds available and they can spend the money on safety . . . The smaller companies tend to look more at the profits; minimize the cost of new building, new machinery, new venture whatever it is. So I don't think they work hand in hand, it's: "how I'm going to do it. Am I going to use the right equipment?" '

Such juggling fits well the conceptualization of Galbraith of using the limited choices they do have in a protective manner, namely to protect the ongoing viability of the company. The wrong choice could spell the demise of the organization if costs exceeded contract price. This reasoning, and the juggling between profit and safety, then, affected the nature of the response. The death at Gemtrench illustrates this well. Gemtrench chose to develop its own safety equipment, which was less than adequate, because the director felt he could not afford the available equipment on the market. After the death the equipment was changed:

'We felt we couldn't afford the Rolls Royce of systems; and we thought the system we had was sufficient. It wasn't. As a result [of the fatality] we changed everything and got the best.'

The need for ongoing and immediate short-term profit in small businesses meant that often only the immediate causes of the fatality were addressed. A comprehensive reassessment of safety was not compatible with ongoing profitability, or 'protection', a reality which formed the context behind their typical blinkered response. This is illustrated by Reid Plumbing where certain safety procedures put in place after the fatality would be used on the site where the death occurred, but not on other sites, due to the increased costs incurred by such processes. With small business the need for immediate returns on profit then overshadowed the long-term consequences of their unsafe practices. The promotion of safety issues depended upon the relationship the particular issue had to profit and survival.

Large businesses also saw a critical relationship between safety and profit. However, this time the emphasis was on the compatibility of profit and safety, not the conflict. Many large businesses were able to see the relationship between profit and safety as positive in the long term, again supporting the theoretical insights in chapter 2 of large business having greater power and control in the market. Unsafe processes by these firms were seen as inevitably inefficient and counter-productive in these firms. The safety executive at Aidans put the argument for a proactive stance on safety this way: 'It concentrates on removing those actions or processes in the workplace that are unproductive anyway.' This particular manager was the strongest advocate for the mutuality of profit and safety, and took his argument beyond the dichotomy between short- and long-term profit by denying that there was any distinction to be made between the two:

'. . . if you are put in a position where you need to take short cuts in order to get your product out of the door and on time, then your process is shonky to begin with, and so is your thinking. You have got a bottleneck somewhere, and that bottleneck may well be caused by unsafe or unproductive processes in the first place . . . or it is greed, you are trying to get things done on the cheap. If you have got satisfactory long-term objectives and then not satisfactory short-term objectives it causes mistiming. Every time that they mistime it they are going to have an accident. It may result in a damaged component, it may result in a tool or a machine damage, or it may result in physical injury; and that is unacceptable. Or a faulty part gets out and goes into circulation; that is also not acceptable because it is going to come back at some time in some way or another.'

With the compatibility of safety and profit secured by their structural opportunities and their cultural ethos, large business could afford to be creative in the resolution of the issues which emerged from the death. Such companies saw their virtuous response as ultimately beneficial to the company in terms of increased profit through lower overall safety costs. This was accompanied by safety personnel who worked hard to show the benefits of improving safety. The safety executive at Aidans again illustrates the role well. He had spent some time convincing a sceptical employer of the benefits of safety:

'I went there and they showed me the accident records, and they thought they were doing it right: any one who went on compo was a bludger, all injuries which were not blood on the floor were manufactured injuries. It was really a lack of knowledge, once they got [*sic*] the knowledge, their attitudes changed dramatically. Once it was put on the monthly report of profit and loss; safety and accidents, monetary return, then they began to realize there was money to be made out of good safety. That is why I aimed at that. I analysed the corporation; the way it stood, and then attacked the most vulnerable point, which was cash flow.'

What is clear here is the difference in the terminology and line of argument between the small organizations and the large concerns. In large organizations safety is all about the law of averages. If a process has a high risk associated with it, in a large organization an injury or death has a high likelihood of resulting at some time within their organization. If a death highlighted a risk, it made sense to eliminate that risk company wide, and any ancillary risks that were uncovered by the death. Thus Mightysteel, for example, instigated a regime to mandate harness use throughout the company, not just on the site where the death occurred.

The differential impact of profit constraints on large and small business then fleshes out the theoretical link between size and constraints to virtue. When a firm is small and profit margins tight, the focus is necessarily short term. Long-term survival is directly related to short-term survival. The larger organization has more space between the demands of profit and the need to act. Constraints on behaviour are present, yet they are not so pressing as to preclude choice, and choice which includes virtue. Within such organizations it could be argued that the managerialist culture as proposed by Berle and Means can come into play. Managers are in the position to present a strong case for the mutuality of safety and profit in the long term.

This section has illustrated then that size may indeed influence virtue, as shown here by the virtue of responses organizations make to the deaths they experience. Size affects the way the relationship between profit and safety is perceived, with small companies viewing profit in the short term and emphasizing the conflict between the two aims, and large organizations emphasizing their compatibility. This view on the compatibility or otherwise of safety and profit then affects the breadth with which they view the implications of the death. The perceived conflict between the two aims results in a blinkered response, their perceived compatibility results in a virtuous response.

The Influence of External Constraints on Virtue: Position in the Contracting Hierarchy

An analysis of the effect of position in the contracting hierarchy on response allows us to explore further the influence of

TABLE 7.2. Responses of Organizations by Position in the Contracting Hierarchy

Response	High Position	Low Position
Virtuous	5	2
Blinkered	9	9
Total	14	11

external constraints on virtue. Within a particular worksite the access to power one organization has over another, in terms of determining the conditions or behaviour of another, has implications for the virtue of the weaker party. It might be expected that those higher in the hierarchy are in a more advantageous position to influence conditions of those lower down. Those in a high position within the contracting hierarchy are those who are in a position to influence directly (and indirectly) the behaviour of other organizations through manipulating the conditions of contract. Landowners, major contractors and those who control the productive process are all high position in the contracting hierarchy, since they control the workplace, have direct and indirect influence on others, namely the subcontractors. Those in a low position within the contracting hierarchy were subcontractors of various kinds. They were under the direct control of another organization on site, one high in the contracting hierarchy. They were typically only on site for short periods of time, although the exception here was Haddons, which although on site during the total construction of the dredger, was tightly controlled by both Resource Mining and Stutganst.

It would be expected then that this control over the worksite, being in the position of major contractor or tenderor, would mean that such organizations experience less constraints on virtue. This should result in a more virtuous response than from those lower in the contracting hierarchy. In this section this proposition is analysed more closely.

Somewhat surprisingly the effect of position in the contracting hierarchy on response appeared to have little or no influence on response as illustrated by Table 7.2. The table shows that although companies responding in a virtuous manner were more likely to be in a high than low position in the contracting hierarchy (five as against two), companies responding in a blinkered fashion were equally likely to be in a high or low position. In fact more firms in a high position acted in blinkered fashion. Based in terms of the figures alone, it is tempting to conclude that position in the contracting hierarchy has little effect.

Such an assessment would be premature. Position in the contracting hierarchy needs to be seen in a broader context of either strength or weakness in the overall market-place. What can be well illustrated by the comments on the contracting/subcontracting process is that such a process does clearly influence choice. However, the effect position in the contracting hierarchy has is dependent on overall power in the market-place. The rationalizations on the contracting process reveal the internal decision making of organizations in a position of weakness. For weak subcontractors their continued existence depended on their ability to obtain contracts by undercutting competitors on cost criteria alone. The project manager of Mightysteel/Arcade explained the contractor's dilemma in a highly competitive market:

'... let's say there is a tender out, half a dozen people might quote. In today's economy they want it done as cheap as possible, as fast as possible with a minimum of fuss ... The company will get prices that vary from $100,000 and $80,000. Now, what is the difference between 80 and 100? The difference is how you do the job; do you do it safely? Do you provide all the equipment to do it properly? Or do you take short cuts and you don't get all the equipment? Because your time to do the job is the same from one guy to another.'

Once the contract is obtained by undercutting competitors, the problem becomes one of completing the job within both the cost and time constraints imposed by that contract. Increased safety on worksites had, in some subcontractors' perspective, decreased productivity. For example, where riggers (who act as subcontractors on a building site) used to 'walk the steel' in the frame construction of buildings, scissor lifts are now required slowing the process down. Some find ways around the regulations to complete the job within the budget by working after hours without the scrutiny of the major contractor, as the project manager of Mightysteel/Arcade again explained:

TABLE 7.3. Responses of Small Organizations by Position in the Contracting Hierarchy

Response	High Position	Low Position
Virtuous	0	1
Blinkered	5	9
Total	5	10

'Years ago you'd be able to erect a building; put on the purlins on the roof, or wall girts, and the guys used to walk the trusses[4] carrying them, right? They are not allowed to do it any more. They are not allowed to walk them across [the trusses]. [But] [i]t is still happening. You see the job being done on the weekends . . . You will drive past on a Friday and there is nothing there. You drive past Monday morning—the job is up. Why did they work on Saturday and Sunday? There are no inspectors, there are no safety reps. There is no unions around. That's the reasons it happens at the weekend because people are taking short cuts. It takes longer, you are supposed to have safety nets underneath so that if the guy falls off he falls into a net, they are all costs. People are taking short cuts for those reasons. To save money.'

The Combined Influence of Size and Position in the Contracting Hierarchy on Response

If it is indeed overall weakness in the market-place which constrains virtue, a more useful analysis may be to look at the **combined** effect of size and position in the contracting hierarchy on response. Recasting the effect of position in the contracting hierarchy on response (Table 7.2) according to both size and position in the contracting hierarchy reveals interesting insights. Table 7.3 shows the response of small (i.e. weak) organizations according to position in the contracting hierarchy. Table 7.4 shows the response of large organizations according to position in the contracting hierarchy.

Table 7.3 shows that **no** small organizations which were in a high position in the contracting hierarchy responded in a virtu-

[4] Roof timber which sits under the roofing material.

TABLE 7.4. Responses of Large Organizations by Position in the Contracting Hierarchy

Response	High Position	Low Position
Virtuous	5	1
Blinkered	4	0
Total	9	1

ous manner. The conclusion from this is that the weak position of small business in the market-place as a whole constrains virtue, irrespective of position in the contracting hierarchy. If the compatibility of profit and safety is not altered by their worksite position in the contracting hierarchy, it is unlikely that their response would alter. The influence of external constraints extends beyond the confines of the single worksite, namely that the position of small business in an industry as a whole needs to be addressed. Small business may only obtain contracts where a conflict between safety and profit is inevitable.

The responses of large organizations sorted by their position in the contracting hierarchy, shown in Table 7.4, is equally instructive. Those large organizations in a high position in the contracting hierarchy were more likely than small business in the same position to act in a virtuous manner. In addition, no large companies in a low position in the contracting hierarchy responded in a blinkered manner: however, there was only one company that was both large and low position in the contracting hierarchy, so this figure must be treated with caution. This suggests the primary constraint on virtue is size, which the interview material shows is mediated by the ability of large business to see profit in the long term.

This overall weakness resulting of small companies in high position in the contracting hierarchy is well supported by the interview material. Small companies as major contractors were seen by most subcontractors as less concerned about the safety of the site overall, being more concerned with low cost, when compared to their larger counterparts:

'The bigger companies are becoming more and more safety conscious; they don't want any flak whether it be from the media, unions, whatever . . . it's public money. Public companies or big private companies they want the job done at the right price, but they want it done right.' [Project manager Arcade/Mightysteel]

This was supported by the owner of Service Cranes. When asked about the concern contractors and building owners had for his workers' safety, he stated:

'With their concern for your safety, well yes and no. Some reputable builders yes, they don't want to have an accident on site, they tend to be the bigger ones. Some of the smaller operators have no concern, they just call you in and expect you to get on with it. Where does it start? It comes back to the man on the site. The small builders they don't have any concern about your safety. They just want to know how quickly you can do it and at what cost. The small builders, they have not been educated they are always trying to push.'

Constraints on virtue then differ according to size of the organization, and the ability of the organization to obtain profitable contracts. How an individual organization is positioned in both the workplace structure and the broader industry determines the degree to which safety, and virtuous behaviour, is incorporated into business reality. Those able to obtain the profitable contracts, usually large organizations, can accommodate safety, which is bolstered by their large workforces and corresponding decreases in compensation costs. In turn their responses to the death are likely to be virtuous. Those more marginalized, and lower in the worksite hierarchy, are forced to choose between safety and profit. This choice is pushed towards minimizing safety procedures because of their small size and lack of influence of compensation concerns. Even when small organizations are in a high position in the contracting hierarchy, they may still be marginalized when seen in light of the structure of the industry as a whole, rather than the single worksite. These constraints result in a blinkered response to the deaths experienced. This general trend would appear to support the theoretical analysis of Marx, but also that of Galbraith and Berle and Means.

Limits to Structure? The Anomalous Cases

The tables above, however, reveal a less than perfect picture. While there is some support for the hypothesis that marginalization (measured by small size and low position in the contracting hierarchy) leads to a blinkered response, and access to power (measured by large size and high position in the contracting hierarchy) leads to a virtuous response, there are clear exceptions to this possible trend. One small company which was in a low position in the contracting hierarchy undertook a virtuous response to the death. Four organizations which were large and in a high position in the contracting hierarchy had a blinkered response. The concern in this section is to explore these anomalies and uncover the implications they hold for the theoretical analysis developed in this chapter that constraints on virtue are most acute on those organizations which are both small and in a weak position in the contracting hierarchy.

The first anomaly, that of the small subcontractor responding in a 'virtuous' manner, extends but does not contradict the major argument developed so far in this chapter. That is, such organizations experience the greatest constraints on virtue due to their small size and weak position in the worksite. The difference here though was the way this company reasoned about its future success given these constraints. It saw its strong commitment to safety and the ensuing virtuous response as part of its success strategy. Like other companies in the 'virtuous' category this company saw profit and safety as compatible. This small company, however, showed different reasoning concerning this compatibility from the large organizations in this category. They argued that a good safety record increased competitiveness in the tendering process, particularly in submissions to reputable firms. This is explained by the owner of the company:

> 'In the long term the effect of [our] increased focus on health and safety is a good one . . . If you are here to stay, then to work safely increases your profit. Just recently a reputable firm wanted to see our safety records before they would give us a job. We were really worried because of the accident, but we did get the job . . . We can't take short cuts and we won't risk people, in the end that will help you succeed.'

The compatibility between profit and safety for this company then revolved around using safety as a commodity. A good safety record could be used to enhance their chances of gaining contracts from the large respectable organizations whom they saw as their future market. As the owner of Service Cranes continued: 'In the long term the effect [on profit] of the increased focus on safety is a good one . . . We are here for the long term, if you are here to stay then safety increases your profit.' The owner also indicated the influence tenderors had on this belief, stating that reputable firms wanted to see his safety record before awarding the company a contract.

This company though was not exempt from constraints on virtue. It was entirely dependent on those awarding contracts deeming safety to be a pivotal issue in deciding which tender to accept. If this was not the case, such a strategy undertaken by Service Cranes could well result in its demise. Service Cranes was constrained, as were all small subcontractors, by those awarding contracts demanding, and paying for, high safety standards. Not all were willing to do so. In the discussion with the director of Service Cranes it became clear that he lost some contracts because of his attitude towards safety; as he stated: 'If I decide it is too dangerous I tell them [the contractor] to get someone else . . . it seems they are able to do so'.

There were, however, examples of organizations in the data which made a conscious effort to influence the safety of their subcontractors. They chose contractors on the basis of their safety record, and built up preferred contractors who would abide by their safety rules and comply with the company standards. The following heavy engineering company, Aidans, was one such organization; as the personnel manager stated concerning one favoured contractor, 'we have had our ins and outs with Reid Plumbing and they were well and truly indoctrinated in what working at heights was required'. This was extended in the case of International Paper where the profitability of the contracts they awarded was directly related to the safety of the contractors, safety which was policed by International Paper themselves. International Paper set up a point system of fines, where a contractor not performing work in a safe manner, or without safety equipment, would lose points, which would then affect the amount of pulpwood accepted from that company. The system was policed by three employees of International Paper who would rove the region dropping in on contractors unannounced. The safety officer explained:

'If a contractor loses more than ten points; which you can see is not that hard, not having one piece of safety equipment loses those points, that means they get a 10 per cent cut in their contract quota [for pulpwood]. They have a quota that they contract for, they deliver so much timber per fortnight which they tender to us for the job [now that fluctuates on demand from the mill]. If they lose more than ten points, they get a 10 per cent quota cut for a quota period, which is a fortnight. That amount comes out to between a $5,000 and $10,000 fine.'

These examples serve to illustrate why regulatory theory can no longer be content to theorize about the actions of a single organization in isolation. Within the dual economy the relationships between organizations, and the way they affect each other, to good or ill, need to be a central issue in debates about regulation both in the literature and in the policy room. As production is increasingly fragmented and the use of contractors increases, how to effect the relationship between various players in the market becomes of paramount importance. This is not to place the sole burden on the overt regulator. Creative ideas of how one company improves the behaviour of another, such as is the case with International Paper, illustrate what is possible out in the market, and supports Grabosky's (1994a and b) work that regulators look to the market to assist in dealing with corporate harm. However, the case of Service Cranes would suggest this is only possible under certain market conditions, namely when the major player has the competitive freedom to insist on safety as part of the contractual obligations. The call to look to the market as a regulatory strategy needs a means by which to assess the viability of a given market in sustaining corporate virtue.

A solution is to look to a Weberian analysis to assist us in taking account of how relationships between organizations either enhance or undermine virtue. Such an analysis would suggest that large organizations demanding high safety standards, and who award preferential treatment to chosen subcontractors, are attempting closure. That is, they are trying to create a closed market where only those with the requisite safety standards may succeed in the tendering process. A pertinent analysis in the case of Service Cranes then would be that this organization was putting its faith in the large organizations succeeding in their attempt at closure. That is, that Service Cranes saw their future lying within sites with restricted entry, where an entrance requirement is high safety standards. The existence of International Paper and others of like mind indicates that some large firms, at least, sought closure based on virtue, or safety.

The dependence of the subcontractor on the attitude of their contractor and the willingness to form such status groups regarding safety nonetheless placed subcontractors in a vulnerable position, with most small subcontractors agreeing that contractors had a limited concern for their safety, and consequently they concluded that safety and profit were ultimately in conflict in their own organizations. This was despite an increased formalization in the contracting process with contracts containing specific instructions regarding safety levels. Formal specification was not a guarantee of safety, it depended on the attitude of the major contractor and the contract price, despite what was specifically written in the contract. This was explained by the demolition contractor employing the previous owner of Better Demolitions:

> 'The way you get a job is a person buys a place, then draws a map of it, and gets in a demolition contractor. The contractor is told to do the job whichever way they [*sic*] can. Originally the contract had no aspect of safety in it, now there is getting to be more. But you are not given the extra money in the contract to make it safe, it's just window dressing.'

The practice of small companies who were in a high position in the contracting hierarchy lends support to the scepticism expressed by the small subcontractors above. For the majority of small business who were in a high position in the contracting hierarchy, safety on site simply was not an issue when putting a contract out for tender, although price may not be the sole determining factor in deciding to whom to award the contract.

The analysis of the small business high in the contracting hierarchy is also supported by a Weberian analysis. A Weberian analysis would suggest that small business is unable to arrange its business in such a way that it is shielded from the full effect of competition for work based purely on cost considerations. Unable to create market closure, it is bound by constraints which push it to compete primarily on cost considerations. It is therefore unable to shield the subcontractors it employs from the same rules of competition. The presence of large organizations able to undertake closure of the market and form preferential arrangements with subcontractors based on virtue, on the other hand, can raise the standard of that worksite. This data tentatively supports Gunningham's (1991) findings that brokerage (or virtue) was improved by high status organizations maintaining ethical standards of a particular stock market through restricting entry to those considered appropriate to compete in that market. This data has similar evidence. Some large organizations in the data attempted closure by creating virtuous criteria as an entry mechanism into their market (i.e. to gain contracts). Such criteria could improve the virtue of the whole site.

The four anomalous large organizations which responded in a blinkered fashion highlight the complications in nurturing virtue in those organizations which are less constrained in terms of choice regarding behaviour. While size and position in the contracting hierarchy may afford these companies more choice, in terms of ethical behaviour, it may not determine which choice, virtuous or non-virtuous, they may take. In the four cases below what is revealed is the way organizations in a position of power can avoid virtue. They do this by using legal definitions of responsibility to argue that they are either not responsible, or not a unitary organization, and so their responsibility is diminished. As Kolko (1965) and others (Bachrach and Baratz, 1970; Lukes, 1974) point out, large organizations are further in a position to dictate the rules of acceptable business practice, either directly, by lobbying government to change legislation in their favour, or indirectly, by the threat of closing down operations if conditions are 'onerous'. They thus dictate to some extent the market within which they operate, and the definitions of responsibility they will accept. The four companies below illustrate some of these elements found in this literature: the first one, Bigland, was able to avoid responsibility by dictating the rules of responsibility; the second, Stutganst, used its power to avoid the implication of being held responsible; and the third and fourth, Mightysteel and Nettles Builders, illustrate how challenges to the concept of the unitary organization were used to deflect responsibility away from the central organization. So, while large size and high position in the contracting hierarchy **may** provide the freedom to respond in a virtuous manner, the **same** preconditions of size and position in the contracting hierarchy provide the power for such organizations to avoid their responsibilities.

The first of these companies, Bigland, was able to continue to distance itself from the need to respond due to its contractual relationship to those involved in the fatality. Rather than being an active part of the productive process, in this case logging, it was the landowner where the operations took place and as such saw it had no role to play in the safety of those using its land for productive purposes. It did, however, place stringent controls on those working the land so as to protect the environment, some of which placed loggers in danger when felling timber. The position to dictate one set of rules while avoiding responsibility for the effect of those rules on those affected by them it strongly defended in court, winning major common law claims in its favour. The situation was explained by the safety officer of International Paper:

'We recently had a contractor who called up and said that he was being forced to put his faller in an area which he considered too dangerous to harvest. But Bigland wanted it harvested and were forcing him to go in there. I went to have a look . . . and I declared it unsafe . . . In the finish I couldn't get any response from Bigland so I contacted the DOL, and they settled the issue once and for all . . . Bigland, even though the land is theirs they don't want to know about it. A court case has just been decided in their favour and it shouldn't have been.'

As long as Bigland was able to maintain total separation between owning land and involvement in the production process, even where the land held inherent dangers for those working on it, it saw no need to make any correlation between its own profitability and the safety of those using the land for productive purposes.

The second company of large size and high position in the contracting hierarchy but blinkered response was Stutganst. This company was an aggressive player at inquest challenging all references to its responsibility for the death which resulted from the collapse of a dredger which it had designed. The strength of legal response which was able to be mounted in this case correspondingly allowed it to continue to deny responsibility for the collapse and the subsequent need for safety changes. Business concerns independent of safety predominated in the case of this company in the way it responded to the fatality and conducted business after the death. Some time after the death the company was involved in restructuring and as part of this process it decided to sell off the arm of the company responsible for constructing dredgers. This process was independent of the experience of the fatality. The imperatives of business in this case overrode the need for a discussion of safety and profit. The primary concern here was to use its power to avoid legal liability and to allow it to continue with its business concerns, which included selling off the part of the company responsible for dredger design. Its size and the multinational nature of its operations allowed it to achieve this end.

The final two large organizations who were in high position in the contracting hierarchy yet responded in a blinkered manner also show the importance of definitions which concern the nature of the unitary organization, and the nature of organizational responsibility. Both these organizations challenge a neat definition of a unitary organization with discrete boundaries which is able to be held as **the** organization which is responsible for the harm that emanates when a death occurs. Both companies illustrate the fluid nature of organizational boundaries and with this the possible shifting definitions of responsibility and responsiveness within and between those boundaries.

The first of these, Mightysteel, was encountered in the previous chapter. As was explained in that chapter it was only through the interviews that it was discovered that the building of the steel mill was under the control of Mightysteel, not Arcade as written in the inquest documents. The two departments of Mightysteel, the site and the central organization, exhibited very different responses: the warehouse construction site exhibited a blinkered response, while the main steel mill exhibited a virtuous response. The warehouse construction site was part of Mightysteel, not a separate unit, with this sub-unit of Mightysteel exhibiting a blinkered response in contrast to the main office, which had a virtuous response. It has long been recognized that different departments within the same organization can act in separate ways (Gross, 1978; Fisse and Braithwaite, 1988; Hawkins, 1990). An added insight from this data concerns where differences in behaviour emanate from. In this case it appears that the difference in response, i.e. behaviour, may be explained by the functions of these different departments in that construction of the warehouse was a short-term concern, and as such was a peripheral operation to the major process of steel making. The construction manager explained the peripheral nature of the project:

'When it [the death] actually happened we were working on the extensions to the existing warehouse . . . We had finished the factory, that is the production site, and we realized our existing warehousing was too small and we would have to extend it.'

Those in control of the peripheral operations may be left to their own devices, as was the case here, and thus may control their operations in such a way which is counter to the prevailing ethos of the company. The construction manager was in this position:

'It [the health and safety on site] was pretty much left to me. I knew there was a health and safety department over the road at the Mill . . . Mightysteel got quite heavily into the retraining, the Health and Safety Act, the whole [safety] department there.'

'But as far as the construction site went it was pretty much left to you?'

'Left to me, yes.'

Here what is illustrated is that a large organization may focus on its core operations, while projects at the periphery may receive less attention. Those in control of the peripheral operations may then choose to run the operation according to their own view. This project manager held a very different view of the mutuality of profit and safety, arguing that there was conflict between the two, in direct contrast to the main mill operation. When asked if an increased emphasis on health and safety improves profit, after a long pause he said:

'I think they don't work hand in hand personally. That's my personal opinion. Let's face it safety does cost money . . . at the end of the day **possibly** a job that is done safely could work out cheaper or the same cost maybe. . . . [But you have to ask] "How am I going to do it? Am I going to use the right equipment?" . . . [that means] more cranes, more cherry pickers, travel towers, working platforms so they are working safely.'

Here then one organization can exhibit different responses, depending on the department concerned. How to encourage the **whole** organization to adopt a virtuous response and a virtuous outlook thus becomes important. This may involve innovative sanctioning, to make the 'buck stop' at the right place within an organization (Fisse and Braithwaite, 1988), or the encouragement of subcultures with a proactive ethos within the organization

(Sinclair, 1993). It may extend beyond this, however, to an investigation of the structure of the particular organization and the structure of the industry to ascertain those structures which encourage a proactive approach to safety (Haines and Sutton, 1997).

The fourth and final of the four large, high position in the contracting hierarchy blinkered respondents, Nettles Builders, illustrates again the problem of definition of 'organization', this time the need for a definition which takes into account a network of relationships between organizations that make up a business conglomerate. Inquest documents suggested Nettles Builders was an independent medium sized organization with approximately 100 employees. From other research, however, it was discovered that in fact Nettles was majority owned by a large conglomerate, which had a stake in a range of companies involved in a variety of productive processes from the manufacture of electrical goods through to ice cream production. Furthermore, that conglomerate was in considerable financial difficulties. Around the time of the interview this holding company was undergoing liquidation. An issue in this case then is the degree of pressure the holding company placed on Nettles in terms of a push for short-term profit, which would in turn affect Nettles' view of the profit/safety nexus and thus their work practices.

This complicates our understanding of the necessary target of regulatory pressure. Current regulatory frameworks would tend to focus on the activities of individual firms. While this is indeed warranted, the question remains regarding the effectiveness of regulation of this nature in light of possible continued pressure for short-term profit from a holding company. As the economy becomes more complex with greater numbers of organizations dedicated to redefining their boundaries and their responsibilities these issues become more acute.

Taken as a whole, these exceptions to the general trend of large size and high position in the contracting hierarchy corresponding with virtuous responses point to the need to investigate the continuing pressures on all organizations to act in a blinkered manner. What seems clear is that the capacity of small organizations to act virtuously, when they are in a low position in the contracting hierarchy, is very much dependent on the attitude of the major player in a worksite. To nurture virtue it may be necessary to encourage closure of worksites so that compliance with high safety standards is a precondition of gaining contracts.

For a major player to attempt closure in this manner, however, they need to be convinced that awarding contracts on this basis is viable, if not vital, to overall success. It is clear that small organizations who are in this controlling position do not see this as viable to their long-term success. Rather, cost forms the controlling variable in the decision to award contracts. With the case of small business who are major contractors, it may be necessary to look at their ability to act virtuously, and to encourage virtue within their subcontractors, in light of the broader constraints they face within their own industry. If their sole competitive edge lies on decreased costs and increased flexibility their capacity to encourage virtue in the broader industry may be severely limited.

With large business the suggestion emerging is one where closure needs to be encouraged. However, the criteria for such closure needs to be carefully scrutinized. Closure increases the power of the organization which has the controlling influence on the worksite. Such power may not necessarily be used to improve standards. The cases of the four large firms which acted in a blinkered manner illustrate that power could be used to avoid responsibility and shift blame rather than promote virtue. Choosing to use power in this negative fashion was made possible by the international nature of some organizations, and the complexity of the unitary organization where extensive cross-ownership between organizations occurs.

The analysis of worksite dynamics in this chapter reveals considerable challenges for regulators. Even so there are indications that the analysis may need to extend more broadly. Structure of industry, structure of capital and the structure of the organization itself may each have a role to play in production and maintenance of virtuous organizations. If this is so, then the current shifts within contemporary capitalism aimed at increasing competitiveness through flexibility have considerable implications for nurturing virtue. The methods by which this is to be achieved, for example industrial restructuring and contracting out, may become central concerns for regulators in the upcoming century. These issues are explored more fully in chapter 9.

The Relationship between Structure, Culture and Response

It has been argued in this chapter that the driving force behind the companies' attitude to the profit/safety nexus is the degree to which their choices are constrained. Where there is choice there is greater possibility that the relationship between profit and safety will be seen as positive. Where choices are limited, the relationship between profit and safety is more likely to be seen as ultimately detrimental to ongoing success. The organizations which were most likely to see this relationship as positive were both large and had high position in the contracting hierarchy. Those which were most likely to emphasize a negative correlation were small and low position in the contracting hierarchy. Exceptions to this pointed to the way in which access to power may enable choice, but that choice includes a choice not to be virtuous.

The concern of this section is the interplay between culture and structure. In particular, what is explored is the degree of dependence or independence culture has from structure. The first question concerns whether large organizations in a high position in the contracting hierarchy have a virtuous culture which leads to a virtuous response; and small organizations in a low position in the contracting hierarchy have a blinkered culture which leads to a blinkered response.

For the majority of organizations, workplace structure, culture and response were linked. Large organizations in a high position in the contracting hierarchy were more prone to exhibit a virtuous culture and respond in a virtuous manner. Conversely, small organizations low in the contracting hierarchy were more likely to adopt a blinkered stance and respond in a blinkered manner (see Figure 7.1).

One possible way to conceptualize the link between structure and culture is to use the concept of organizational or industrial character. Organizational character incorporates both culture and external constraints on organizational choice (Selznick, 1992). Philip Selznick writes:

> The character of an organization includes culture, but something more as well. A pattern of dependency—for example, on a specific labour force, a market, or particular suppliers—may have little to do with symbolism

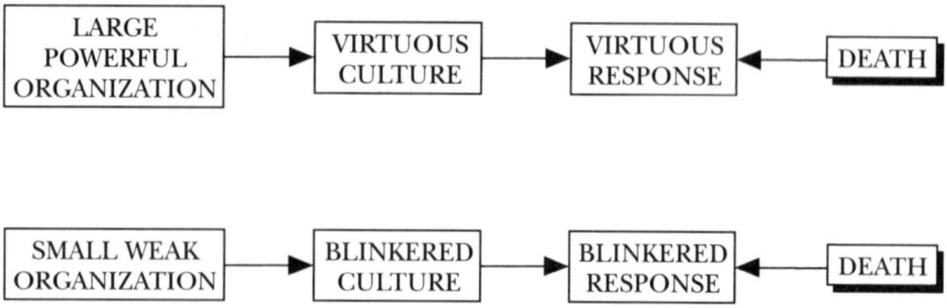

FIG. 7.1. Relationship between Response, Culture and External Constraints

> or belief. *The character of a company* or trade union *owes much to the structure of the industry*, the skills of employees or members, the alliances that can be fashioned, and many other practical limits and opportunities. Attitudes and beliefs account for only part of an organization's distinctive character. [Selznick, 1992:321, emphasis added]

What this suggests is that the character of a particular company, or indeed an industry, is a combination of both the structure of the industry and the associated culture.

Of particular interest to a discussion of structure, and of character, are the anomalous cases in the data. Was the culture of those which did not respond in the way predicted by their size and position in the contracting hierarchy related to that size and position in the contracting hierarchy or related to their response? Specifically, which of the two cultures did the one small, low position in the contracting hierarchy virtuous respondent subscribe to, and which culture did those companies which were large and high position in the contracting hierarchy but responded in a blinkered fashion have, a virtuous culture, or a blinkered culture? In other words was their response consistent with their culture, or was their position in the workplace structure, i.e. their size and position in the contracting hierarchy, consistent with their culture? Where structure did not predict response, was culture related to their structural position, or their response?

In the cases where size and position in the contracting hierarchy did not correlate with response, culture was consistent with response (Figure 7.2). The small organization with a low position in the contracting hierarchy which exhibited a virtuous response, Service Cranes, had largely a virtuous culture. Of the four that were large and had a high position in the contracting hierarchy

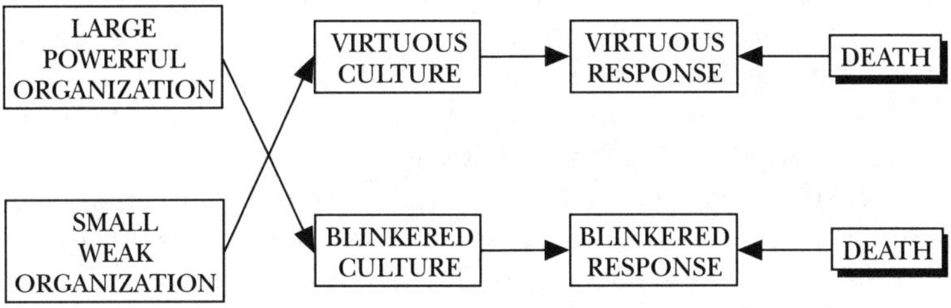

FIG. 7.2. Relationship between Response, Culture and External Constraints in Anomalous Cases

with a blinkered response, three had cultures consistent with a blinkered culture. The fourth did not have enough material available to make a cultural assessment.

What this suggests is that organizations respond or act in manners consistent with their culture, and borrowing from Selznick (1992) act 'out of character' when compared to their industrial peers. This suggests some independence from external constraints or structure and indicates some power to culture as an independent factor in explaining behaviour. However, while the actions of these companies were consistent with culture, they were also consistent with the logic of profit and safety. Their rationalizations on profit and safety were a precondition of culture. This suggests either the influence of broader structural influences, such as the structure of the industry, competitiveness within an industry; or alternatively the influence of a subjective assessment within organizations regarding beliefs about the compatibility of safety and profit, which was only partially dependent on structure. While the data has only limited insight into the influence of the structure of industry directly on culture, the data lends some support to the existence of an element of 'faith' or subjectivity in the assessment of the relationship of safety to profit.

The case of Service Cranes illustrates this point. They were convinced their long-term viability would be improved by their high standard of safety. While the interviews revealed contractors who were concerned for the history of safety of subcontractors, some of whom were discussed above, it was also true that Service Cranes had lost contracts due to their refusal to take unsafe jobs. It was a matter of some faith regarding how many they had obtained due to their proactive stance on safety, and how many they had lost, as the number was impossible to calculate. I am not saying here that this faith was unfounded, rather to suggest that there is both an objective and a subjective component to the belief in the compatibility of safety and profit.

The subjectivity of the belief regarding the compatibility of safety and profit is also seen in the arguments of those whose response was consistent with both their size and position in the contracting hierarchy and their culture. Large virtuous respondents, such as the central division of Mightysteel, pointed to the 'hidden' costs of accidents to support their argument:

> 'Accidents cost them a lot of money. Indirect costs that are never accounted for; the stoppages, industrial stoppages which you have as a result of the serious accident. The fact that you have to bring a new employee in and retrain him. A lot of costs which are never ever measured in any accident. They only ever measure the direct costs which are your hospitals and workers compensation . . .'

For those arguing **against** the compatibility of safety and profit the existence of more immediate and 'visible' costs proved their case. They cited time spent on safety as an important component of costs, illustrated here by the ex-owner of Daytons Rigging: 'You had to have harnesses, nets, you weren't allowed to work off the ladders. He'd keep catching us every five minutes and then you tell the guy to get down. Three days . . . now how my boss makes a profit I don't know.'

Within the constraints imposed by size and contract price then, there was an element of a philosophical perspective on the safety/profit debate which could direct individuals to look for hard evidence to support their perspective. The safety officer of Mightysteel had a strong belief in the compatibility of the two aims, and used compensation and rehabilitation costs to argue for changes in the steel mill:

> '. . . to justify getting the robotic arms I had to go back to the manager of one of the processes. We went through five years of accidents on the first floor and justified it, because the family[5] sign the cheque. They say how is it going to save us money? . . . We had five years of accidents to show them; and we costed them, and then justified it. [So you can't

[5] The organization in this case was a large family business.

really separate OHS from cost?] No, all part of it isn't it? Part and parcel of the saving.'

However, the 'ground rules' remain the same for both perspectives, which directed the logic used by key individuals within the organization in their argument for or against change. Independent of the side of the debate, safety is justified by '. . . cost, dollars and cents, the bottom line!'

Safety is thus essentially a commodity within both arguments and as such susceptible to justification on economic grounds alone, which is itself informed by economic debate. Structure, including workplace structure of size and position in the contracting hierarchy, set the ground rules for the debate concerning profit and safety. The organizations then use these ground rules as bounds to their rational 'debate' about the compatibility of profit and safety. This then determines how they see success is to be achieved which then becomes expressed through the organizational culture. It is from within that cultural context, and the normative controls it exerts, that response ensues.

Conclusion

This chapter has highlighted how virtue may be constrained by the size an organization is, and the position it holds in the contracting hierarchy. To a large degree the analysis above is consistent with the Marxist thesis of capital accumulation constraining the choices of smaller weaker players in the market. This chapter shows it was the smaller organizations which acted in the least virtuous manner as shown by their predominantly blinkered response to the death. A virtuous response was largely restricted to large organizations higher in the contracting hierarchy. Access to power by virtue of an organization's size and position in the contracting hierarchy gave greater choice of response, choice which included a 'virtuous' course of behaviour. Lack of power constrained choice and could be seen to force a blinkered response.

It should be clear though that a virtuous response by powerful organizations arose out of an assessment of where future success lay, rather than obedience to any intrinsic quality of the virtue itself. Debates about the relationship between profit and safety formed an intrinsic part of the cultural assumptions of the organization. From these cultural assumptions concerning future success, behaviour resulted. Where safety was seen as integral to future success, cultural norms (namely a virtuous culture) flowered which inculcated the value of safety within the organization. These cultural norms provided the assumptions which lay behind decisions from which behaviour followed. Where safety and success were seen as ultimately in conflict, cultural norms (in this case a blinkered culture) emerged which placed a priority on 'getting the job done' and dichotomizing choice. Such cultural norms provided the rationalizations which lay behind the blinkered response.

The data suggest some modification of the Marxist thesis may be appropriate. In particular there were some attempts at closure by some large organizations with a virtuous culture. These attempts at closure consisted of building exclusive contractual relationships with subcontractors who knew, and were willing to abide by, these large organizations' high standards on safety. Nurturing virtue in such contexts would then involve encouraging closure, where such closure encourages and maintains virtuous practice.

The data presented here also suggested that there was a need to extend the view of constraints to virtue as extending beyond those internal to a particular worksite. The presence of the behaviour of four large organizations inconsistent with their lack of constraints to behave virtuously leads to further questions. Are there, for example, conditions in the broader economy which preclude the formation of virtuous cultures within these companies? Further, is this due to the level and nature of competitiveness in these industries? At the very least regulators need to be looking in the direction of industry structure when forming policy.

Again this is both consistent with, yet extends, a Marxist analysis. A Marxist analysis would certainly see the need to extend analysis beyond the single worksite in isolation. The augmentation of the Marxist analysis is by the need to include in regulatory theory an understanding of the way in which certain industrial structures may allow the actors to act virtuously, while others preclude the choice to act virtuously. The concept of closure, of drawing boundaries around acceptable behaviour at the level of industry, again may be important here. An industry may need to exclude those organizations which seek to compete by cutting corners. Industry needs protection from competition, or control of competition, where that competition is based on premises which undermine virtue. Protection from such competition may by afforded by virtue of the size and power of some organizations, or by government regulation, or both. The government, and perhaps even international forums such as GATT, need to support these attempts.

Finally, there was some indication in the analysis of the data in this chapter of a subjective element concerning organizational views on the relationship between profit and safety. Here the normative cultural assumptions could play a vital role. Cultural assumptions directed the individuals within organizations to seek examples as evidence to support their stance. Hence those imbued with the virtuous view pointed to 'hidden' costs, while those from a blinkered perspective gave examples of the short-term 'up front' costs of safety. Within this limited subjective space, companies could act 'out of character' with respect to comparable organizations.

What is necessary to ascertain at this point is the role legislation plays in producing virtue either by reducing the constraints to virtue, by impacting on the rules of competition, or by influencing those with fewer constraints and more choice to take the virtuous path. From the above analysis, it is unlikely that legislation aimed at improving safety is able to increase the choices smaller weaker players have in acting virtuously. However, from the above analysis one possible avenue may be to encourage closure in industry where safety forms the basis of that closure. Further, legislation may be effective in influencing the choices the larger, more powerful organizations have. This chapter argued that while large, powerful organizations have the choice to act virtuously, they do not always choose this path. Legislation may encourage this choice.

8 How is Virtue Produced? The Role of Law and Law Enforcement

THE aim of this chapter is to review how the contemporary Victorian regulatory structure concerned with health and safety pushed organizations towards, or away from, virtue. The data presented thus far suggests that to undertake such a review adequately may involve taking account of how response to regulations is affected by the size and particular culture of the organization concerned. Further, it is necessary to look at the full range of regulatory schema targeted at maintaining and improving safety at work to look for signs of success. The key areas of law in occupational health and safety which are addressed in this chapter include occupational health and safety law, but go beyond this to look at the regulatory effect of common law liability and the effectiveness of compensation law in producing virtuous organizations.

Certainly the most direct regulatory apparatus concerned with safety at work is the specific occupational health and safety legislation, both in terms of its content and the enforcement of that content in terms of prosecution for breaches under the Act. It is this aspect of regulation (or its mining equivalent) which forms the basis for much discussion of regulation in the area of health and safety particularly by sociologists and criminologists (Gunningham, 1984; Braithwaite, 1985; Braithwaite and Grabosky, 1985; Grabosky and Braithwaite, 1986; Carson and Johnstone, 1990; Hopkins, 1989b and c, 1994b; James, 1992). Further, the focus by many writers tends to be orientated towards a discussion of law enforcement and compliance, rather than discussion of the architecture of the law itself (see for example Glasbeek and Rowland, 1979; Pearce and Tombs, 1990; Hopkins, 1994b). Review of the data presented in this chapter begins with analysis of the health and safety legislation in producing virtue, i.e. giving rise to virtuous responses to the fatalities which improve safety.

Discussion of structures set up by health and safety legislation and the effectiveness of the structures is an important part of the ability of legislation to improve safety at work. In the enthusiasm to analyse compliance with legislation, exploration of the actual effectiveness of the statute in improving safety tends to be missed. A comprehensive analysis of regulatory law requires both. The relevant Act in Victoria operating at the time of the research (and still in a modified form currently) was the *Occupational Health and Safety Act* 1985 (Vic.) (hereafter 'OHSA'), an Act which promotes a tripartite approach to safety between employers, unions and regulators.[1] It incorporates suggestions put forward by Lord Robens in his 1972 report on health and safety concerned specifically with placing a primary duty of care on employers, as opposed to employees or regulators (Robens, 1972). It is considered a comprehensive Act, as it requires contractors to be responsible for the safety of subcontractors' employees as well as viewing the involvement of employees as integral to safety, and legislates for their involvement through health and safety representatives and committees.[2] Such committees have been found by some research to be very important for raising safety levels (Biggins, Phillips and O'Sullivan, 1991). Further, the legislation in Victoria has provided for a system of Improvement Notices and Prohibition Notices to provide for adequate enforcement of adherence to safety legislation, whereby authorized officers, including worker representatives[3] and safety inspectors, can demand safety improvements where workers are at unacceptable risk. The Act is underpinned by legislating a common law duty of care (known as 'general duties') on employers. Employers are required 'as far as is practicable' to provide a safe workplace

[1] Recent changes in Victoria have seen a removal of the role of the unions, while the role for safety representatives remains. This means workers can still influence safety in the workplace, but are not formally party to the setting of regulations or general guidelines outside the workplace. At the time of the interviews they had this ability through the now disbanded Victorian Occupational Health and Safety Commission. The activities of the commission, in diminished form, are undertaken by a ministerial advisory committee.

[2] The actual definition and role of these safety representatives and committees varies. The points of difference revolve around the role of unions in the appointment of safety representatives, and the power they can wield in terms of cessation of work. For a useful comparison see the Industry Commission Report (1994, Appendix C).

[3] Worker representatives are only empowered to place a Provisional Improvement Notice (or PIN) on a machine or process. This has to be ratified by the government inspector.

(section 21). Such a requirement encourages the use of written procedures to clarify correct safe work procedures. Prosecution of health and safety offences has been increasing, admittedly from a very low base (compare figures in Braithwaite and Grabosky, 1986, with those in Hopkins, 1994a). However, within the deaths analysed for this study only one prosecution resulted (Perrone, 1993; Johnstone, 1994).

However, legal liability extends beyond liability under health and safety legislation or the criminal law. An important part of liability for organizations comes from the common law, with individuals taking direct legal action to recover damages from their employers. How organizations respond to legal liability then, can be explored by looking at how organizations respond to their common law liabilities, as well as response to enforcement action under health and safety legislation or criminal law. To some extent the impact on an organization taken to court for damages (either compensatory or punitive) can be seen as an approximation for criminal prosecution, particularly in the way the organization defends itself against such a contingency, and the impact that has as a spur for virtue.[4]

The second area of the data which is discussed in this chapter concerns the impact common law claims have on safety, and by extension virtue. Unlike fines, which have tended to be low (for a current overview see Hopkins, 1994a), common law claims can lead to substantial financial outlays by the organization. For this reason they could be seen to have a **greater** impact on organizational behaviour and response than criminal penalties. Unlike criminal penalties, however, common law claims can be insured against. The role of the insurer in protecting their own assets needs to be considered here.

Finally, the effectiveness of compensation law in improving safety is explored through the data. The use of compensation law as a regulatory mechanism has become increasingly important in recent years. Compensation law is no longer considered only as a mechanism to compensate workers for illness and injury, but also as a method of altering organizational attitudes to safety.

[4] The common law, in particular the drive for punitive damages by lawyers, has been seen as a useful way to get organizations to improve their safety standards. It has been used as a quasi-prosecutorial measure by legal firms with an expertise in bringing negligence claims.

This has been achieved through moulding the costs of compensation more directly to reflect the actual health and safety standards within a particular workplace, rather than purely acting to compensate a worker after illness or injury has occurred. Varying premiums apply depending on an organization's past safety performance (Industry Commission, 1994). What this provides for is positive financial inducements through lower premiums to those companies with a good safety record, as measured by the numbers of claims.

To the list of formal legal measures for encouraging virtue needs to be added the potential effect of publicity and the role of the media. While it is not a legal mechanism, the role of the media as a regulator has often been posed as a useful adjunct to governmental mechanisms, as a way of shaming organizations in a public manner into compliance (Clinard and Yeager, 1980; Coffee, 1981; Fisse and Braithwaite, 1983). Its high profile as a proposed regulatory mechanism warrants its inclusion here.

What was suggested by the previous chapter, and needs to be kept in mind here, is the way that external economic constraints faced by an organization form the context within which this regulation takes place. Health and safety mechanisms, as well as the mechanisms open to the media, are limited in their ability to alter constraints such as organizational size and the access to power the organization has in the market. These constraints faced by the various organizations may affect the way they respond to regulatory pressure. Different responses organizations make to regulatory techniques may depend upon who they are, in terms of size and power, and the position they hold in the contracting hierarchy.

Organizations and Safety: The Importance of a Safety Focus and the Role of Health and Safety Legislation

The data illustrates that the various aspects of OHSA were viewed differently by the two cultures. One clear example was raised in chapter 6, since it also formed an aspect of the inclusive or dichotomous nature of the two organizational cultures. This was the attitudes towards section 21(3) which defines employee broadly to include responsibility for subcontractors' employees, in the context of the employers' general duties as outlined in section 21(1) and (2). According to this section primary responsibility for safety of the subcontractor's employee lies with the major contractor. This can be seen as crucial to improving safety at a worksite level (Haines, 1993) since it begins to recognize the influence companies have on each other within multiple employer worksites, in particular the power the major contractor has over the conditions of subcontractors. Contractors with a blinkered culture in the data, however, did not see their subcontractors' employees as their responsibility despite the legislation. When using subcontractors these firms saw responsibility for the safety of the subcontractor's employee lying with the subcontractor, not themselves, as 'he's the one who employs them'. In contrast contractors with a virtuous culture saw the ultimate responsibility for the safety of all workers on site resting with them.

This example tends to suggest that 'virtuous' organizations with their inclusive culture **actively** used OHSA to improve safety. Further, such companies had a well developed safety bureaucracy, often related to legislative requirements, which reflected a high priority on safety. This bureaucracy included safety officers or other safety personnel who had direct access to those in power, use of written procedures as standard, and a safety committee structure and health and safety representatives that involved both management and workers. In addition, the organization was supportive of key individuals who were committed to use the bureaucratic structure to improve safety. In this way a high priority was placed on safety, one which was able to challenge individual attitudes and manipulate the immediate organizational context in the interest of safety. Within these departments were individuals with a commitment to safety and a willingness to pursue safety issues. The aim of these individuals and departments was to build up knowledge and consciousness of safety issues within the organization. These usually included extensive use of written procedures,[5] but were not limited to those procedures, as it was

[5] The exception to this was the one small business with a virtuous culture, which had written procedures in place, but relied far more heavily on verbal communication to get the message of safety across.

recognized that these had to be translated into practice. This they did by a combination of training, knowledge testing and various consciousness raising exercises within the organization.

Organizations with a virtuous culture had an active role for both worker safety representatives and safety committees in the investigation and learning process arising out of the fatalities. Such committees have been shown to be of great benefit to workplace safety (Biggins, Phillips and O'Sullivan, 1991). The safety representatives and safety committees were seen as a major resource during investigations into the fatalities, a view exemplified here by Resource Mining:

'One of its positive side effects, in the production group at least, was that it was the first major investigation that we carried out with employee reps., because we hadn't had a fatal since 1978. This was the first time in which employee reps. came in, and were formally part of the process. Prior to that they had been there sort of as part of local initiative, because there weren't formal health and safety reps. . . . They made very positive and useful contributions. So that was a learning curve for managers to say that there was a resource out there, that people can provide us assistance. The outcome of it went right through that health and safety structure. . . . Up to that stage they tended to be relatively superficial, the sort of worn stair tread or the debris round the corner or whatever. This tended to get people to say "well let's step back and [ask] what are the things that are potentially the most hazardous". Because we have worked with them for 10 or 15 years, we have come to regard them [as normal]. It had that effect for a period of time. . . . Certainly the fact that the report[6] became generally available showed we've got some hundreds of health and safety reps. Health and safety reps. not only have the sort of legal power coming down, but they have by virtue of their knowledge of the workplace, a sort of personal authority in those sorts of investigations that they have something to contribute. Probably that was the first time that most of them had seen a formal outcome of an investigation.'

Here the benefit of having worker representation on safety issues, required by legislation, was amplified by the organization's receptiveness to learning from such worker committees.

[6] This report was internal to the organization. It was extensively referred to at inquest, and relied on heavily by the Department of Labour in their own investigations. Another company involved in the same fatality commented that this sort of comprehensive report was highly unusual.

Safety representatives and committees were also used to disseminate information and allay fears throughout large organizations, essential in maintaining credibility and trust. The safety executive at Aidans explained how support of the legitimacy of the worker representation by the company, through providing them with details about the death, assisted in building trust between management and workers:

'. . . the plant [at Aidans] is a fairly large building and this occurred in one particular zone. People working in other zones were able to make quite legitimate inquiries, get rid of their apprehensions and get back to the job. So it was a two-way flow of information. It reinforced the role of the safety nominees in the workplace. They were an authority figure in the role of safety; whether they be safety reps., shop stewards, or foremen, because they had this information and they were told they could share it.'

What is being illustrated here is the way a proactive stance on safety, one which is able to produce a virtuous response to a fatality, is bolstered by well designed health and safety legislation.

However well legislation is designed though, it is not sufficient to ensure its use. The data illustrated that written legislation alone was not enough to improve safety in itself, there needed to be the will to make it work. As the manager at Haddons commented, 'it requires everyone to get together to make safety work'. The Act could prescribe formal change, but not necessarily substantive change. Virtuous respondents with their characteristic cultural emphasis on inclusiveness and harmony were then the most receptive to provisions in the Act which also emphasized inclusiveness and a joint approach to improving safety. Some of these indicated they had certain structures in place, like the safety committees, before they were required by law, illustrating that the motivation to improve safety may well anticipate good legislative change.

In the absence of the will to promote safety, such as found in the blinkered respondents, the effort of the organization was weighted towards **compliance with legislation, rather than focusing on safety**, yet total compliance was seen as impossible. Requirements under legislation, and even internal company procedure, retreated to a formality with the meaning behind the documentation lost. The written word remains the same, but the meaning attached to it changes from safety improvement to compliance. The focus then becomes one of compliance where necessary and avoidance where possible, since total compliance is seen as an unnecessary burden on profit. The director of Nettles Builders reflected on the perceived impossibility of compliance with all legislative requirements: 'I think there is a genuine feeling that if you did comply with everything that you couldn't get anything done. Productivity would drop to substantially nothing.' Without the desire to improve safety each additional written requirement becomes an increased burden, where the only solution is selective evasion of legislative requirements.

The power of legislation then is not only related to its content, or even its enforcement, but the willingness of the target organization to implement its statutes. For example, the effect of legislation may take time to filter down to those with a lower priority on safety issues. The current Act, although enacted in 1985, had limited influence on blinkered respondents in 1987 (the year of the deaths). The safety officer at Roadtech commented on the lack of its effectiveness at the time of the death: 'The Health and Safety Act made a big difference, but not in 1987 it was only just getting going.' Knowledge of relevant legislation due to its 'newness' therefore had an impact on its usefulness, a problem which appeared to be the most acute in the small business arena. For some on small business worksites, such as the Leafytown Council site, there was a degree of uncertainty regarding the status of the 'new' Act which had been brought in in 1985: 'At that time [1987] it was no one's role [to supervise] now they have just brought the Health and Safety Act in, it was a draft then.'

Even when there is knowledge of the relevant legislation, compliance by blinkered respondents was not necessarily assured. A logging contractor, Adams Logging, knew of the possibility of appointing a health and safety representative under the OHSA but stated: 'It is practical but I don't really see the necessity for it [a health and safety representative] . . . I should nominate someone but I don't know if anyone would want to do it.' This was despite their written contract with the mill, with a requirement of that contract being their full compliance with the Health and Safety Act. While this company complied with the letter of the law, then, their adherence to the spirit could be doubted.

Without the motivation to embrace legislation as a means to improve safety, those with a blinkered culture focused on formal compliance with legislative requirements. Formal compliance though could simply be used as a tool to further organizational politics unrelated to safety. The submerging of safety aims to the political is illustrated in the case of Leafytown Council. The architect of Leafytown Council was on the safety committee (required by legislation) of the council, not because of the dangers or safety responsibilities she might encounter when on building sites, which were considerable, but for political reasons. Her presence on the committee was primarily 'to keep another lady off [the committee]', who was presumably considered a troublemaker. Further, this committee did not see the safety record of contractors they employed to do building work for them as their responsibility, and the architect was frustrated with what did get discussed:

> 'We have a health and safety committee here and more or less by default I am on that committee. But it always strikes me the sort of injuries we tend to have at local government are terribly trivial . . . sometimes I feel a bit cynical. I feel a lot of people can make a claim for very trivial things.'

There was access to first aid courses, which may have helped her prevent the fatality at the council site, but she stated: 'I've applied several times for the course but they are usually shunted towards the outside staff which is after all pretty sensible . . .'.

There was some limited indication that the OHSA could promote change within the blinkered group. The Act was seen by some blinkered respondents as a positive force for safety, even if they also viewed the number of safety regulations as an excessive burden. However, in the case of this group the organizations were less wholesale in their approval than their virtuous counterparts, taking on board only those aspects they felt would not impact too hard on their costs.

There were, to be sure, some problems with legislation brought to notice by the virtuous respondents. In particular, responsibilities under the OHSA were seen as ambiguous in the multiple employer workplace with respect to the responsibility of the owner versus the occupier of a premises. This uncertainty was explained by the project manager of Resource Mining:

'The Health and Safety Act in Victoria is a bit vague in that respect. In terms of the occupier, if we would hand the site over to the major contractor, it becomes the major contractor's site. What that means in respect to legal obligation, I suspect, is that despite the definition of occupier, the major contractor still has the front running at the end of the day. He [*sic*] is familiar with unsafe practices on his site then, although the sub. might get picked up, he is also liable for those issues. [You would see that as unclear?] Yes.'

The relative liabilities of the owner versus the occupier become important when the site holds dangers for the occupier in trying to complete the work. Of particular relevance here is the situation many loggers find themselves in when logging land not owned by them or the mill they are contracted to. For example, Bigland, a landowner but not a mill owner, considered its primary responsibility to be conservation of the land, not the safety of those logging the forest. Some complained that the conservation requirements of Bigland created a dangerous environment, for which the company felt no responsibility. The safety officer of International Paper, a mill which also owned land, explained:

'If they [the loggers] have the problem it's generally with Bigland where they are being hit with the environmental constraints and so on. [For example] where they are not allowed to fall a tree down in a gullied area and so on or whatever, there is a boundary on the coops that they are allowed in. Then Bigland comes in and says this tree has to go. There is only one way for it to go . . . down, into where its not supposed to go, unless he takes a hell of a risk to get it to go out the other way. So he will call me, and I will go and see and say, "There is only one way to fall the tree and that is down that way." He [the logger] says "They won't let you do it that way", so I tell him to leave and refer Bigland to me. Then I say [to Bigland] "Listen here Charlie, read [shows the safety manual] . . .".'

Interviewer: 'In a sense they are in a similar position to you.'

'They are the occupier. . . . We have had a lot of discussion with them over their role in relation to creating a safe workplace, and they just completely won't have a bar of that as being their problem.'

The effectiveness of health and safety legislation in improving safety then is constrained in a number of ways. First, it has to be good law, that is it has to be workable and understand the way organizations, as opposed to individuals, behave. This, OHSA appeared to do. However, there are limitations beyond this concerning the degree to which this legislation can effect cultural change. To stimulate cultural change, legislation is needed to alter the direction in which organizations perceive their future success to lie. This was a difficult task in the case of small organizations who were dependent upon short-term profitability for survival, as outlined in the previous chapter. Health and safety law was not able to alter these constraints, and so its ability to influence cultural change was limited.

Even where the structural position allowed a long-term view on profit and so a virtuous approach was tenable the Act needed to provide motivation for cultural change. Without sufficient motivation those with power litigate about their responsibility under ambiguous sections of legislation, exemplified here with Bigland, or, in the case of smaller weaker players, exploit their invisibility to escape compliance.

It could perhaps be argued that motivation can be provided by adequate prosecution for breaches of statutes. In this sample there was only one prosecution, that of Gemtrench. Gemtrench it will be remembered was a small plumbing subcontractor. Prosecution in this case was a simple matter since there was no complex bureaucracy to deal with or confusion in terms of who to hold responsible. However, the effectiveness of the prosecution needs to be questioned, since it could be argued that prosecution in such cases simply punishes, but does not alter those in a marginalized position (Haines and Sutton, 1997). Further, penalties in this case were small ($500 fine and a good behaviour bond), further questioning the effectiveness of prosecution.

Discussion by the organizations in the data dwelled little on prosecution under OHSA. The lack of discussion regarding prosecutions may have been partly due to the limited nature of prosecution activity. Other charges against companies in the sample were considered by the regulatory agency, including one prosecution for manslaughter, but no charges were forthcoming.

There have been recent increases in prosecution both in the number and level of the fines (Hopkins, 1994a). This study is not in a position to gauge the impact of these measures. What **can** be explored, however, is the impact of legal liability on virtue in the organizations, through analysis of the organizations' response to their liabilities under common law.

Organizations and Defensiveness: The Fear of Legal Liability and the Common Law

Organizations in the study had a real fear of being held liable under common law for the deaths they experienced.[7] The organizational concern to limit such liability could build directly on defensive sentiments associated with the blinkered culture, resulting in curtailment of the safety focused response and in some cases resulting in a response solely concerned with the reduction of liability, as demonstrated in chapter 3. While the effect on the actual response to the issues raised by the death was found predominantly in the blinkered group, the aim of reducing or eliminating legal liability was seen as necessary by both blinkered and virtuous respondents.

In companies with a proactive safety ethos the limiting of legal liability had the potential to clash with their virtuous culture which lay behind the virtuous behaviour responding to the death. To maintain a virtuous culture the company had to resolve such conflicts. Part of this friction was expressed through the different legal imperatives within different aspects of the law, the demands of OHSA on the one hand and the need to protect the organization against common law actions, on the other. The project manger of Resource Mining explained:

> 'There is conflict in Victoria really at the moment, between the requirements of the health and safety legislation, your common law liability in terms of how you protect yourself for that. . . . We are trying to resolve some of those issues from a recent incident.'

However, it was also clear that the conflict between safety and liability did not reside solely in legislation. The aims of reducing

[7] It is this concern with the common law liabilities which appeared as a strong undercurrent to the inquest process. This is despite the inquest being inquisitorial in form, and set up for the purposes of future prevention of similar harm. Many organizations at the inquest saw the process as a precursor to downstream litigation. Further, organizations did not clearly distinguish between the various legal purposes of the inquest process, OHSA prosecutions, and compensatory damages. Fear of court processes was more generalized. Nonetheless, the section here focuses on fear of legal liability as it was experienced during and after the inquest process; for this reason the conclusions drawn may need to be interpreted with care.

legal liability and the aims of promoting a safe workplace **after an event had occurred**, revealed inherent problems. This was exemplified in the interviews in two ways. The first relates to the written word, in this case the written information emanating out of accident investigations, the second concerned experiences in court. For those in the safety arena, written information should be used to improve safety and prevent further trauma. It should be widely disseminated for educational purposes. Those concerned with liability viewed an investigation differently, the purpose being to elicit information and orientate it in such a way that it placed the company in the best possible light. Potentially prejudicial information was jealously guarded, and revealed on a 'needs to know' basis. This was clearly seen in the following case at Roadtech[8] in which the safety officer was currently involved:

'There is a real problem with document discovery. You can't tell the truth on paper, in case the document gets found and used against you. Its not people at the coalface, 99 per cent of the time the company is at fault. They don't want the coalface to know exactly what is going on. As the safety officer I was rapped over the knuckles for going too far with the internal investigations. I felt I had to say the facts like they were, but I was rapped over the knuckles in case the document ever came to light. . . . I get into all sorts of trouble, I am seen as the nasty safety person. . . . It had to go to the solicitors. The report is the summary of the truth, of what we failed to do. . . . Legal concerns weigh heavily on the company.'

As the safety officer, the purpose of an investigation report was to detail what the company failed to do in order to prevent a similar occurrence in the future. From a legal point of view such a document is a hazard, the purpose of documentation is to place 'fact' in the best possible light to avoid future liabilities. Importantly though, both legal and safety perspectives see the written word as an important tool in the promotion of their specific goals, namely for the one protection against liability, and for the other the promotion of safety. The form for both might then be the same, an internal investigation report, yet the substantive effect demanded by the two departments may differ, and conflict arise over how the document is to be used.

[8] Roadtech had been taken over by a large multinational since the fatality. This example then, reflects the culture of the multinational, not the original small business.

The second example where the friction between liability and safety became apparent was through the experience of those in court who came with a 'naïve' view of the primary purpose of the investigation being prevention. They were confronted in court by lawyers attempting to manipulate blame in order to reduce their own clients' liability. Information became jealously guarded and the competitive edge of the business culture became caught up in the adversarial nature of the legal system. This was clearly demonstrated at the inquest of the dredger collapse:

'It was a little like the Nuremberg trial. I think everyone just claimed they were just obeying orders. . . . What we did, people either side of us were doing something else. . . . Everybody sort of sees areas in which they are quite prepared to be helpful in, and areas in which they are not so prepared to be helpful in. . . . Everybody sort of wants to fight on the ground that they are best able to fight on, and ignore the ground they are least able to. . . . It was a preliminary to potential downstream litigation.'

In court, written documentation was clearly presented by various parties as a means to protect themselves from liability as the interview indicated. Any ambivalence regarding this view by those called to court as witnesses became a magnet for lawyers aiming to exploit their clients' position at the expense of other players. This case of the dredger collapse contains a graphic illustration of the conflict of perspectives regarding the purpose of information. The project manager of Haddons (the engineering contractor) saw the inquest as a forum to understand the death and prevent its future occurrence. Because of this he was initially untroubled at the prospect of being jointly represented by the barrister retained by Stutganst, the designer of the dredger:

'I asked [my] company do you just show up [at the inquest]. We had letters [from Stutganst] indicating we should be covered by them, but I soon found out that I was being attacked by them.'

This initial trust then proved to be a grave mistake. Almost immediately once in court he found out that the primary aim at the inquest was to cover yourself and your company's interests. The proactive safety perspective on information which the project manager held to be important in understanding the death became submerged by issues of liability in court. The project manager of Haddons again illustrates this point:

'. . . the note which I received [from the coronial court] just asked me to be called forward and to give evidence. Now, never being in court before I just rolled up and I saw all these Queen's Counsels. I think there was five or six there at the time. I thought, hell what am I in for? I was called up as first cab off the rank. Well being open and honest, I guess that I tried to describe the situation to these people. But the QCs just wanted to go in a specific direction, [and] not being briefed how to answer questions . . . , that's the part that really shook me up more than anything, because I was just so vulnerable at the time. I just wasn't expecting that you know. . . . I was in the box there for six or seven hours, and then they called me back there the next day. . . . I came out of that totally shattered. I got to the point when I really questioned what was I saying, was it correct? . . . I really had to gather myself together again. I found that more harrowing than the actual incident, because I was barrelled from different sides . . .'

The manager had realized that the sole purpose of the inquest from the point of view of the organizations present was to prevent liability at a later stage. There was little point in attempting to show the intricacies of the problems on the dredger site. The court was a battleground with the ground rules clearly laid out. These ground rules precluded neutral inquiry concerning safety. The only option was for the manager to obtain his own ammunition, which required the services of his own barrister. The next day he went and got his own representation and was able to re-enter the court battle with the same perspective as the other organizations:

'I went and got representation. Then I was recalled and you know from my own QC's point of view [who went through the incident again] and said, "what did you mean by this?", "did you really mean that?", so I could then respond to those answers.'

The inquest had clear limitations in its ability to understand the issues which led to the death. The limitations stemmed from the ground rules of the court context, protection against liability. This produced a very distinct perspective on the information which surfaced through the court investigation. This perspective precluded differing perspectives on the same information, particularly a perspective which saw safety as the central issue. This conflict of perspectives is illustrated again by Haddons:

'. . . I also [saw] they were coming at it from more of a legal sense than more of a practical application of what really happened. The "ifs" and the "buts" and the "commas" and all this sort of thing. I am not attuned to that, that is totally foreign. . . . They'd say, "We don't want to hear about that just answer my question." In trying to explain the complexity of it you then become exposed . . . Now the next time I go through they will get a "yes" or a "no" answer, it is as simple as that.'

Here the intervention of external legal counsel to support the project manager of Haddons came as welcome relief. The lawyer acted as a translator, to change the safety discourse into a legal discourse and present the information Haddon's had according to the ground rules set in the court scene. This final quote from the project manager illustrates how the information was realigned to fit the legal discourse: "now Paul, my boss, sat down with me for hours and we went to the solicitors after and we got all these things straightened out'.

The reduction of legal liability involved organizations outside the immediate workplace environment as well as legal departments within organizations. The major organization to have influence outside the work environment was the insurer. From both the primary stance was reactive and defensive. The insurer had a vital interest in the outcome of liability issues, and was a strong influence on companies' actions. At the most extreme, when an event occurred the insurer could take over from the company as they rush in to protect their own assets. In the case of Lynden Hydraulics their insurer instructed the company to speak to no one regarding the fatality, and all enquiries should be directed to the insurer. It was the insurance company's lawyer that represented the company at inquest. The researcher was the first person to speak to the company directly. In other cases interviews were refused because of fear of losing insurance, for example in the forklift fatality involving forklift hire companies: 'If they say "You've mucked things up", we face enormous legal costs. We may have done everything right, but there are legal ramifications of insurance, so we can't talk because there are difficulties there.'

Here defensiveness and avoidance become paramount, with the possibility of a merry-go-round of litigation, which validates a cautious attitude to investigation of incidents within companies. A director of Nettles Builders recounted his experience at inquest, and his willingness to initiate retaliatory legal action if needed:

'I felt the response of Postens[9] [at the inquest] was totally over the top, a flagrant attempt to deny responsibility and push it onto me. Their barrister was trying to blame me in person. I felt that we had no responsibility. If we had been taken to court for compensation, then we would have tried to recover the money from the demolition contractor . . .'

While both blinkered and virtuous respondents were faced with the need to protect their organization against liability, virtuous respondents also had to resolve the conflict that emerged between the demands of reducing liability and the demands of a proactive safety orientated response inherent in their virtuous culture. Naïvety in this conflict could lead to the problems experienced by the project manager at Haddons above, and leave the company as shouldering the majority of liability for the death which may bear little relation to their actual contribution.

To avoid these problems the conflict was resolved by such companies in one of two ways; either to place a priority on safety to avoid future long-term liability, or to separate safety and legal concerns within the organization. Resource Mining chose the former route and resolved the potential conflict by asserting that their proactive safety stance was ultimately in their own best (long term) legal interest:

'. . . but our view is that if we don't comprehensively investigate [we get into more trouble]. Despite the fact that that information might subsequently be used to beat us over the head, in the event of a repetition because of inadequate fact finding the first time, we would be doubly liable at that point. That is the conclusion we have reached.'

Other virtuous respondents, such as Aidans, resolved the conflict by separating responsibilities for the two, safety and liability, within their organizations. The personnel manager at Aidans

[9] I was unable to interview Postens for the research. Initially they agreed to an interview when requested over the telephone, and the initial conversations related to the need for safety and the need for emotional sensitivity. However, when the request was put in writing stating specific details, the company refused the interview stating they did not deal with specific deaths, even though this was understood to be the case during telephone contact. Given the vigour of their legal response, it is possible that their refusal reflected a concern with the legal ramifications. After this experience all appointments were made by telephone only, with written consent being obtained just prior to the interviews.

showed the problems associated with the close relationship between issues of liability and safety, where liability issues could discriminate against employees with safety concerns:

'When I joined the first thing I recognized was that people were being discriminated against, because they had an action against the company for WorkCare.[10] . . . The litigation was taken out of the workplace. Even the processing of the claims was drawn out of the workplace, out of the foreman's office, and taken upstairs so it was them and us. That allowed us to be much more constructive in what we did, and had much more benefit over time. And that was one of the first changes I made in the place.'

This separation of roles and cultures had benefits in terms of safety for the above company, the legal issues here were divorced from the safety issues to allow safety to flourish.

The separation of roles did not necessarily mean a diminishing of legal defences of the organization. Further, the strength of legal defences could be viewed as an asset to safety. Some reported an increase in avenues of communication about safety when they knew they were protected from legal liability. Here the project manager at Haddons when asked about the impact of increased recourse to legal representation pointed to the benefits for safety in terms of increased flow of information:

'. . . I know now even if there was a problem, I would get support, full support from the company, they would back me to the hilt. So it gives me, it takes the added pressure off. . . . It opens the doors of communication a bit better, you have a tendency more to talk over these things. Not that you wouldn't before, but you know that it is there and you would refer to it. That has happened in recent times on other projects we have had within the company, where the various site managers have felt exposed, management have said we will support you. That has come out as a result of this particular fatality.'

However, in some cases the separation of the legal and the safety realms could also have some dubious effects, particularly if a legal process, such as an inquest, aims to promote safety within the company or prevent similar occurrences in the future. With a separation of safety and legal cultures within an organization, the legal orientation could become the sole influence on the

[10] The (then) name for workers compensation claims. Now known as WorkCover.

company as it appeared in court. When this occurred, a distorted view of the safety efforts of the company was presented to the coroner, with the recommendations coming out of the inquest bearing little relevance to the actual safety response within organizations. This was illustrated in the data by Jedd's death, which was due to rolling logs and the collapse of the skyline used to drag logs uphill in high lead logging. At inquest the question of the safety of high lead logging was raised. The contractor, Adams, was logging for a high profile pulp mill, International Paper, with the consequence that the mill feared litigation. To forestall this, the mill produced a report on the fatality with recommendations for action to remedy the problem and submitted this at the inquest. The coroner accepted the recommendations and congratulated the company on its swift action. The report was written without consultation with the safety department of the mill, whose safety officer was scathing of the report in terms of its real effect on safety:

> 'This document wasn't written by me, it was written by a, if I can use the word, another clown in the company. The recommendations in that, according to the experts that I happened to let see this, are very wrong and in fact quite dangerous. So that was ignored, 'cause it is a useless piece of paper. . . . My report, I don't think would have even got to the coroner, and that was the important one.'

Fortunately the recommendations endorsed by the coroner in this case were not implemented; changes were made, however, in consultation with the safety officer. From the safety officer's perspective, the inquest was 'a non-event'. With the separation of legal and safety concerns, those promoting safety could see the inquest and legal process as holding little relevance and simply something 'off to the side'.

The separation of the legal and the safety concerns then, and the adversarial nature of the legal culture and its concomitant logic, could distort the reality of what is 'safe' and 'unsafe'. The purpose of documentation presented at the court is to reduce the legal culpability of the company in question. It needs to address legal issues such as 'due diligence' and 'general duty of care' in ways that lawyers and the judiciary accept. What matters for safety is the stereotypes of lawyers, and legal precedents. Acts are interpreted with these issues in mind. The imperatives of the safety culture, well recognized by the safety officer at International Paper, are set aside, and the 'decontextualization and homogenizing effect' of the law comes into play (Johnstone, 1994).

This was despite the inquest being inquisitorial in itself which aims to overcome some of these problems. The wider legal culture was adversarial, and it was this which influenced the inquest process. This was exacerbated when those in court felt under threat and had the resources to employ considerable legal support, or there were major issues at stake. Aggressive lawyers backed by companies which saw the inquest as a precursor to downstream litigation would seek to put their company in the best light. This would lead in some instances to those at Inquest feeling like the process was being run by the bar table rather than the coroner, as the project manager of Haddons suggested:

> 'I got the feeling that perhaps, I don't know if it is possible that the QCs may have been more authoritative than the coroner, I don't know if that can be. I feel that some of the counsels there may have had more rank than the coroner, in hindsight. I don't know, . . . I am not critical of the coroner in any way, perhaps I felt for him a bit. There were a couple of hairy questions put there, and I could see that he [the coroner] had a difficult job at times.'

The separation of the safety and legal cultures is therefore not an advantage in itself, but depends on the strength of the safety culture within any organization, and its ability to function almost despite the legal process. Law enforcement may unwittingly serve only formal ends, such as accountability, while distorting or even destroying substantive improvements in safety. This poses considerable problems for those wishing to maximize external accountability of the company for their safety record. There may well exist a paradox as suggested by Sitkin and Bies (1994a:28–31) where accountability and substantive improvements (in this case in safety) may not be compatible. Accountability is usually considered to be achieved through the legal process. However, it was the legal process which could distort actual behaviour within organizations in this study, thus reducing accountability. The dynamics of the legal process, coupled with the legal astuteness of an organization, could produce a protective shield and an impression of that organization to outsiders which may not have borne any direct relationship to safety levels on the factory floor.

Such paradoxes may not however be consistent across contexts. The data also indicated that **without** a strong safety focus the integration of legal and safety issues within an organization may have beneficial effects, particularly in the prevention of incidents. Most blinkered respondents had little separation of the legal and safety concerns, and the fear of future liability could drive safety improvements. The architect of Leafytown Council remarked:

'I think on the whole councils are very conscious of safety, cynically enough, even from a point of view of who's going to sue them. If we do various repaving we are very careful to make sure they are very even, because if people fall over they will say its the council pavement. Even pop up sprinklers in lawns can be considered hazardous and the public is becoming much more aware. They mightn't ask for much money, and council I'm sure normally denies responsibility entirely, but you know I'm sure we keep our legal firm quite happily engaged on council peripheral work.'

This fear could also push employers to reinforce safe work practices, as was the case with Ben Adams:

'. . . it makes you emphasize to the men that if they say, "I'll be right", in what they are doing, that they won't be right, they have got to go about it a different way.'

Interviewer: 'Because you might have to pay for it?'

'Yes. I joke with them that it's not them I am worried about it's their wife.'

But virtuous respondents argued working out of fear because of non-compliance and possible prosecution creates resentment and ultimately gets bogged down, as the safety executive from Aidans commented: 'if you do things from fear of prosecution you would never do anything'. Safety in these contexts can regress to a 'cat and mouse' affair, with primacy of safety relegated to legal interpretation, and defensive manoeuvring. Pressure can also be brought to bear on those injured not to report their injuries (James, 1993). This then feeds back into the reasons why some organizations with a strong safety focus choose to separate the cultures in the first place.

What this suggests is that 'virtuous' organizations are those most caught in situations of paradox where resort to legal mechanisms may undermine virtue. Virtuous organizations which change to non-virtuous over time would then pose particular problems to the regulator. Legally astute, as they had to be originally to protect their virtuous culture, they are now in a unique position to defend themselves from unwarranted intrusion. While this is to some extent speculative, it does raise serious concerns regarding the easy shift from virtue to non-virtue, once an organization has already the structures to protect virtue in place.

Legal Liability and Small Business

Of course separation of legal and safety concerns is only a possibility when organizations are of a certain size. The structure of small business, the small number of employees and the consequent lack of multiple layers of management, means that such businesses rely heavily on the character of the owner/directors who run them to promote safety, in contradiction to immediate demands of self-protection. Small subcontractors have to juggle all orientations, the defensiveness needed in the legal arena, with the proactivity and honesty required to improve safety.

The potential for conflict and the inability of small businesses to protect themselves from liability is augmented by their major mode of communication, verbal as opposed to written. Small businesses were less likely to shield themselves from legal intrusion by mountainous manuals and safety procedures. When the interviewer asked one small business about written procedures, the manager dug around in a filing cabinet until he found a single sheet of typewritten statements. The purpose of the sheet was not to improve safety, but to fulfil requirements under a contract with a major local contractor; 'real' safety training remained verbal. As the manager of Lynden Hydraulics stated:

> '. . . it [the written document] is very general and is used to go into contracts we tender for. A lot of safety is self-evident. The written policy is necessary only in the tendering process.'

The verbal communication relied on by small business is more open to distortion under legal scrutiny than if a company can point to comprehensive written procedures. The possible protection afforded by the written word was highlighted by the safety officer of Mightysteel:

'In the second fatality[11] it probably saved our arse that we do have these bloody procedures in place, and do have a lot of procedures around. That's what the coroners say, we are a model of the installation of the OHS Act.'

The vulnerability of small business combined with a lack of legal sophistication could result in small business being disarmingly honest to their own detriment at inquest:

'Well I've got nothing to hide, I was willing to wear it. The attitude of the court was, well someone has to be answerable. I went to the court willing to be open. They were willing to believe the Department of Mines over me, I was made to feel a liar. We were railroaded. OK we were complacent. . . . We could have hidden everything but that is not my way. If we had perhaps we could have got away with things.' [Owner, Gemtrench]

On the other hand small businesses had advantages over their larger counterparts, both in terms of their structure and the workings of the system. In terms of structure their most notable advantage was that of invisibility. Small businesses can hide more easily from public scrutiny and are likely to receive little public attention (Sutton and Wild, 1988). In addition, the nature of their business, in many cases as a subcontractor, often means they require a good relationship with the larger businesses which give them contracts, not a glowing relationship with the public at large.

Finally, the way the reactive systems, both state and private, worked after the fatality could also be to their advantage. First, inquests involving only small businesses were often very low-key affairs, occurring some months after the event. Secondly, insurance companies could take over from small business and take the role of the legal departments of larger companies, thus shielding them from the full impact of the process.

Taken out of the context of their potential vulnerability and their reliance on verbal as opposed to written communication, the steps small businesses take to limit their liability appear almost callous. Their responses ranged from increasing insurance cover, changing from a partnership to a limited liability company to the most extreme, changing the whole identity of the organization. In the case of the Constructotech, a small business which manufactured the hydraulics in the dredger collapse, when the

[11] This company experienced a second fatality in 1990.

interviewer asked about the involvement of the company in the fatality she was told:

'You have got the wrong company. We are a totally different company, that company was wound up four years ago [around the time of the fatality]. This is a brand new company, all new documents payroll and so on, only the personnel were moved over. . . . The old company was liquidated and there is no relationship between the old and the new company.'

While it is not necessary to condone such action, it is necessary to see it in terms of a particular set of vulnerabilities, such as lack of protection from an extensive bureaucracy, and opportunities, such as flexibility and invisibility, which push small business to such measures.

The threat of legal liability was a powerful motivator for the organizations in the study. The primary motivation though was one of protecting against such liability, not necessarily to improve safety. This primary motivation in achieving such protection being defensive could conflict with the proactive stance required to improve safety, the stance associated with the virtuous culture. Indeed the data showed cases where safety improvements could be hindered by the threat of legal liability, by limiting the investigation into the death, particularly the written investigation.

Rather than stimulating cultural change, the threat of legal liability caused the majority of virtuous respondents to separate out functions within their organization. Safety became isolated from legal issues in order to protect the viability of safety and the proactive ethos. What was argued in court bore only a limited relationship to the actual situation within the company due to the distortions by the court process and the isolation of safety personnel from the court process.

Legal liability had a greater effect on safety with respect to the blinkered culture, but did little to alter their overall cultural perspective. While it could alter specific practices the motivation it provided to improve safety could not engender widespread cultural change. In the case of small business separation of legal and safety concerns was not possible. The response of these companies to their legal liabilities, changing insurance cover, changing the status of the organization from partnership to limited liability company and in one case changing company name, is made understandable, although not acceptable, as a response to the liability pressures they faced.

Manipulation of Insurance Premiums: The Role of Compensation Legislation

Use of compensation premiums to encourage safety in the workplace has become a major policy focus of state governments in recent years (Industry Commission, 1994). The aim of this policy is to tie the premium paid by the individual organization to their actual safety performance. The worse the record, the more is paid in insurance premiums. Such a system is able to act directly on organizations, and bypass issues of legal liability and the problems associated with the legal process, described above.

Despite its importance, the influence of compensation legislation on safety has not formed a large part of the criminological debate on health and safety regulation. Since it is an incentive to improve safety which acts continuously on organizations, it is difficult to see where this fits in terms of a hierarchy of sanctions, or regulatory pyramid for example. Compensation measures form part of the overall context within which an organization acts. As such they hold greater potential than measures that depend upon enforcement processes and direct regulatory intervention, such as inspections.

Compensation legislation acts to modify directly the profit/safety relationship in favour of safety. The previous chapter argued that the two organizational cultures revolved around this profit/safety nexus, with the virtuous culture pointing to the congruence between the two aims, and the blinkered culture their ultimate friction. Tying compensation premiums to safety levels appears to be an effective way to affect the calculation between safety and profit. The data tentatively showed that compensation law can effect powerful change by altering the profit/safety equation. The improved profit gained through the comprehensive attitude to safety at Mightysteel was seen as resulting from safety bonuses from WorkCare,[12] explained here by the safety officer at Mightysteel:

'Last year we got an 18 per cent [safety] bonus and I think it worked out to something like about $300,000 last year, the bonus. We've got a

[12] This is the name of the scheme under the previous Victorian Labor Government. The revised legislation is now known as WorkCover.

$22,000 million payroll. So the way the WorkCare is, works. If you can save 1 per cent you are doing well.'

Tying compensation premiums to safety record then, appeared to play a central role in tipping the balance in favour of the compatibility of profit and safety in the eye of the company. Well crafted legislation which affected the calculation between profit and safety can provide the needed justification for virtuous responses and comprehensive safety programmes.

Education of large-scale employers regarding the monetary gains available from such comprehensive safety programmes, however, was important to the effectiveness of such measures. Education about the benefits of improved safety on profit, however, reflected a logic of large organizations rather than small concerns. The safety executive at Aidans, a large organization, explained the process of education, and the way it was intimately linked to a debate concerning profit and costs:

'I walked in in 1984 and they had forked out an horrendous amount for workers comp. renewal, and I said look I want 10 per cent of the savings spent purely on safety. That was to be my budget in the first year. I saved 560 grand, they nearly screamed, they couldn't renege on it, so we had a self funding budget from day one. I said I want an advance on the first 10 per cent, and I drew $20,000 into a budget. That is how I ran safety in the first year, which was fundamentally to get into the workplace and find out where the accidents were happening and why . . .'

However, the effect of compensation on safety, like other influences, was mediated by the organizations themselves. Size affected the ability to view the consensus between the two aims of safety and profit. Large size allowed the requisite calculations involved in savings to support safety as part of an overall long-term view. The savings in compensation rest on an argument of cost reduction through lower claims and lower premiums involving large numbers of people:

'The process of occupational health and safety that I have been involved in, over sixty programmes, saves money. Compensation was $873,000 in 1984, at the end (seven years later) it was $403,000, including all medical equipment and training. You could scale that against inflation if you like; our payroll had moved from 2.4 million to 12 million dollars in the same period.'

In large businesses the savings from safety impacting compensation premiums and rehabilitation costs can be graded, calculated and translated into large sums. The same could not be said of small organizations, where compensation premiums were not mentioned to influence safety. No small businesses mentioned the rise in compensation costs, either present or future, as an issue in stimulating their response to the death and the safety improvements they made. When mentioned by one firm, compensation was seen as a burden, and a reason for not taking on extra employees, rather than a spur to improve safety. The potential influence of compensation on virtue was thus limited by the size of the organization. Small business was not pushed out of its reactive response to safety issues by compensation legislation.

This can only be understood by appreciating the assessment of risk undertaken by small businesses. Even if they are in reality less safe than their larger counterparts, the actual risk of an incident occurring to a particular business is much lower simply because they have few employees. This leds to situations where small firms can have patently unsafe procedures or equipment, yet no accidents result. Gemtrench, a small plumbing contractor, had used his shoring equipment for a number of years before the poor design of this equipment led to a fatality. No problems had arisen to alert the company of the risk before the death, despite the investigator's report stating that the equipment was 'patently dangerous'. Safety for small business can be seen as a gambling exercise, with each individual business gambling high safety risks for the necessary profit return, due to their small size and small numbers of employees. This high risk though was not necessarily evident since small business does not necessarily see the fatal result which inevitably comes from high-risk practices. Large businesses, with many employees, on the other hand are far more likely to see the tragedy that follows high risk.

This goes to the heart of the problem of the dual economy. Such an economy creates the conditions whereby a different logic applies dependent upon which sector, core or marginal, a company inhabits. Core organizations plan for both short and long term and this synoptic calculative capability moves them to shun short-term corner cutting in favour of building a virtuous culture which can serve the company well into the future. The effect of limited liability is muted for these organizations which seek to limit damage not only in terms of monetary loss, but also reputation which is valued highly. Hence, virtue approximates notions of virtue which exist outside the organization and the immediate industrial environment.

The secondary economy stands in sharp contrast. The short term is the only term of importance. The future is simply more of the hand to mouth survival techniques employed to survive in the short term. The visible effects of the immediate environment become the sole concern. Opportunities for making quick profit are seized upon, in the expectation that good times only last until the next economic downturn. High-risk, low probability events, such as a death, simply do not figure into the equation. Such firms simply have to gamble with the expectation that they will not occur. Even when they do occur, limited liability ensures the cost is not borne entirely by the gambler, the small business person. Limited liability is essential to the existence of this sector, since it provides the backdrop for such gambling to take place. When good times return, the secondary economy picks up again. Crucially the virtue of this economy is the vice the regulators attempt to eradicate, gambling on the short term, cutting corners and so on.[13]

One solution is to shift the control of the secondary economy to the core organizations. As we have seen this has some potential, as illustrated by the case of the points system of International Paper, cited above. Another possibility relevant here would be to transfer the responsibility for compensation onto the major contractor. Under the OHSA in Victoria, the prima facie responsibility for ensuring a safe workplace lies with the major contractor, making them responsible for the safety of the subcontractor, and the subcontractor's employees. However, subcontractors are responsible for their own compensation premiums. This could be seen to encourage contracting out of risk.

Research by Claire James (1993) and Andrew Hopkins (1995) in the area of variable compensation premiums shows additional problems if such a mechanism is to be considered as some sort of panacea to raise safety levels. This research into reporting of work related illness and injury fleshes out the picture presented

[13] The development of the above insights was enhanced greatly by informal correspondence with John Braithwaite.

here. Lower compensation premiums depend on lowering of reporting, not necessarily incidence of injury and illness. To obtain compensation, employees have to be willing to report injury. Yet studies show that employees of certain organizations, namely those which are small or which are family businesses, are reluctant to report. Small organizations can pressure employees not to report injury (James, 1993) and the experience of death (where reporting is inevitable) is so unusual that its effect is severely limited. Again this highlights the broad conclusions of Galbraith (1973) in terms of the inherent exploitation of small and family business. Compensation law alone cannot overcome broader structural issues and is then unlikely to engender positive change across the whole spectrum of organizations.

Publicity and Organizations: The Role of the Media

Although not strictly relevant to the effect of legislation and legal liability on organizational behaviour, the media has often been cited as a way to bolster the responsiveness of organizations and increase compliance with legislation (Coffee, 1981; Fisse and Braithwaite, 1983). According to these writers it has the potential to overcome some of the problems of forcing accountability through the legal system, some of which were illustrated in the previous section. As such it is of interest here, particularly if there was an effect the media had on the type of response the organization made. It is theoretically possible, for example, that the media could bridge the separation between legal and safety cultures in some organizations, making organizations both accountable and virtuous, or could reduce the ability of small business to hide. In short, the media could be used to augment accountability of both small and large organizations.

Unfortunately, the role of the media in encouraging virtuous responses through increasing organizational accountability was minimal. While media involvement may have influence on some large high-profile incidents, the feedback from companies in this sample was not encouraging. Media involvement in the fatalities and the follow-up was minimal, and was usually restricted to a brief 'factual' account in the local newspaper, or a brief news item on television; as the manager at Aidans commented, 'it was too scant to be wrong'. The overall impression from respondents was that scant information was given by the media in terms of what actually happened, as explained here by the owner of Reids Plumbing:

'It was on television at night—an industrial accident, and there was certainly a clipping of some sort in the newspaper. Just the facts, like an industrial accident, someone falling, a fatal accident.' [Reids Plumbing]

In addition, where television was involved the lasting memory for some was the attention of the media on the trauma and the 'gore', not the actual contributing factors to the death, as noted here by the project manager at Resource Mining: 'they really did want to get in and have a blood on the floor thing . . .'. Understandably this was upsetting to some, such as the director of Nettles Builders who commented: 'If anything [it was] upsetting at the time the fact that there was media there.' The resources of the media were also compared to those of the police in the case of Leafytown Council:

'Channel 7 or 9 sort of arrived immediately, I'm not sure who it was actually, complete with extra helicopter and video camera. I found that quite upsetting. The resources the police had were very limited compared to the media. At first I thought, well that's a good idea, that's [a] detective sort of photographing this, that and everything. In fact it wasn't [the police] it was the media. . . . I felt that it was unnecessary and intrusive. It said there had been a fatality on the job because of this and this. It didn't lay blame, and it didn't comment. I thought there are many more newsworthy items really than someone who has been killed, and yet I think it can be awfully intrusive of relatives.'

Rather than help the public understand the contributory factors to the death, or provide a picture to help the public at large understand and analyse the events (by, for example, providing a profile of the toll of industrial deaths), media reporting was focused on the human drama and tragedy in a sensationalist and intrusive manner.

In one case, the logging fatality involving Adams, the police helped those involved escape the scrutiny of the media: 'They [the media] probably got there four hours after it had happened, we just cleaned everything up and we heard they were coming, so the police said just go, we will handle it, and we shot through.'

The media were not seen to affect the way the companies were perceived; their interest was too transient and too focused on the human emotion surrounding the particular event. In addition those reporting the event did not link the fatality to the action or non-action of the companies involved; they remained an unwelcome intrusion on private grief. Use of the media may produce positive results in high-profile cases; however, in the routine harm perpetrated by companies illustrated here the influence waned. In these cases the traditional sensationalist orientation of the media came to the fore (Ditton and Duffy, 1983; Kiel, 1989) with typical demands for oversimplification of the issues (Coffee, 1981) and so threatened more harm, in terms of trauma for the relatives, than good. The interest of the public by such media was assumed to be fickle: issues of health and safety captured the imagination of the public for brief periods; however, the interest diminished as new issues gained ascendancy.

Conclusion

The aim of this chapter was to see how legislation and the regulatory climate influenced virtue, by producing virtuous responses and encouraging a virtuous culture. The record card for the influence of legislation was mixed, and continued to illustrate how the context within which an organization operates, and constraints on the way success could be achieved, affected the response to death and the promotion of virtue.

Health and Safety Law had considerable value in terms of content, particularly in the responsibility it places on contractors for subcontractors' responsibility, and the emphasis it has on inclusiveness to promote safety. It placed responsibility on government, business and workers to work together to improve safety. As such it has much in common with the virtuous culture and was often taken enthusiastically on board by companies with such a culture. However, its ability to motivate was limited and although it had some impact on blinkered respondents, they sought ways to minimize its impact since total compliance was considered antithetical to business success.

The ability to persuade organizations that safety is in their own interest then, is enhanced by good legislation. However, to leave the debate about the ability to persuade at the framing of legislation would be a mistake. It is clear that legislation only forms part of the context of the organization which influences safety and its impact depends on both the external constraints an organization is reacting to and their cultural perspective. Different organizations react differently to legislation and regulation depending upon who they are, the choices they have in terms of long term success and their culture which is underpinned by their view concerning that future success.

To promote virtue in the long term then, a regulatory framework needs to be able to influence and direct organizational culture, or at least alter the premises which lie behind decision making. If culture undermines compliance, compliance (and virtue) are likely to be sporadic, contextual and short-term. Law and law enforcement may thus need to be aware of culture as well as monitoring actual behaviour.

The effect of fear of common law actions allowed some insight into how organizations respond to threat. Limiting legal liability, with its defensive orientation, had most in common with a blinkered culture, and could threaten the virtuous response and the integrity of the virtuous culture. Organizations with such a culture needed to protect themselves against liability most often drawing boundaries between 'inside' and 'outside' the organization, where legal departments could wage war in the courts and have as little damage as possible to the integrity of the 'inside' culture. In these virtuous organizations the paradox between increasing accountability and actual change was raised. Increased accountability mechanisms could produce adverse outcomes for safety. The threat of legal liability, on the other hand, did appear to have an impact on those from a blinkered culture although did not appear to shift them towards 'virtue' in terms of cultural change, rather shifted them to minimal compliance.

Attempting to produce cultural change through law and law enforcement though is problematic. Law may produce formal change with little or no change in substance (Sitkin and Bies, 1994b). Processes and procedures may be modified, yet safety and a culture which promotes safety may remain absent. Rationalization and bureaucratization of procedure, whether undertaken by self-motivated organizations, or as a result of regulatory pressure, does not necessarily produce substantive change. There are many instances where formal change and formal processes produce little substantive change (Weber, 1991:216–21; Macaulay, 1969; Van Maanen and Pentland, 1994). Further, increased formalization may be used to maintain the status quo, the very definition of duties and responsibilities in procedures and legislation allowing key organizations and individuals to avoid blame (Sutton and Wild, 1980) and take health and safety backwards rather than forwards (Johnstone, 1994).

The use of variable insurance premiums under compensation legislation held much promise in promoting improvements in safety and maximizing virtue since it altered the milieu in which such companies act and tipped the profit/safety balance toward safety. However, its impact was largely limited to those organizations which had the greatest choice, namely those which were large and high in the contracting hierarchy. The impact on smaller weaker players appeared minimal, and could be explained by their lack of choice forced by necessary short-term success goals. Their small number of employees meant they could often win by gambling on safety, since they were unlikely to see the traumatic result of high-risk procedures. A regulatory strategy emphasizing only compensation law is therefore risky.

Finally, suggestions that the media should be used as a tool to stimulate compliance need to go beyond an appeal to the various forms of the media as they are currently constructed. In this study the media's own agenda, in terms of sensationalism and the need for 'good copy', overrode any public interest aspect that may have arisen from their involvement.

The future of regulation and the ability to maximize virtue depends as much on the choices forced on organizations by the structure and context of the worksite, and the changing shape of organizations, as it does on law, legal change and law enforcement. An environment which undermines the 'benevolence' of large organizations with a virtuous culture, or progressively devolves costs so that only a narrow view on profit prevails, will diminish the space within which the regulator can argue that safety is in the self-interest of the organization. It is the changing shape of the business and regulatory environment which is the subject of the final data chapter.

9 The Broad Context of Response: Competing Demands and Prospects for the Future

THE aim of this chapter is to extend the analysis of the data beyond the responses the organizations made, to an analysis of their perceptions regarding the place of safety in the contemporary economic and political environment. What is of central concern here is the organizations' long-term commitment to safety within such a climate. The previous chapters could be seen as presenting a 'snapshot' of virtue and its production. This chapter aims to explore the system in motion, giving attention to the particular dynamics facing organizations at the present time. A response may have been virtuous, with a culture supportive of that virtue in the short term, but what are the chances that such a response will remain influential in the long term? While these are certainly important issues it must be recognized, however, that the conclusions drawn in this chapter are necessarily more tentative since the data explored here concerns attitudes and behaviours only indirectly associated with the actual deaths.

The challenges facing the organizations within the contemporary economic and political climate could be encapsulated in two groups. The first group was increased competition in the marketplace. This increased competition had three aspects: the challenges brought about by economic rationalist policies specifically aimed at increasing competition, such as restructuring and contracting out; the effect of the recession then being experienced; and finally, changes to the nature of competition brought about by mergers, acquisitions and bankruptcy.

The second group of challenges pertains to changes in the regulatory climate which could be seen to place organizations under increasing pressure. Both the number, and more importantly the complexity, of legislation was increasing, despite the deregulatory rhetoric of government. Primarily the complexity was introduced through new Australian and International Standards confirmed by Standards Australia. Such standards, although not automatically binding in a legal sense, may be incorporated into regulations.[1] This was compounded by greater pressure by government to improve safety through new health and safety legislation enacted in 1985, the *Occupational Health and Safety Act* 1985 (Vic.). Central to this legislation was the general duty of care on all employers, placing in criminal law duties previously only found under common law.

The Demands for Competitiveness

While increasing demands on organizations regarding health and safety standards then, government was simultaneously increasing the level of competition felt by organizations. This it was doing through both macro- and micro-economic reform (INDECS, 1992; Battin, 1991). The prevailing logic of government in making such changes is based on the perception that competition, within a 'free' market, is, by definition, efficient and good. The central tenets of 'economic rationalism', the philosophy of current government (Pusey, 1991), include contracting out, downsizing, and an increasing emphasis on the small operator as opposed to the 'large inefficient' bureaucratic structure. All are aimed at increasing such competition. Competition is seen not only as the engine for economic development but also for the greater social good. This sentiment is well captured by the National Competition Policy (hereafter 'Hilmer Report'), a key report which increasingly informs government policy at both national and state levels:

> If Australia is to prosper as a nation, maintain and improve living standards and opportunities for its people, it has no choice but to improve the productivity and international competitiveness of its firms and institutions. Australian organisations, irrespective of their size, location or ownership, must become more efficient, more innovative and more flexible.
>
> Over the last decade or so, there has been a growing recognition, not only in Australia but around the world, of the role that competition plays in meeting these challenges. Competition provides the spur for business to improve their performance, develop new products and respond to changing circumstances. Competition offers the promise of lower prices and improved choice for consumers and greater efficiency, higher economic growth and increased opportunities for the economy as a whole. [page 1]

[1] In 1991 there were 4,500 such standards, 1,500 of which were taken up into legislation (Standards Australia, 1991).

Regulation, on the other hand, is seen to threaten the free market, and so must be kept to a minimum (Friedman, 1962, 1988; see also the Hilmer Report and a discussion in Battin, 1991, 1992; Dollery, 1992). To ensure regulations are kept in check most states and territories, as well as the Federal Government, put in place various offices of 'Regulation Review' to reduce the number and scope of regulations (Hilmer, 1993:203). New regulations in Victoria, for example, have to be scrutinized by the relevant office through a 'regulatory impact statement' process where the regulatory agency has to argue that the benefits of the new regulation outweigh the costs. Further, all regulations in that state now have a 'sunset clause' after ten years, meaning they will cease to have effect unless that relevant government agency puts in train a process to ensure the regulation stays in force (Regulation Reform, 1992).

Since the underlying aim of economic rationalism is to increase competition, other effects which also increase competition can be seen to give insight to the long-term influence of economic rationalist policies on virtue. One such effect acting at the time of the study was recession. Just as economic rationalist policies increase competitiveness between organizations, so too does recession. Since competition is central to the rationale underlying economic rationalism, increased competition such as that experienced under recession allows exploration of the premise that increased competition is an unmitigated good. The fundamental question that needs exploration through the data, then, is to understand the effect increasing the level of competition has on organizational virtue.

Recent economic changes, as well as increasing competition, have resulted in greater levels of mergers and acquisitions between organizations. While mergers and acquisitions are an integral part of the capitalist economy, and arguably part of the inevitable process of capital accumulation (Harvey, 1989), the deregulation of the financial markets can be seen to have increased the numbers of mergers, acquisitions and takeovers (Pritchard, 1994). Since not all capital ventures of this nature are successful, however, there is a reverse side to capital accumulation, namely bankruptcy and divestment of companies. As part of the analysis of broad economic changes, this chapter will explore how such activity, namely mergers, acquisitions and divestment, influences virtue.

The effect of economic rationalist policies, and the faith in competition, hold considerable implications for the production and maintenance of organizational virtue, and require analysis. Is it the 'free market', as argued by the rationalists, which will ensure not only the most equitable space for competition, and the most efficient allocation of resources, but also long-term gains in terms of economic virtue?

Increased Regulation

The second group of challenges facing organizations, that of increasing social regulation, is less discussed, but certainly present (Head, 1991; Bradmore, 1993). This increased emphasis on social regulation can be seen at a number of levels in the safety sphere. At the level of health and safety legislation, the social responsibility of employers to the safety of their employees was emphasized in Victoria by the *Occupational Health and Safety Act* 1985 (Vic.) placing the common law 'duty of care' in legislation. Secondly, there are increasing regulatory standards, as well as at the time of the interviews an increased government campaign regarding prosecutions, including prosecutions for manslaughter. Alongside such legislative increase in standards was the increased expectations of corporate behaviour and social 'virtue', made visible by an increased emphasis on 'Best Practice' (Ewer, Hampson, Lloyd, Ranford, Rix and Smith, 1993) and the growth in use of Australian and International Standards on 'Quality' (see for example AS 3901; AS 3902; and ISO 9001 and ISO 9002). Much to the chagrin of various Offices of Regulatory Review around Australia, effective regulation has increased.[2]

What is of particular interest here is the way the organizations in the study responded to these challenges of increased

[2] It appears this has largely arisen because of non-legislated standards, such as those put out by Standards Australia. These standards are not subject to the same review as regulations. Further, principal Acts, such as the *Occupational Health and Safety Act* 1985 (Vic.), are not subject to review. These Acts can draw directly on Australian standards, thus bypassing the constraints of the review process. There is some indication that the shift to a general duty of care has increased the number of documents a given organization has to consult before being assured of compliance with the law (Rex Deighton Smith, Director, Office of Regulation Reform, Victoria, personal communication).

competition and increased emphasis on safety. Did they, as might be expected, look to their underlying philosophy and culture, or did they look to other resources to solve the dilemmas posed by the competing forces of increased social regulation and the promotion of competition outlined above? In short, this chapter explores broad influences on the organizations which have implications for safety and draws tentative conclusions regarding the constitutive nature of regulation, to borrow Shearing's (1993) term.

The data outlined here highlight the importance of understanding regulation within a given economic and political context. The context here involves organizations coming to grips with expanded demands for social regulation at a time of increased competition within a progressively uncertain economic climate dominated, some would argue, by the needs of short-term capital (Pritchard, 1994; Sykes, 1994).

The Promotion of Competition: Economic Vicissitudes and Economic Rationalism

The focus of this section is on an analysis of how increased competition, whether brought about by economic vicissitudes or economic rationalism, affected safety and the commitment to safety by the organizations in the sample. The effect of competition on safety can be explored through analysis of the impact of recession, and the effect of the contracting out process. While there is some overlap with the previous chapter, the focus here is on the effect of competition on safety, as it is this which forms the focus of the rationale underpinning economic rationalism.

Policies promoted by an economic rationalist view include greater recourse to contracting out aspects of business, and progressively reducing the size of core business operations (Harvey, 1989; Drucker, 1992). This is seen to increase competition within the particular business and increase the overall efficiency of production while decreasing costs. The effect of this process on safety can be explored to some extent through the data. While the areas of contracting out occurring in the sample were primarily in the traditional areas of construction and logging, it is the effect of the **process** that is the focus here. This process of contracting out is similar whether in a traditional area, or in an area only recently subject to contracting out.

What the data illustrated was that increased competition **could** result in safer performance by those which remained in business, but only if those in positions of power were either willing or able to pay for the upfront costs incurred by increasing safety. Those in a weak position dependent on winning contracts were more likely to see competition as a negative influence on safety. This finding should not be surprising since it is consistent with the findings of previous chapters. Increased competition, whether brought about by economic vicissitudes, or a concerted campaign of economic rationalist policies aimed at increasing efficiency through competition, will affect organizations differently in terms of their calculation of the profit/safety nexus. Size and position in the contracting hierarchy influenced outlook, with large organizations high in the contracting hierarchy pointing to the value of competition for safety, while the small subcontractors pointed to the way competition directly and negatively affected safety.

However, this chapter goes one step further. It looks at what may happen when the crank of competition is wound higher, both on those with a virtuous culture and those from a blinkered perspective. The experience of recession allows some insight here. In the recession experienced, costs had to be cut, and expenditure controlled. Recession had a pivotal effect on the competitive nature of the contracting process by increasing the power of large organizations high in the contracting hierarchy, at the very time they themselves were vulnerable by the same push for competition and increased efficiency. In recession the number of replies received for a given call for tenders rose dramatically. As the number of contracts dwindled and the number of subcontractors bidding for each rose substantially, 'these days if we put [a contract] out for tender we get 30–40 replies, which is a nightmare' (Leafytown Council).

In recession some continued to see the competition as beneficial for safety: 'It's terrific at the moment they are knocking down your door to try and get a job.' For them, it meant they were able to dictate stringent safety standards on site, 'kicking subcontractors off site' for non-compliance. Replacement of subcontractors was no problem; when asked about replacing them the safety officer of Mightysteel replied: 'We'll get another subcontractor, don't you worry about that . . . they are knocking down your door to try and get a job.'

While there was a clear buyers' market in terms of awarding contracts, the buyers (i.e. the tenderors) were also keenly concerned to minimize costs. If safety was used as a criterion for accepting or rejecting subcontractors it had to be fully justified in terms of the cost implications for the organization. As the safety officer at Mightysteel commented when making the argument for safety in terms of contracts: 'With profit squeezed I have to justify myself more and better . . .'.

In such an environment safety becomes progressively aligned with efficiency and performance, rather than safety being an issue in its own right. This focus is illustrated by the project manager of Resource Mining:

> 'It's a far more competitive tendering environment. There is an economy in downturn, people are trying to prove they are efficient and their organizations are efficient. So the performance of the contractors generally has improved significantly.'

With increased competitiveness then, major players were in a very powerful position, leaving very little bargaining power to those tendering for contracts. However, those with power, the tenderors, were under financial pressure themselves and so had to decide how much they are willing to pay for the safety of subcontractors and their employees. The resultant competition, for the subcontractors could mean reduced profitability of contracts and increased temptation to cut corners, explained by Daytons Rigging:

> '. . . there is a lot of people in this industry now who have only just come in in the last four years, and their prices are just too low. I can't compete with them. . . . They are cutting corners. Like the safety officer might go home on a Saturday. If they find out he's not working, they'll be in there Saturday and Sunday cutting corners. [The construction company knows what goes on?] Oh yes, but they want the job up quicker too.'

The owner of Daytons had decided not to trade during the recession, since the prices paid for contracts were simply too low: 'I could find a job but they want it done too cheap you see, and when they are cutting corners you don't make any money.' Other organizations, such as the owner of (the now defunct) Better

Demolitions, also alluded to the two sides of large organizations which would seek out operators desperate for work in order to cut costs: 'The big companies know the ones that will take the risks. They get them on side and get them to come in at 2.00a.m. and do it for $10,000. . . . Some people have the money to be safe and some don't.'

For companies in a vulnerable position in the contracting hierarchy increased competition impinged directly on safety. Unless the company was a preferred subcontractor for a particular organization putting out the contract the profit margins, and thus the margins for safety, were very tight:

> 'Where you are a recommended subtenderer, in other words you are going to get the job whether you are $10,000 dearer or not, then you can put all the safety parts in you like. But if you tender for a job, particularly at the moment, you might be one of 150 people who are tendering. So you have to keep the quote as low as you possibly can. There is only a 10 per cent mark up, so if you do the job for half a million dollars, and you get the job for $410,000, there is something wrong. You have done a mistake somewhere in your calculations. [All the quotes] should be around $480,000, $470, $465, $490,000. So therefore the safety part comes into it. . . . There are certain short cuts you will do to win the contract, and save money.'

Subcontractors, therefore, were made more vulnerable by increased competition, the more intense that competition the more safety becomes an issue. In this context the confluence of 'efficiency' and safety becomes critically important. This nexus, and the pitfalls associated, were well illustrated by one organization which had experienced the direct effects of economic rationalist policies of downsizing and contracting out to increase efficiency. Resource Mining was undergoing considerable downsizing and was set to shed a further 1500 positions at the time of the interview. It had split its operations into three units in order to promote competition between the various open cut operations it owned. The project manager felt that such competition improved both safety and efficiency, in line with the espoused virtuous philosophy it held:

> 'It [the restructuring] casts pressure on each of our open cuts to keep their costs as low as possible, so we can compete with other producers. . . . I think competition is probably more positive than negative, in the

sense that the better operations integrate health and safety into their day-to-day activities.'

In addition, the restructuring was seen to bring health and safety into closer alignment with the needs of the restructured operation: 'We . . . have only one corporate health and safety person left now, . . . we are linking up accountability and responsibility . . . so they [the safety people] are now closer to where the decisions are being taken'.

However, closer analysis reveals the possible differential effect competition can have. Safety and 'efficiency' were seen to coincide where safety could be seen as an integral part of the job, not as an afterthought. Where an existing operation was modified to include safety, the result of competition was potentially destructive to the safety effort, as the same manager at Resource Mining explained:

'If you can integrate health and safety at the stage when a job is being designed, so that people are neither being harmed in the long term due to exposure, or in the short term because of injuries, then you have an efficient way of operating. Where we have an existing operation and then said OK, what are the health and safety implications, and added them on [it is not so good]. Add-ons are always the first thing that tends to get disregarded.'

This may explain the difference between the various organizations in the sample regarding the attitude towards competition and safety. Competition may affect safety in a positive way up to a point and as long as safety is seen as an integral part of the job at hand. However, where safety is an 'add-on', which has a tangible cost and is a negative drag on winning a contract, for example use of a scissor lift to replace a roof, competition and safety are competing bedfellows.

Here it is necessary, however, to address the effect reducing staff may have on safety, particularly in those companies which seek to integrate safety with their other operations. Again the effect may not be a simple one. Reduction in staff numbers may not inevitably lead to a lack of safety. It is clear, however, that safety personnel play a critical role in maintaining safety at work, particularly in the long term, as the project manager of Resource Mining commented: 'The proactive stuff comes from your health and safety people.' Safety personnel, however, also represent a quantifiable cost, and may be squeezed by a company looking to cut costs. The 'integration' approach to health and safety could result in an increase in roles within an organization, with no increase, or perhaps a decrease, in staffing. The fulfilment of a total number of roles expected of one individual may become impossible, and choices between roles are forced on middle management. Such was the experience of the following safety officer at Roadtech: 'I have two hats, one is safety and the other is I am an engineer. That is secondary but I can't do half a job.' The people in such positions are forced to make choices and have an ambiguous relationship with their employer. This ambiguity is illustrated by the safety officer at Roadtech, who on the one hand was very positive about the company:

> 'The company is very good in that they have never knocked me back when I have requested something for safety, in terms of it being too expensive or too hard . . .'

However, later in the same interview he stated:

> 'It is very rare an employee is in the wrong. It is a breakdown in the process or the system. It may well be that there is not even a system in place, no job description, no training, its not like the way things should be done, second nature. . . . It's a shame companies have to be forced to take training seriously. You would think they would do it off their own bat, but they are now forced through government incentives otherwise they are taxed.'

The above quote is full of 'doublespeak': on one hand the 'company has never knocked me back' and on the other 'It's a shame companies have to be forced to take training seriously.' The overall feeling is one of uneasiness, where the safety officer is unsure whether the company is really interested in safety or not.

Increased competition and (cost) efficiency then are not an unmitigated good for safety. Where the company size is large and high in the contracting hierarchy, and where safety can be easily integrated into the job, safety may benefit from competition. However, where competition and efficiency are the sole focus and the costs of safety easily identifiable (such as personnel or equipment costs) then competition and efficiency threaten safety. These identifiable costs become more problematic in the contracting out process where securing of contracts depends on a competitive quote. Extraneous costs, safety included, may simply be too high in the short term for business survival.

Mergers, Acquisitions and Bankruptcy

Mergers, acquisitions and bankruptcies are an integral part of what Schumpeter describes as the 'creative destructive' impulse of capitalism, particularly in the wake of financial deregulation (Pritchard, 1994). The amount of such activity in the sample was high. Six of the twenty-six organizations in the core sample[3] had been subjected to a takeover or sell off. However, the dramatic shifts in virtue (gauged by company culture) which occurred in these cases need to be seen in light of a range of influences, including changes to company size and profitability. Takeovers could inject large amounts of much needed capital which elevated the status of the target organization from a small to large business.

Most of the takeovers in the sample involved large companies with well developed business philosophies taking over small companies working off a survival approach to business. In these cases changes made have to be seen in light of the changed size and profitability of the target company. The influence of these 'other factors' is strengthened by one case in the sample where two equals (in terms of size and position in the contracting hierarchy) were battling for control of a steel mill. In this case the influence on safety was minimal, which indicates that the size influence may be the major one in the event of takeovers.

Size changes also influence safety when the reverse occurs. The late 1980s saw the dramatic collapse of a large number of holding companies, and this sample was not exempt from that influence. In follow-up work on Aidans, the company had been drastically affected by the dramatic collapse of one of Australia's largest corporate giants. This company had been the embodiment of a virtuous ideology at the time of the fatality and the immediate response. The sell off occurred at the time of the interview. The particular business where the fatality occurred continued to operate, and in the short term maintained the same safety

[3] The number includes Sergensons, the company which did not contribute to a death and so was not subject to an analysis of virtue in its response.

philosophy which had been achieved when part of the large corporate empire. However, the same organization two years later revealed a very different picture, with the company reduced to a small backyard business with incredibly tight profit margins.

The new owners, previous managers under the large corporate structure, had purchased the company, but had found that without the resources of the corporate structure they had been forced to move to premises with cheaper rent and of a lower standard. The new owner was attempting to re-establish a viable business with a total of two employees, with the owner working alone on weekends to construct an office separate to the warehouse where the machinery operated.

The process of dramatic decline such as this is hazardous for safety levels. While for some the ultimate outcome of this process is to go out of business (four businesses in the original sample of thirty-eight went out of business) for others it is a temporary phenomenon and recovery is the ultimate outcome. Yet others remain locked in a marginal status drifting in and out of business when conditions change. There is no doubt that this marginal status, whether long- or short-term, is accompanied by a conflict approach to priorities. The choice for these companies may not be between virtuous ideology or a blinkered approach, but between conflict and non-existence.

Mergers, acquisitions and bankruptcies are then yet another illustration of the way the dynamics of capitalism continuously challenge virtue. Such activity forms the backdrop of regulation, constantly threatening to change and in some cases undermine the rules of regulatory activity.

The Effect of Increasing Social Regulation on the Profit/Safety Equation

The purpose of this section is to illustrate how the increase in regulation in the area of occupational health and safety was perceived by the organizations in the study in terms of the effect on their ongoing economic viability and the push for competitiveness. It is important to remember that the increase in social regulation extends beyond the specific act targeted at occupational health and safety and includes compensation legislation, coronial inquiries, common law actions, regulations and standards.

Through all these mechanisms modifications to workplaces can occur. The director of Reid Plumbing illustrates how such moves influenced both behaviour and attitudes. He complied with some new standards while remaining ambivalent to the push for increased safety in his underlying attitude. The death of one of his subcontractors involved 'walking' the ladder like a pair of stilts. The director freely admitted the value of this practice in making work flow more smoothly; but for the written procedure and the push of the government and safety officers, he argued, the practice would still be accepted:

'[I]t would have been fairly common practice fifteen or twenty years ago, . . . you couldn't do it now. There is certainly a lot of work places now with safety officers and safety rules that the DOL push. So we now have a new awareness that the State Government push as well.'

While this particular measure which banned walking the ladder was reasonably well accepted, each change could be challenged and was challenged, with relation to the increasing costs it imposed. For example, this same director was equivocal about the positive influence of the push for safety when it came to directions for use of mobile scaffolding during re-roofing operations. The preferred practice used by this company was to 'skate' the new roofing over the old, a now banned practice:

'Quite often you will skate over the roof and put the new sheet on with nothing [no scaffolding] underneath. Now the DOL would ban that, they would want a mobile scaffold underneath.'

The reason for this preferred practice revolved around the issue of cost:

'The job would normally cost $40 per hour, say a total of $60 including the cost of the sheet. With the scaffold it could cost you $700. . . . Some of the safety procedures are felt by a lot of contractors to be too heavy, so there are short cuts taken.'

The increased regulatory demands then could be seen as incompatible with survival. This feeling of being overburdened was common to the blinkered group. At the time of the interview the Department of Labour was involved in a campaign to increase safety in logging. The effect of this was felt by the owner of Adams Logging with a fearful look to the future:

> 'It's going alright at the moment but with the government policies coming up it could create a lot more cost. . . . DOL are coming in, they seem to have a lot more red tape and paraphernalia you have to go through.'

For large organizations with a virtuous approach the increased demands of social regulation went beyond addressing the effects of specifically targeted legislation. These companies were seeking to capitalize on their attitude and commitment to safety; one avenue of doing this was through accreditation with the Standards Association of Australia. In a sense they could be seen to be imposing increased standards than those required by legislation. However, although such accreditation could only be attained through addressing some issues relevant to safety, such as equipment design and training, the primary focus for this is the quality of the **product or service** and thus valuable in terms of the marketing. Accreditation was felt by Mightysteel to increase the quality of the product, as well as the status of the organization, and therefore its competitiveness in the market. While accreditation of the product then did not directly influence safety, it certainly had an indirect effect, as explained by the safety officer of the plant:

> 'We've just had the Australian Standards Commission [*sic*] here, and now we are an Australian Standards approved organization with respect to our products. . . . We are melting down scrap, and you have got to add additives. We had to bring the steel up to the Australian Standard [with respect to the quantity of additives], [so] we now have an automatic additions system [which means] people are now working in air-conditioned consoles. . . . We [previously] had a process which is a fairly dangerous one. You are melting down steel at 1,600 degrees Celsius and hand shovelling in the additives. Standards approval looks at things like not only your quality of product, but also customer supply and training.'

Increased emphasis on social regulation then is multifaceted, including both the influence of targeted legislation and the push generally for 'increased quality', which includes reference to health and safety. The effect of this was felt across all companies studied. The increased emphasis on safety received a mixed reception, with those with a blinkered culture emphasizing the costs involved in such regulation, exemplified here by Reid Plumbing and Adams Logging. Virtuous respondents such as Mightysteel sought to include the increased emphasis on such regulation within the win/win solution of promoting safety as improving competitiveness.

However, the increased demands for safety had a limited effect when stimulating major contractors to pay more for the contracts they needed filled. While regulation had increased the costs of contracts, the increased price of safety was not matched by the increase in pay for the contract, as explained by the owner of Daytons Rigging: 'it's gone up but not that much, the reason I am doing what I am doing now [working for someone else] is simply because of that, you can't compete with all the people round you'. To win contracts and stay in business for many involved cutting corners, such as utilizing times of the day and night when regulators, both from government and the major contractor, were not present: 'They sit there with their tail lights shining up on the ceiling then walk around at night because the DOL is not there' (ex owner, Better Demolitions). In the highly competitive market described above, not only did some small business cut corners, but also avoided reporting injury, as this may have resulted in job loss: 'Some of the smaller organizations are too frightened to make a claim because they might lose their jobs. That happens.' (Project manager, Mightysteel.)

The general effect of increasing social regulation then is mitigated by the shift to contracts combined with the increased focus on competition. Ultimately those employers in secondary labour markets have little to gain from global increased standards. In the current climate they are most likely to resist changes to safety levels as these have a direct and negative impact on profitability. Legislation has some, albeit partial, effect in protection of the subcontractor. Health and safety legislation takes account of contracts, with a broad definition of employee to include subcontractors' employees. However, compensation legislation does not have such a definition, yet it was illustrated in the previous chapter that this had the most direct effect on the profit/safety nexus.

The solution provided by most large organizations to solve their dilemmas with respect to increased regulation and safety improvement, namely to push for quality accreditation, is weakened through the contracting out process. Safety officers in major corporations felt this lack of control, which they saw as a key issue in maintaining safety overall, and they resented the increased use of contractors for work such as maintenance. Contractors were seen as less reliable and less committed to the company as a whole. The safety officer of Mightysteel was one such officer: 'I'd like to eliminate contractors. You have much more control over your own workforce.'

Keeping Their Own House in Order: Business Programmes

The discussion so far has illustrated the considerable tension between the demand for increased competitiveness within the current rationalist structure of capital, and the increased demand on social regulation. These competing pressures saw certain organizations look outside their boundaries for solutions. One prominent solution for five of the companies studied[4] was adherence to the principles of Quality Assurance.

This section will study one of these organizations, Resource Mining, in some detail in order to highlight the strengths and weaknesses in relying on a programme to resolve long-standing issues associated with the promotion of safety. Quality Assurance is the current manifestation of a long history of programmes such as Management by Objectives in the late 1960s and 1970s and Quality Circles in the 1970s and early 1980s (Terry, 1981; Robson, 1982; Hill, 1986). The attraction of these business programmes is the way they promise to solve a wide diversity of problems, including employee safety, under one aegis. Organizations in this study attempted to improve their safety levels not only by using the structure outlined in legislation, but also by Quality Assurance procedures which attempted to lift the business 'game' as a whole with safety as part of a wider package of measures.

Quality Assurance works through promoting a consensus from within the organization. It aims to achieve this by a 'customer focus' which places a priority on doing the job right first time. The programme aims to minimize or eliminate conflict within the organization with an emphasis on a unified process being a common solution to multiple problems found within the organization. Quality Assurance challenges the perception that the primary cause of mistakes is malcontent, complainers or bludgers. The solution promoted by these packages in contrast sees complaint

[4] Resource Mining, Haddons, Lynden Hydraulics, Mightysteel and Roadtech.

as positive, particularly when complaint arises from customers. In this view, what the customer wants is by definition right. From this point the scheme unravels into identifying correct processes (as opposed to people), using symbols and distinct language[5] to highlight correct process. The ideal result of this process is a systematic and comprehensive programme of checking and cross-checking aimed at raising standards throughout organizations, including contractual relations. Included in the 'Quality' approach is adherence to regulatory controls, since non-compliance, it is argued, ultimately causes more problems, and wastes valuable time and resources to clear up mistakes.

In terms of substance, Quality Assurance and similar strategies such as Total Quality Management, attempt to subsume 'soft' goals, such as safety, under measurable criteria, such as standard of product, with the ultimate aim of increasing the viability of the organization. The practice of Quality Assurance is labour intensive in the short term, with the establishment of in-house training and formal procedures, although they may argue that in the long term they save time, that time historically spent on rectifying mistakes. The attraction of these programmes, especially to organizations which have a virtuous ideology, is obvious. There are clearly similarities between what is promised under a 'Quality Management' scheme and what is desired by the 'virtuous' organization. Such programmes promise increased efficiency and cost savings, while allowing organizations to comply fully with regulations and improve customer satisfaction (however defined).

The challenge to create a coherent culture which was able to solve a diverse range of issues, including health and safety, and improve the long-term viability of the organization, was thus argued to be provided by the implementation of Quality Assurance. Quality Assurance was argued to be a preventative to future safety incidents in that its major focus was on correct process, and fatalities often resulted from a breakdown in process. This was true of Resource Mining:

'We have moved across to a QA approach, which sort of instead of focusing on the end, goes back and looks at how things are designed, then

[5] For example, employees are asked to identify 'Poncs'. These are the 'Price Of Non Conformity' or the mistakes that result from incorrect process which cost the organization time and money.

how are they manufactured, how they are assembled, and how they are tested. [There was] an integrated approach. There was a measure of it here, but it certainly wasn't QA. We have built into the new tender documents a full QA approach which would enable the tenderer to go back and justify even perhaps the expertise of the designer . . .'

The reality of the implementation of these programmes and the decisions of the subscribing organizations, however, illustrate how competing influences of increased competition and increased demand for safety cannot always be eliminated by a 'programme', however good that claims to be. This particular case of Resource Mining highlights the way programmes can slip into the realm of the symbolic, replacing the actual substance learnt from the death, thus sidestepping the potential key to improvement. Resource Mining had investigated the fatality which resulted from the dredger collapse thoroughly and instituted a number of changes, in a response classified in chapter 4 as virtuous. Since the time of the fatality they also instituted a major Quality Assurance initiative. The project manager expressed considerable confidence in the new Quality Assurance process, to the extent that he felt it would have prevented the fatality had it been in place during the construction of the dredger that collapsed. In terms of future dredger contracts he also felt that because of the experience of the fatality they had gained much expertise which would be of great use in future projects. However, the bad experience of the collapse, and liability and other monetary concerns, also pushed them towards a 'turnkey approach' of simply buying a 'ready made' dredger, which would minimize their active involvement in the construction process. They would shift from using their own experience and learning from the collapse to rely on the Quality Assurance process of choosing contractors to ensure the 'right' choice of contractor.[6] Ultimately then the knowledge gained from the fatality and subsequent investigation was largely lost in the upcoming purchase of a new dredger, at least in part due to monetary concerns, and transferred to a heavy reliance on a Quality Assurance programme to ensure the virtuous ideology of the contractor. The contractor who won the contract for the new dredger would have an arm's length relationship

[6] It is interesting to note that the manager was reminded of another dredger collapse in the 1960s which had been forgotten.

with the buyer 'rather like buying a car in a car yard'. The ability of Resource Mining to influence the contractor, and to ensure the safety of the selling company's employees, relies entirely on a Quality Assurance document under a 'turnkey' contract. In effect the 'substance' of learning from the fatality was exchanged to the 'symbol' of using a Quality Assurance package. This is not to criticize the content of such a package, but to point to the shift that can occur between substance and symbol when companies are faced with underlying conflicts. As chapter 7 showed, companies with a blinkered approach were willing to sign contracts, yet not comply with the stipulations of that contract, which exacerbates the problems associated with such a shift.

Additional problems of this 'package' approach arise in organizations under times of stress, when the organization seeks to cut costs; priority is placed on time and soft goals become collapsed as qualitative aims are measured by quantitative criteria. The problem of multiple roles placed on an ever dwindling pool of staff is relevant to the promotion of schemes such as Quality Assurance, as it was relevant to the discussion of 'downsizing' above.

Programmes such as Quality Assurance hold considerable promise for organizations keen to harmonize the multiple and competing pressures placed upon them. However, such programmes do not immunize participating organizations against the economic vicissitudes described above, and can be seen to be combined and distorted with other pressures on the organizations responding to the competitive environment by cutting costs and cutting staff. As the case of Resource Mining showed, adherence to such programmes may provide a convenient solution to organizations wishing to divest themselves of ongoing responsibility for their subcontractors. Learning from the fatality may be replaced by promotion of adherence to process.

Conclusion

The current climate of competitiveness holds considerable challenges for the maintenance of virtue. The dual structure of contemporary capitalism made up of large core organizations and a periphery of secondary organizations (Harvey, 1989) forms a backdrop to this competitiveness. The impact of competitiveness combined with the dual structure of capitalist enterprises lends support to the argument developed in the preceding chapters that it is this structure which has a controlling role to play in the determination of, and the maintenance of, virtue. The analysis of this chapter continues this argument. Competition was not, as might be expected, an unmitigated disaster for safety and virtue. It was mediated by the degree to which the dilemmas of competition could be resolved by the guiding philosophy of the company, and the power it had to enable it to maintain the faith in the virtuous approach to the resolution of problems. The dilemmas were most easily resolved by large 'core' organizations.

However, for those in the secondary labour market increased competitiveness holds considerable threat. The organizations in this 'space' are less amenable to the arguments put forward by the virtuous philosophy for increased virtue increasing competitiveness. With increased competition their position of a blinkered philosophy appears vindicated. Virtue is totally dependent on context. Where context allows for safety (where they are paid for the increased immediate costs of safety) virtue will result, where costs are not forthcoming safety will suffer.

The creative destructive impulse of capitalism works at a number of levels, one of which is the effect of competition, in particular the effect of competitiveness on safety. Increased competition has both positive and negative aspects. When competition is combined with access to power and a regulatory climate which supports virtue, it can increase virtue. However, the current trend of economic rationalism contains within it a conscious effort to curb individual companies' access to power within any market. The result is that the freedom to be virtuous is also curbed. Taken to extremes, extremes that I would argue are present in the writing on economic rationalism, competition is ultimately destructive of virtue.

Yet another level to this creative destructive impulse is the impact of mergers, acquisitions, bankruptcies and sell offs on regulation and compliance. This level of business activity is usually ignored by those writing on regulation, but this study shows it can have considerable influence on safety levels. From the data above the influence of mergers and acqusitions was positive or neutral, and depended upon the cultural philosophies of the organizations concerned. On the other hand bankruptcies and the subsequent sell offs were more hazardous for compliance levels. Bringing into the regulatory debate the dynamic nature of capitalism, and the impact of that dynamism, remains an important challenge.

This chapter has also highlighted the need to take account of the state of regulation, beyond a view that the current impulse is purely deregulatory. On paper at least there is an argument that social regulation is increasing (Ayres and Braithwaite, 1992; Head, 1991; Bradmore, 1993). While enforcement policies may shift from prosecution to self-regulation independent of the actual letter of the law, studies have shown that the majority of organizations will attempt to comply with regulations independent of enforcement measures (Ayres and Braithwaite, 1992). This state of affairs encourages those with access to power to be virtuous. However, the existence of a stable or increasing secondary labour market within contemporary capitalism, aimed at increasing flexibility and competitiveness, is structurally resistant to policies which increase social regulation. Compliance in these markets is necessarily partial and context driven.

The policies of economic rationalism actively seek to break down the barriers some organizations build as protection against the vicissitudes of competition. Organizations which build such barriers are essentially large and in positions of power over the market. These are the organizations which have the space to be virtuous and comply with increasing social regulation. If economic rationalist policies are successful, and such barriers eliminated, the possibilities inherent within the increase in social regulation fall away. Since the overriding demand of the organization is for profit, when safety and profit are incompatible, then safety will suffer. The extremes of competition promoted by economic rationalism would seem to promote just such a situation. This chapter and the chapter on organizational culture point to the vulnerability of the virtuous approach when faced with extremes of competition.

Large organizations in positions of power have not been complacent regarding the oncoming onslaught. Primarily the response has been one of seeing 'Quality' as the ultimate solution, and the ultimate way in which competition and virtue can combine. While there may be some reason for optimism in certain circumstances, the analysis of the case of Resource Mining shows that such programmes are not immune from problems. The increased focus on form and procedure of Quality Assurance as a solution to safety was in tension with substantive learning in this area. Reliance on bureaucratic procedure to encapsulate substantive learning, as Weber identified, has inherent problems. Over time the reason for the procedure is lost, and observance of form prevails over the pursuit of value, in this case the value of safety improvement.

10 Conclusion

THE concern of this book has been to understand organizational 'virtue' and the possibility of nurturing virtue as the primary aim of regulatory action within the contemporary capitalist economies. The vehicle used to examine good corporate conduct has been analysis of how organizations respond to the harm they contribute to, namely the death of a worker, within complex worksite structures. The response of each of the companies involved in the death gave an opportunity to assess virtue within the complexity of worksite forms which characterize current economic life.

Chapter 3 highlighted the range of contexts within which the death at work occurred, and suggested the need to go beyond the causes of incidents in search of an adequate 'test' of virtue. In chapter 4, the data showed that responses to the deaths experienced provided a useful tool with which to explore virtue, and established through analysis of the responses that they could be characterized as either 'virtuous' or lacking in virtue. Chapters 5 to 9 explored various factors which lay behind corporate action or inaction to the death, in order to understand how virtue arises and how it may be 'nurtured'.

It appears from this study that while there can be some optimism that the exercise of nurturing virtue may be fruitful in certain arenas, the undertaking may be far more complex than previously suggested. In particular the data presented in the preceding chapters suggest greater attention needs to be paid to dynamics both within and outside the organization in order to ascertain their capacity for 'virtue' before deciding upon a particular regulatory strategy.

Chapter 5 explored techniques of neutralization as a means of distinguishing organizational virtue from non-virtue. The findings illustrated that identification of virtue requires an understanding of organizational dynamics, not just rationalizations of individuals in organizations, since the defensive nature of the rationalizations was not associated with the actual response the organization made. Chapter 6 tackled the issue of organizational dynamics leading to virtue or non-virtue, and explored the important mediating role that organizational culture could play in determining how organizations reacted to the death they experienced. Culture was a 'touchstone', or web of assumptions, which provided the basis for deciding how success for the organization was to be achieved. This web of assumptions then provided the various justifications for action (or inaction) which followed the death. Consistent with the differing route to success, organizational culture differed between the two sets of respondents, the virtuous and the blinkered. The blinkered culture dichotomized choices within the organization (safety *or* profit) which led to their restricted and defensive 'non-virtuous' reaction to the death. Safety initiatives were perceived as a threat, and so these companies were wary of regulators and suspicious of unions. The 'virtuous' culture on the other hand aimed to harmonize the various imperatives they faced. Safety and success were not only seen as compatible, but safety was an integral part of success. Here the input of unions, regulators and safety committees were for the most part welcomed and incorporated into an overall safety strategy.

Crucially, chapter 7 indicated that culture and the ensuing response to the death bore a strong relationship to structure. The context within which the organizations acted was central to understanding how an organization behaved, and the extent to which it could be virtuous. In particular, the size of organization bore strong relationship to culture and behaviour. Large organizations tended to act in a virtuous manner, small organizations tended to lack virtue. However, there were exceptions. Within the exceptions, such as large organizations responding in a blinkered manner, response was related to culture, not structure. Exploring these exceptions further, it was clear that access to power could be used either to improve virtue, or to avoid responsibility. A multinational fought legal battles off shore, and argued their English was not good enough to understand what was going on in court, for example. Further there was some indication that broader structural relationships affected culture, such as the degree of competitiveness within an industry, and the degree to which contract price was premised on cost considerations alone. Overall, structure was seen to be intimately related to capacity for virtue individual firms had.

Chapter 8 explored the role of law in moulding response to the safety issues raised by the death in light of the influence of structure and culture. The range of relevant legal mechanisms impinging on issues such as safety is broad: encompassing coronial inquiries, compensation law, the common law, as well as health and safety law which has been the traditional focus of research. The response to law was differentiated according to an organization's size and culture. Further, in terms of law enforcement, chapter 8 argued that concerns about legal liability had the potential to trigger considerable changes within organizations, not all of which could be considered as desirable from the point of view of improving corporate accountability.

Finally, chapter 9 explored the way current political and economic factors both increased competitiveness within industry and changed expectations about safety standards. Findings suggested that increased competition and increased pace of industrial activity held considerable threats to virtue in the long term. There was no simple relationship between increased competitiveness and increased threat to virtue, however. 'Virtuous' organizations looked to their strengths to incorporate raised ethical expectations, and used programmes such as Quality Assurance to help harmonize the conflicting imperatives they faced. Nonetheless, an inability to shield themselves from extreme competition could mean that such programmes could become a face-saving exercise while safety was undermined by recent policy changes aimed at increasing efficiency and competitiveness.

In concluding, it is useful to consider the implications of this study for current writing in the area of regulation. Two key themes have emanated from recent writing on regulation. First, Ayres and Braithwaite (1992) argue for the need to 'transcend' the deregulation debate, and build trustworthy organizations through use of judicious and imaginative sanctions. Organizations need to be given space for virtue, in the sure knowledge that if they fail, a hierarchy of sanctions waits to be applied (Braithwaite, 1985, 1991, 1993; Ayres and Braithwaite, 1992; Fisse and Braithwaite, 1993). A second theme emanates from the work of Shearing (1993) and argues for intervening into the market in creative ways in order to sustain corporate virtue (Shearing, 1993; Gunningham, 1993; Grabosky, 1994a and b). This chapter will explore the implications of the data presented here for the themes of trust and use of market forces to encourage virtuous organizational behaviour.

An important focus of this study has been to link the work of current theorists (such as Braithwaite and Shearing) back to the formal theoretical traditions of Marx and Weber. The data has been used as a heuristic device, a way of making some sort of overall conceptual sense of recent theorizing. The latter half of this chapter will bring together the work of recent theorists and evaluate them in light of the insights provided by the data and these broader theoretical traditions.

Braithwaite and Beyond

The Regulatory Pyramid

Research into deaths on multiple employer worksites confirms that Braithwaite (1991, 1993), Shearing (1993), Grabosky (1994a and b) and Gunningham (1993) are correct in their assertion that greater numbers of more intrusive and punitive measures against organizations is unlikely to be the ultimate solution to corporate harm. While an argument can be made for applying severe sanctions in the case of flagrant breaches of the law (Polk, Haines and Perrone, 1993, 1995), criminal penalties against organizations and their members may have several negative side-effects, which work against the ultimate goal of regulation.

The crucial issue is where the debate goes from here, and the underlying framework to be used as the primary tool in ordering regulatory priorities. Perhaps the most commonly cited paradigm is that of the regulatory pyramid (Braithwaite, 1985, 1991; Ayres and Braithwaite, 1992; Braithwaite, 1993; Fisse and Braithwaite, 1993). It has proved a popular ordering structure for government policy documents on regulation, one recent example of its use being the Industry Commission report into Health and Safety (1995:694–5, Vol. II: 421). It is thus a useful paradigm with which to begin discussion. Braithwaite (1991) describes the pyramid in the following way:

> My contention is that compliance is most likely when the regulatory agency displays an explicit enforcement pyramid . . . Most regulatory action occurs at the base of the pyramid where initially attempts are made to coax compliance by persuasion. The next phase of enforcement escalation is a warning letter; if this fails to secure compliance, civil

monetary penalties are imposed; if this fails, criminal prosecution ensues; if this fails, the plant is shut down or a licence to operate is suspended; if this fails, the licence to do business is revoked . . . The **form** of the enforcement pyramid is the subject of the theory, not the content of the particular pyramid. [page 24. Emphasis added]

The pyramid acts as a paradigm for regulation in that it suggests that regulators must have recourse to a wide range of sanctions, which should be applied in strict order of escalating severity and intrusiveness into the internal working of the organization. Fisse and Braithwaite (1993) are keen to point to the motivational and dynamic nature of the pyramid paradigm:

A central idea behind the pyramidal enforcement is the game theoretic postulate that actors, individual or corporate, are most likely to comply if they know that enforcement is backed up by sanctions which can be escalated in response to any given level of non compliance, whether minor or egregious. The pyramid proposed is tall rather than squat, the theory being that the taller the enforcement pyramid, the more levels of possible escalation, then the greater the pressure that can be exerted to motivate 'voluntary' compliance at the base of the pyramid. Compliance is thus understood within a dynamic enforcement game where enforcers try to get commitment from corporations to comply with the law and can back up their negotiation with credible threats about the dangers faced by defendants if they choose to go down the path of non compliance. [page 143]

While the pyramid metaphor may have considerable merit in bringing some order to bear on the internal strategies of a single regulatory agency, it also can make the task of regulation appear deceptively simple. At the very least the data here suggest that escalation and de-escalation of penalty may be far more difficult than previously anticipated. While escalation of sanction may be a perfectly reasonable response to non-compliance, analysts and practitioners should be aware that this produces important effects in companies, which, in response to threat, aim to reduce their vulnerability to scrutiny, and so, to liability. It is, therefore, sensible to suggest, as Fisse and Braithwaite (1993) do, that breaking down the corporate veil may be less effective than ensuring a penalty structure which demands internal disciplinary action. Nonetheless, to maintain credibility, intrusive sanctions, where warranted, must be used, as Braithwaite (1993) has pointed out. When escalation of penalty occurs, motivation for corporate compliance shifts from co-operation and trust, to deterrence and mistrust.

Measures aimed at increasing public scrutiny and legal accountability in order to secure compliance may paradoxically create chronically distrustful organizations which comply with minimal requirements when under scrutiny, yet retreat to non-compliance at the earliest opportunity. Defiant organizations, like defiant individuals, may prove the most difficult to deal with (Sherman, 1993). In some of the cases examined in the data, the relatively minor threat of public scrutiny through the coroner's inquest (when compared to criminal prosecution for example) produced substantial changes aimed at reducing the courts' capacity to scrutinize activities internal to the company. Fear of legal liability, in this case primarily fear of common law actions, in certain cases directly affected internal company mechanisms which aimed to improve safety. In one company, for example, power given to company lawyers meant they had the power to vet safety officers' investigations into incidents, limiting the scope and nature of the inquiry into safety issues. In order to avoid such negative side-effects and preserve the integrity of safety functions within their own organizations, large virtuous organizations had to find creative ways to respond both to the demands of safety, and protection from legal liability. Many of these companies underwent a type of 'schizophrenia', splitting the functions of one department from another, legal from safety, to ensure both that liability was protected, and safety could continue unhindered by the gaze of the courts. In these organizations there was a paradox where demand for increased accountability through the courts could produce less virtue. The point is that organizations can change qualitatively when faced with the threat of legal liability. Such qualitative changes may not easily be reversed when penalties are de-escalated and the regulator attempts to re-establish trust. Legal astuteness gained through involvement in a court process is unlikely to be abandoned once the threat is past. In the data Haddons had qualitatively changed their attitude to the threat of legal liability through their appearance at inquest. The danger is that once such 'schizophrenic' processes are put in place, organizations whose standards drop will be adept at hiding their internal processes from public scrutiny, precisely because they have previously felt the weight of that legal liability. Building trust with organizations who have never experienced legal threat is one thing, rebuilding trust may be an entirely different matter.

Such paradoxes are well documented by Sitkin and Bies (1994a) and pose considerable dilemmas for those criminologists advocating penalties or public accountability as the prime motivator for safety improvements.[1] Even for those advocating a gradation of penalties, ordered according to a sanctioning hierarchy or a regulatory pyramid, the problem of such paradoxes remains. If organizational practices change in response to the threat of legal liability in a way that inhibits long-term virtue, such as legal vetting of all safety and environmental reports, further organizational change is needed after the legal threat has subsided in a direction that will allow continuation of positive change. A single regulator, or regulatory agency, however, may not be in a position to effect such changes.

Part of the strength of a regulatory strategy may in fact be the way regulatory techniques act in tandem, to complement one another. The pyramid model recommends 'ranking' the various regulatory techniques in some sort of hierarchy to allow for orderly escalation of penalty in the face of non-compliance (Braithwaite, 1985; Ayres and Braithwaite, 1992; Fisse and Braithwaite, 1993). This study suggests that, in the arena of safety at least, this may be of limited value as a tool to understanding regulation or a blueprint for organizational control. The range of legislation which influences a given area may be diverse, such as health and safety legislation, compensation legislation and the common law in the case of health and safety. Each of these act with different but related purposes, and, crucially, all at the same time. That is they each act independently (or at least semi-independently), not in a sequential form. To reiterate, while the pyramid may be a useful metaphor to assist a single agency to understand its enforcement policy, it has limited use in understanding the nature of regulation in the market-place, where multiple legal constraints and opportunities shape organizational behaviour.

Further, it cannot be assumed that a single regulatory response, or range of responses, will be equally effective against all organizations, large or small. Who the company was, in terms of size

[1] I have argued elsewhere (Haines, 1994) that there may well be a justification of criminal sanction based on criteria other than deterrence and improving company behaviour. Other elements of criminal law enforcement, such as equal sanctions for equal harm against society, the public need for retribution against those who wreak great harm, and the need to wield the symbolism of the criminal law, may be an important factor in the decision to prosecute.

and culture, in this study determined how they acted in response to a particular legal threat. Equally as important, then, as the paradoxes created in organizations by their response to legal threat (or threats), are the findings here that the threat of penalty is mediated by who the company is, in terms of their size and access to power, and company culture premised on either a harmonizing or dichotomizing imperative. This finding dovetails nicely with research into differential impact of penalty on individuals (see Sherman, 1993). Whether individuals and organizations respond to measures aimed at deterrence may reside, to a far greater extent than currently recognized in theoretical models, in this case regulatory theory, with who the individual or organization *is*, and their position within the broader social structure.

A good example of the way regulatory techniques affect different organizations in a different manner is provided by the differential impact publicity has on organizations of different size and stature. Publicity as a sanction has been suggested by many as a useful regulatory technique (Clinard and Yeager, 1980; Coffee, 1981; Fisse and Braithwaite, 1983). Loss of prestige through adverse publicity, whether formal or informal, is seen to be of grave concern for organizations, who, it is argued, go to great lengths to maintain their public image (Fisse and Braithwaite, 1983). This study suggests, however, that it may be only large high-profile organizations which are sensitive to public image. In contrast, small organizations thrive on their invisibility to the public at large, and to the regulators, and so may be little affected by public impression of their activities. This was particularly acute when the profitability of a small business was determined by their ability to gain contracts from other organizations in their industry. In such situations a good relationship with potential contractors was far more important than a good relationship with the public at large. Publicity as a sanction may then only be successful against large organizations with a high public profile. Small business with a low stake in public approval may be little affected.[2]

[2] Additionally such sanctions must go further than the private media sector. They are simply not interested in the daily grind of corporate misbehaviour. In their search for the sensational, it is unlikely that media would take the space for the reality of everyday breaches. A good example of the sensational is the recent prosecution of the 'Denbo' company for manslaughter (*The Queen* v. *Denbo Pty. Ltd.* Victorian Supreme Court, Teague, J June 1994). A prosecution for manslaughter is newsworthy, while the more mundane deaths that were the subject of this study received little or no attention.

Part of understanding that the effect of sanctions may differ depending upon the size of organization, is the understanding that the response of different organizations varies precisely because of the opportunities afforded by their size. The response of small organizations to legal threat in this study included changing their identity, which was only possible precisely because of their small size. However, it was difficult for small organizations to hide internal processes from scrutiny because there were few in the organization, while large organizations with multiple departments had the option of hiding internal processes from external examination.

It is possible to argue from the data that small business may be far more responsive to punitive sanctions. Further, this response to harm is relatively straightforward for the regulator, since wading through multiple layers of management to ascertain culpability is not necessary. Such a response, however, does little to change the reasons behind such offending behaviour, since it only serves to punish, but not alter the often marginal status of small business within the wider economy (Haines and Sutton, 1997). If success for small business lies in directions antithetical to virtue, sanctions are destined to be effective only in the short term.

The differential effect of regulatory techniques dependent upon size goes beyond possible sanctions to be imposed, and extends to other legal arenas, such as the use of compensation premiums as a regulatory tool. The current study suggests that compensation legislation motivated large business to improve their safety levels, but for small business this was not the case. Following James (1993) the data presented here suggests that, for small business, excessive reliance on compensation legislation may not be advisable.

It is necessary to take the analysis of structure beyond that defined by size of the organization and the imperatives brought to bear because of size. This study suggests that it is not possible to target regulatory strategies at single organizations working in isolation. The worksite 'mix' in terms of the combination of large high-profile organizations and small dependent organizations, in any one site, is itself integral to understanding useful regulatory strategies. The data suggested that regulation was easier if at least one company on site was large and high-profile. By targeting this company, it was possible to influence the behaviour of others on the same site. Where all companies on site were small and not well-known, the ability to influence behaviour was more complex, since no organization at a particular worksite was sensitive to public gaze. It is possible in such cases that a more heavy-handed regulatory approach is necessary,[3] and prescriptive as opposed to open-ended 'duty of care' regulatory standards should apply.

It is difficult to conceptualize the challenges to regulation presented by structure within the paradigm of the pyramid. This is because it is what companies bring to the regulatory arena which prefigures their response to the regulators' attempt at control. An organization's size and ability to alter the circumstances under which they trade or produce, determine, to a greater or lesser extent, how they will respond to the various overtures of the regulator. A regulator who gives a company space to be virtuous as Braithwaite (1993) suggests may either appear very wise, or very naïve, depending on who the company is. Creating 'space' for virtue is a hazardous exercise; such space is not a blank page, but is full of pressures and dynamics which may either promote or destroy virtue.

In understanding how to regulate, I would suggest that a useful starting-point is to understand the structural and cultural imperatives that organizations bring to the regulatory equation. To borrow Selznick's (1992:321) term, the *character* of organizations needs to be the focus, where the nature of the *regulatory space* that individual firms inhabit has a strong influence on that character. Mapping dynamics within, outside and between organizations, which influence the organizational behaviour, is a necessary starting-point to regulation (for a useful example, see Grabosky, 1989:298). However, these dynamics need to be mapped in a way that brings issues of power within the regulatory space into sharp relief. This provides essential insight into what regulatory

[3] Braithwaite has suggested that incapacitation (e.g. licence revocation) is appropriate with certain operators, and it would seem that small operators who act as a high-risk gambler would fit into the category of operators where such measures would be appropriate. This does not come without risk, however. Organizations are quick to react to measures seen as unfair and differential treatment of different groups of firms may produce considerable outcry. A different enforcement regime may therefore need to be tied to a different regulatory regime. For example, operators may be able to develop their own regulatory schema subject to approval. Large operators with a capacity for virtue would be encouraged to undertake this approach. Those who did not choose to do so would be subject to prescriptive legislation. Under these conditions differential enforcement practices may be possible.

strategies might be effective and how organizations might respond to regulatory attempts to influence organizational behaviour in need of regulation (such as behaviour which threatens the well-being of workers). By first mapping industrial dynamics it may be possible to identify 'points of entry' into the worksite where a regulatory strategy, ordered around the concept of a pyramid, may be possible.

Tripartism

Before leaving Braithwaite, it is necessary to take account of a second major contribution he and Ayres (1992) have made to the regulatory debate. This concerns the concept of tripartism as it applies to regulation. Tripartism involves bringing a third party into the regulatory arena occupied by organization and regulator. This third party ideally consists of those essentially affected by the actions of the organizations, such as unions in the case of health and safety, and environmental groups in the case of pollution of the environment by industry. By involving a third party in this manner, Ayres and Braithwaite argue regulatory capture can be avoided, and communication enhanced to the benefit of corporate virtue. Ayres and Braithwaite (1992) argue that benefits accrue to regulation by way of co-operative communication cultivated under a tripartite framework:

> . . . co-operative open communication may produce more efficient regulatory outcomes because bad arguments and bad solutions are less likely to go unchallenged. And genuine communication means that when challenges are advanced, they are listened to. Furthermore, three heads are better than two in ensuring that all the arguments are properly considered . . . [page 87]

What light is shed on the concept of tripartism by the data presented here? The data presented on organizational culture in chapter 6 suggested that the virtuous culture was enriched and responses to the death improved by the input of third parties, namely health and safety committees and unions. From this then, the data would support Ayres and Braithwaite's (1992) contention that a tripartite structure to the regulatory arena is a useful aim of regulatory policy.

How successful though is such an aim likely to be? Again the data throws some light on its potential success. In the case of both unions and health and safety representatives, size and culture of the organization had a strong influence on the likelihood of acceptance of input of the third party. Small organizations, and others with a blinkered culture, resisted the input of groups 'outside' the workplace. Outside intrusion was resented as it was seen as politically motivated, and likely to increase costs. Further, tripartite effectiveness could not simply be legislated into existence. For example, while for some workers of small organizations union membership was compulsory (in essence mandating a tripartite structure), the effective 'voice' of the union into business affairs was minimal, as membership tended to be tokenistic. Similarly, although health and safety representatives were allowed for under the *Occupational Health and Safety Act* 1985 (Vic.), in practice they rarely existed within the small organization.

This suggests that the effectiveness of an interest group in raising the virtuous behaviour of an organization may depend upon the structure of the industry or worksite which is the focus of attention. This observation can be fleshed out using David Harvey's (1989) work on the role of the unions (see especially pages 147–55). Harvey argues that the influence of the unions on conditions of work depends upon the structure of capital. In the postwar boom years, Harvey suggests, the stability of capital meant that co-operation with unions was consistent with overall corporate success. A quiescent workforce represented by a union which worked together with management was preferable to an unrepresented and unpredictable workforce which could threaten stability. The key to understanding the impact of unions is to understand that it was the structure of capital, dominated by large stable industries, that allowed the space for union involvement in management decision making.

If Harvey is right, it would seem that it is only those organizations which retain some sense of certainty concerning their future which can be expected to be open to regulation through tripartite structures. The data supports this to a certain extent. Large organizations were, in fact, more likely in this study to have worked constructively with unions to improve safety levels.

Harvey (1989) argues, though, that the structure of the economy is changing. Stability no longer characterizes the structure of capital and with the changing economy the space for input of third parties, such as unions, may be decreasing, rather than increasing:

> The labour market has, for example, undergone a radical restructuring. Faced with strong market volatility, heightened competition, and narrowing profit margins, employers have taken advantage of weakened union power and the pools of surplus (unemployed or underemployed) labourers to push for much more flexible work regimes and labour contracts. [page 150]

Utilizing Harvey's argument in light of the data presented here suggests the main focus of attention may need to be to identify regulatory spaces in which third parties may be effective and accepted by a given organization or industry. This may mean, for example, identification of a high-profile group, or status group (such as an industry association, for example), within a given industry, where such a group acts as a standard-bearer for that industry. A status group, similar to the Weberian (1991) concept, is then a formal (or informal) group which encapsulates the values which imbue trade in a particular area.[4] The group exists because of common values and common aims and seeks to exclude those who want to undermine such values (by excluding those who wish to compete through cutting corners on safety, for example), and thus may exert hegemonic control. The interest group then, needs to gain acceptance by that status group.[5] Third party influence at the level of the status group may be enough to raise standards.

Such high-profile groups, however, do not inevitably work to improve ethical standards. This study had examples of large powerful organizations who used their power to avoid responsibility rather than raise industry standards. It is unlikely, though, that

[4] It is important to note that the Weberian concept of status group is that such groups coalesce around values **other than economic values**. The term status group is for Weber, however, an ideal type, which suggests that groups, particularly in the economic sphere, are unlikely to exist totally independent of economic considerations. The point I want to make is that status groups in industry encapsulate values in trade which are premised on considerations other than pure economics. Further, these values can exert an independent influence on the directions the industry will take.

[5] This study suggests that to gain such acceptance may necessitate 'buying into' the success ethic, where to be ethical is to be successful since this was the prime motivator of virtue for organizations in this study.

powerful industry groups which do exert unethical influence will respond positively to simply changing law enforcement practices, or welcome the involvement of the officially legislated interest group involvement. Where status groups act in a way which is antithetical to virtue, and the status group actively rejects participation by third parties, political will may be required, such as direct government intervention to break unhelpful monopolies. In other words, the first question should be about how the structure of the industry can be altered to allow effective third party intervention, the second about how to mould industrial cultures so they see such intervention as assisting long-term success, and, finally, questions may concern notions of tripartism in relation to empowerment of the building of trust (Ayres and Braithwaite, 1992:81–100). Terms such as trust and empowerment have to be seen in context of how the industry is structured, and the way this either assists, or undermines, the empowerment process.

Perhaps the most difficult arena for the effective involvement of third parties, particularly public interest groups, is in industrial contexts which are dominated by small business. In such arenas there may be no 'centre' to work with. In the absence of a strong industrial centre influencing large sectors of a given industry, third party involvement may more easily be marginalized or ignored. Selecting the target for tripartite involvement may need to work on a number of levels, such as working with regional industry bodies, where such bodies adequately represent their members.

The point is that inclusion of third parties does not necessarily guarantee success. As Ayres and Braithwaite (1992) themselves argue:

> We do not imagine that PIGs (Public Interest Groups) can secure the resources to put tripartism into effect across the board any more than we imagine that regulators have the resources to put bipartism into effect across the board. Our concern is more modestly with finding out whether tripartism can work, if and when it can be applied. [pages 99–100]

This book has made a start in trying to ascertain the conditions under which third party involvement may be possible, in light of the data coupled with the theoretical insights of Weber and Harvey. What may be crucial to the effectiveness of third party groups is the location of that third party within the power structure of a particular industry, and its acceptance by status groups in that industry. In light of rapid changes to existing economic structures, however, there is an urgent need for greater research into tripartite structures which are possible in industry structures which lack identifiable status groups.

I would argue that the beginning point to effective regulation is not about finding an appropriate scale of regulatory techniques; it is about understanding the dynamics of a particular industrial context, i.e. the regulatory space, and identifying the way in which virtue either thrives or becomes marginalized within such a space. The primary aim of regulation should be to understand how the scene is set in a particular industry, and to work to alter the context so a greater level of virtue can be anticipated, rather than accept an industrial structure where virtue is marginalized and rely on sanctions which aim to punish or persuade. When sufficiently armed with knowledge about the structure of a given environment, it may be possible to identify entry points into that industry for the purposes of regulation and creative involvement of third parties. Using knowledge of such entry points specific regulatory techniques, possibly ordered according to pyramid fashion, may then be effective against particular cases of non-virtue.

Starting with the Market: Constitutive Regulation and Beyond

As was outlined in the introductory chapters, recent writing in regulation has emphasized this need to take account of context, and the informal controls of the market, when devising responses to social harm. Shearing (1993) using the term constitutive regulation has taken this view, suggesting that the beginning of the regulatory endeavour entails analysis of the market terrain. Regulation must be broadened to extend beyond analysis of the state as somehow central to regulation, in a position to 'command and control' business activity. Shearing (1993) writes:

> ... regulatory space as a whole should be made the subject of regulatory policy. In doing so it decentres the state as a source of regulation and points to the role that can be played by a whole host of regulatory schemes ... Regulation has never been a state monopoly. [page 73]

In moving beyond the state, however, Shearing is adamantly opposed to seeing the market in any idealized sense of 'natural order', instead defining the market as politically constituted, with 'a recognition of multiple sources of regulation and a concern with the conflicts and alliances between them' (page 77). He argues that the opportunities for regulation lie in understanding the market through 'lay' thinking, i.e. understanding how those within a given industry understand their situation. With this knowledge that task is to devise interventions which promote trust and give assurance of certainty. Regulation, then, needs to be broadened to incorporate a vision of organizational social control, rather than the traditional regulatory model of command and control. In this way regulators may be able to uncover the 'multiple sites of regulation' which hold the promise for effective reduction of social harm.

Grabosky (1994a and b) fleshes out a fuller picture of the nature of constitutive regulation, also taking as his starting-point discussion of the market-place. Like Shearing, Grabosky seems optimistic that useful regulation can take place in the market, which he points out is at times more demanding than the overt regulator in terms of standards. For example, if a purchaser of goods requires high moral standards of the seller, the seller is far more likely to comply than when the seller is subject only to statutory regulations:

> The very existence of supplier assessment sends signals to the market-place. As upstream environmental vetting becomes even more common, these signals will be amplified. Of course, prospective suppliers are always free not to cooperate with 'green' purchasing policies. But in defying market forces, they run the risk of losing a competitive edge. [Grabosky, 1994b:431]

Grabosky argues that harnessing market forces for the purposes of improving corporate behaviour is both immediate and effective. Like Braithwaite (1991) and Shearing (1993) he also sees room for third parties to play an active role in regulation. Such groups range from environmental groups to large-scale investors and insurance companies each with unique leverage with which to assist the market to act in more productive ways.

Finally, Grabosky (1994b) is keen to point to the ways in which large high-profile organizations act to increase 'virtue'. They do so in response to a range of stimuli, which include government incentive or edict concerning disclosure, but also in response to the power of the consumer whether as individuals or through institutional investment:

> The power of market forces (with or without a boost from governments or third parties) should not be underestimated and may exceed the capacity of command and control regulation to improve environmental citizenship . . . It is an interesting paradox that just as much environmental degradation is attributed to the profit motive, so too is a good deal of exemplary corporate citizenship. [page 422]

Armed with the knowledge that some organizations can be virtuous it follows that others can be made to act likewise.

An important further insight to this recent debate is taken by Gunningham (1993). While echoing many of the views of both Shearing (1993) and Grabosky (1994a and b), Gunningham (1993) tentatively shifts the analysis to the level of industrial structures as a whole, and the influence such structures have on the behaviour of individual firms. Different structures, he argues, give rise to different methods of informal regulation of behaviour between organizations. While one structure may support virtue, another may not. Industries characterized by a predominance of small businesses and intense competition are less likely to exhibit virtuous behaviour, than those where a few high-profile companies predominate and can influence the behaviour of others. Altering structure may then achieve far greater results than the regulator acting in isolation:

> Sometimes structural solutions can achieve far more than 'policing' e.g., in respect of futures, reduce the size of the trading put so surveillance by large customers, and regulators is made easier; abolish the practice of 'dual trading' where brokers trade for themselves *and* their customers, creating conflict of interest . . . [page 110]

Further Gunningham (1993) suggests that different cultures may require different regulatory strategies. Ultimately, Gunningham argues, like Shearing (1993) and Grabosky (1994a and b), that regulation begins with context, but for Gunningham the emphasis on context is on the structural and cultural imperatives within a given environment which need to be heeded if regulation is to be successful:

Above all, one cannot discuss the virtues or failings of different regulatory mechanisms in abstract terms but only with respect to concrete circumstances. Are we dealing with the long term or short term interests, small or large players, the politically powerless or the powerful, with enlightened self-interest, or 'free rider' problems? What is the previous institutional memory and experience of alternative regulatory strategies? In order to be effective, mechanisms of social control (whether direct government regulations, self regulation, informal mechanisms or whatever) need to be tailored to the structural features of each individual market or institution. [page 112]

This study concurs which much of the thrust of the argument of Shearing (1993), Grabosky (1994a and b) and Gunningham (1993). Regulation is broad, as all three acknowledge, with considerable scope for government to assist in setting the scene for industry. Further, there are a multitude of ways positive commerce may arise through analysis of social control within a specific organizational context.

There are, however, several further issues which are raised by the present findings. The data revealed, for example, large high-profile companies which behaved virtuously, supporting Grabosky's (1994b) observations. However, it is worth emphasizing the reasons behind their actions and the prospects for their continued existence. For the organizations in this study virtuous action depended on virtuous culture. It was this culture which acted as a touchstone or normative framework which interpreted virtuous action as ultimately successful. It allowed individuals to rationalize that short-term costs, such as purchase of new equipment with improved safety features, for example, would in the long term ensure organizational success. Chapter 9 illustrated that in certain circumstances competition may aid ethical behaviour, namely when the cost outlay can be justified on criteria other than virtue (for example, if a new machine, as well as being safer is also more efficient, it will be purchased). As long as virtuous investment is profitable it will occur. If not, it is the virtue, not the profit that will suffer.

The data presented in chapter 9 further suggested that problems for virtue as a success strategy arise where the upfront costs are high, and do not translate into greater efficiency or productivity. A classic example here is the building industry, where the use of scaffolding, hoists and harnesses can considerably slow progress and add to cost. The temptation in these cases is to cut corners, work at night or find other ways around the problem. Such a situation is exacerbated by highly competitive tendering environments where the most competitive tender on strict cost measures is often that which is successful. While the building contract may stipulate high safety and other standards to be adhered to, the reality of the contract price means that corners must be cut and workers exploited in order to fulfil such contracts.

For high upfront safety costs to be accepted they have to be passed on to the purchaser. In many cases purchasers may simply not be aware of the health and safety issues involved when they purchase property, for example. With this ignorance, costs of providing a safe workplace are difficult to pass on. It is difficult to manipulate consumer preference for different products if aspects involved in production are hidden, such as health and safety of the workers.[6]

Further, it is of concern that the conditions which allow for virtue and profit to coexist are substantially challenged in the current economic and political climate. Chapter 6 suggested that it was precisely the virtuous culture that faced the greatest ongoing challenge. The constant push to increase competitiveness in the current era challenged the virtuous ideology of those organizations which sought to harmonize the multitude of demands they were facing. Companies depend upon continued investment. In the present climate, investment is fickle, and countries responsive to the demands of highly mobile capital, through deregulated financial markets, so investment will go where the profit is to be made. Since profit, not virtue, is the driving force behind investment, such companies ultimately have to make virtue profitable.

Reconnecting back to Social Theory

How do we make sense of regulation, then, in light of the proliferation of recent suggestions concerning regulation, and the

[6] I am reminded of the predicament facing the Victorian Trades Hall Council when trying to organize a boycott of Kader products in the wake of the Thailand toy factory fire of 1993. Labelling of the products from the factory was so scant, that short of a general boycott of all toys from Thailand it was impossible to ensure that the Kader company would have been affected.

need to see regulation as constituted by the market, rather than a technical exercise of command and control by the regulator? I would argue that what is lacking from the current debate is the jump from grounded theory to formal theory, to use Blumer's (1978) term. The tendency is for each new study to simply add to the list of empirical research, a list which simply grows longer, more complex, and packed ever more densely with insights that are unable to be accessed easily. Unless this growing list of research touches base with some formal theoretical base, repetition of insight is likely to characterize the regulation debate for some time to come.

The quest for such theory necessarily takes us beyond criminology. As some academic criminologists point out, including Shearing (1989), criminological issues 'sooner or later [lead] us away from crime' to which I would add, away from criminological theory (examples here include Chan, 1992; Garland, 1990; and Sutton, 1994, to name but a few).

The theoretical base I chose to explore as a useful beginning point for regulation used both Marxian and Weberian perspectives, combining these with insights from the organizational symbolists, and more recent historical materialist analyses of Harvey (1989). This was outlined in chapter 2. This chapter took as a starting-point recent regulatory theory, such as that proposed by Gunningham (1993) which argued that to explain regulation adequately requires a sophisticated insight into the way structure and culture combine in the organizational context. In chapter 2 it was noted that such a call was present in the writing of Weber, who argued convincingly a century ago that the key to understanding-regulation lay in the interaction between structure and culture. In turn, Weber was responding to the gauntlet laid down by Marx that analysis of the capitalist structure alone could explain corporate behaviour. In a sense recent criminological debates on regulation have simply come full circle.

To make the link back to formal theory the task facing regulatory theory is to begin where Weber and Marx left off, namely to analyse the ways in which structure and culture interact within the contemporary context. To do this, this book has argued for the need to take seriously the structure of the economy, in particular the relationship between small and large business outlined by Marx (1976) and taken up more recently by Harvey (1989).

If this book is correct in linking the success of small business to the ability to 'exploit the margins' of the economic space left by larger players, then it follows that in at least some instances small business survives partly due to the fact that it is not virtuous (in the social regulation sense of the word). It actively exploits avenues for success which are mapped out by the broader economy. Calls for small business to act like larger concerns without understanding the broader pressures facing such business will fail.

Research into youth subcultures established long ago that exhorting marginalized groups to improve their behaviour was not likely to be a successful strategy (Cohen, 1988). The same is true of punishing marginalized business. As Galbraith (1973) points out, exploitation of small business may mean an exploitation of the self, since many such businesses are run by the owner and staffed by family members. Sanctioning a small family business is problematic, as is drawing a clear line between family loyalty and exploitation.

However, data and theory in this study suggest some possibilities. These include encouraging demands by larger organizations that their contracts only go to 'virtuous' players. The case of International Paper is one such example. They were able to control the safety practices of their subcontractors by way of a 'fine' system stipulated in their contract. Such a strategy is well supported in the regulatory literature (Gunningham, 1993; Grabosky, 1994b) and makes sense since those with the power and the adequate profit margin are those asked to pay the price for virtue.

Rather than simply increasing the responsibilities of larger players, however, it is necessary to analyse the position of such businesses and their ability to sustain demands that they increase their responsibilities. It is at this point that Weberian insights become useful. Weber argued that the ability of organizations to sustain ethical behaviour (which includes increasing their social responsibilities) depends on wider structural support for this position. With such structural support, a culture may be cultivated within such organizations which 'nurtures virtue'.

The implication of Weber's analysis is that to demand organizations nurture virtue requires those organizations be shielded from the excesses of competition. Organizations which encapsulate virtuous values must be allowed to form status groups which have a degree of control over the market. In Weberian terms they must be able to effect closure, that is restrict entry into the market. With a degree of control over the market, such organizations can then ensure that entry to that market, and ability to compete within it, is predicated on virtuous behaviour. The culture associated with such groups acts to limit the effects of the everyday challenges to virtue by limiting such effects to the short term.[7] Without structural support and the control of the market this entails, economic forces ultimately propel short-term considerations (such as the immediate costs of safety equipment) to the forefront. The tyranny of immediate costs dictates that long-term policy and virtuous culture disintegrate.

Further, this study concurs with Weber, that there is a semi-autonomous dimension to culture. For Weber this was exemplified by the Protestant work ethic and the structure of capitalism (Weber, 1974). In the context of the present study, the interaction between structure and culture was exemplified by the influence of large, high status organizations, and their harmonizing 'virtuous' cultures. Virtuous culture acts in a manner similar to rose-coloured spectacles. It reinterprets virtuous action as consistent with future success. Like rose-coloured spectacles, however, the vision cannot be sustained without some basis in (economic) reality. When structural supports disintegrate, culture must eventually fade.

There are of course limits to the formation of 'virtuous' status groups as a panacea to regulatory policy, again well illustrated by the data presented here. First, in locations where small business predominates regulation is far more difficult, and may require far greater levels of direct government intervention. Such locations are analogous to Gunningham's (1991) observations of the highly competitive stock exchanges such as Hong Kong dominated by small business which was unable to prevent cheating by brokers. In these locations the structure (multiple small units in a highly competitive arena) prevents the growth of status groups, so virtuous cultures are unable to flourish.

Secondly, there are examples where status group formation and closure takes place around values that are antithetical to virtue. Weberian closure can be used to exploit consumers by producing

[7] For a vivid example of this in the US nuclear power industry, see Rees (1994:103–10).

cartels, for example. Further, with the power afforded to status groups organizations in such groups can use their extensive power to exploit the letter of the law, as exemplified by Stutganst in this study. In such cases it is unlikely that a law enforcement approach alone will be successful. As Sutton (1983) has aptly demonstrated such organizations feel at one with the law, and are adept at exploiting the letter while avoiding the spirit. In such cases potential for improvement may be more successful by changing the environment (or structure) within which such organizations act. This may include increasing the number of players in the industry, for example allowing non-lawyers to do conveyancing work; empowering third parties, for example mandating consumer groups, or environmental groups, to have access to company decision making; or analysing the industry to locate status groups with virtuous values and supporting them (akin to an internal 'takeover' of the industry).

Fukuyama (1995) reminds us, virtuous culture needs to be consistent with broader cultural values. The possibility of growth of virtuous cultures within industry, even when economic conditions permit, depends to some extent on the degree to which such cultures resonate with like-minded values in the broader cultural climate. The primacy of an individualistic, competitive ethos in the broader society would not be one which would encourage closure to take place around values of co-operation and harmonizing of the multiple demands, including safety, which exist within organizations. To the extent that these cultural values are independent from structure, it may be possible to promote different visions of contemporary capitalism. Commentators from a wide range of backgrounds have promoted the idea of morality within society as a whole (Selznick, 1992) or a 'civil society' (Cox, 1995). In diverse ways these authors seek to reinforce the communal nature of societies, as opposed to the individualism championed by a neo-conservative ethos (see also Hutton, 1996). It may well be that organizational virtue would flourish to a greater extent under such forms of capitalism.

It is important at this point to reiterate the need to look for virtue at an organizational or even a societal level. The direct relationship between organizational levels of virtue and individual virtue are problematic. The work discussed in this book included the insights of Weber, Selznick and a limited discussion of MacIntyre (1995); but there are many other examples. Added to this is the discussion of the data in chapter 5 concerning possible techniques of neutralization, which showed that individual attributes are not easily translated into organizational virtues or vices. Further, simply pointing to bureaucratic procedures as repositories of virtue is limited in its usefulness. The dynamic nature of organizations, and the *persistent* tension between substantive issues and formal rationality or bureaucratic rules, must be accounted for. Organizational dynamics can distort bureaucratic attempts at defining or mandating virtuous behaviour, whether through extensive safety procedures, formal rules of accountability, or quality assurance procedures. The discussion of Quality Assurance in chapter 9 illustrated the way rules and procedures which aim to capture substance can be subverted by antithetical organizational goals, in this case downsizing and restructuring. Organizational character *as a whole* needs be the focus. Reductionism, and oversimplification of the task of nurturing organizational virtue, must be resisted in whatever guise it takes.

A considerable part of understanding organizational character is to understand the demands of capital. To do this we need to revisit the state of contemporary capitalism presented in chapter 2 to analyse the influences this has on corporate virtue. If the theoretical analysis presented in this book is correct, the picture is fairly daunting. For a start the number of small organizations is increasing, and the number of 'flexible' industry structures is expanding. Ours is a time of dramatic economic change. As Harvey (1989:151) notes, even within large organizations the proportion of core employees, those with full-time permanent status, is declining, replaced by part-time casual employees who are both less committed to the organization, and more easily replaced or dispensed with. Flexible workplaces that are both small and exist on short-term contracts which are more easily tailored to competitive needs are increasing. In this environment the possibilities of closure—of an industry being effectively controlled by 'virtuous' firms—are decreasing. The capacity of high status organizations to dictate rules of conduct within industry is being undermined as markets continually expand. In such markets, firms prepared to ignore ethical conduct may win a competitive edge. Where safety is seen to undermine competitiveness, safety is more likely to be sacrificed. Further, establishment of rules of trade by government which prohibit trading in risky processes is more difficult within a flexible dynamic system. Indeed Weber himself argued that in times of rapid change economic considerations become the driving force for action. It is only in periods of stability that the influence of status groups grows.

Following Harvey it could be argued, for example, that the current influence of large organizations with a stake in virtue is a carry-over from the relative economic stability that followed the postwar years. Unless we find ways to value virtue alongside competitiveness, and provide the structural space for virtue to wield influence, the future looks fairly bleak. Such a search may require a rethinking of the way power is exerted in times of economic dynamism, and active rejection of the pervasive culture of economic rationalism, with its primacy on competition as the only solution to economic and social woes, as the only culture which can 'interlock' with the current wave of economic change.

While the total picture may look bleak, with the 'entry points' into effective regulation decreasing, pessimism and nihilism simply play into the hands of an economic rationalist model which suggests that all corporate conduct should be left to the market. Rather, we need to look for economic and political structures in the current order which have the potential to nurture virtue. With this knowledge we may then discern when and how the market can wield positive influence along the lines suggested by Grabosky (1994a and b). Governments may, then, need to foster structures which can effect closure and in this way broaden the influence of those who act virtuously. In such spaces nurturing virtue by judicious actions by regulators as suggested by Braithwaite (1993) makes much sense. First, however, regulatory theory needs to promote a framework which understands the economic and political imperatives impinging on organizations, challenge these where necessary, and work with these in order to promote 'ethical' and safe cultures.

There is an obvious need to work on more than one level. Promoting alternative visions of capitalism may be a good long-term objective. But if the research and use of Marxist analysis in this book has anything to tell us, it is likely that this will encounter considerable challenges. Rather, it may be that hard fought arguments at the level of particular companies or industries about the need to control competition in order to reduce the likelihood of harm may achieve small, but nonetheless important, victories.

Altering markets, and allowing economic space for virtue to flourish are, of course, highly contentious in the current political climate, dominated by the 'Hilmer'[8] philosophy of competition as the solution to social problems. However, regulation is, and always has been, political and intricately linked to the economic and cultural framework of industry. A contemporary example of the political nature of regulation is seen in the recent changes to health and safety regulation in Victoria after the Liberal (conservative) Government won a landslide victory in 1992. No changes were made to sanctions, and the encouragement to prosecute was, if anything, greater than under the previous Labor regime. Dramatic changes were, however, made to three aspects: the compensation system; access to the common law; and involvement of the unions in the health and safety process. This should not be surprising after analysis of the data presented in this study. Compensation costs, threats of civil liability and the strength of union influence were among the 'thorns in the side' of the blinkered culture predominant amongst small businesses. The Victorian Government was simply responding to those aspects of health and safety regulation which hurt such companies most. Politically the Government was astute; however, one could be forgiven for having doubts about the effectiveness of such changes on alleviating suffering in the workplace. Rather, it could be argued that by supporting the dichotomous logic of the blinkered culture, the Government was at the same time undermining the justification for the virtuous to continue.

Simply put, regulation and the promotion of organizational virtue cannot be divorced from the broader political and economic picture. Since regulation is constituted by the market, there is a need for the state to acknowledge that it is a player in that market, and accept an active role in shaping the market to promote the long-term interests of the health of the people in the industry. This demands leadership from government and liaison between various arms of the government sector, since the

[8] Professor Hilmer was the author of an influential document, the 'National Competition Policy', commissioned by the Australian Federal Government in 1993. The document has been used to justify many changes aimed at increasing competition within the national economy.

conditions which support or weaken organizations' abilities to promote social values are created by the structure of their market and the constraints and opportunities it provides.

Getting structural constraints and opportunities right, however, is not sufficient in itself. Analysis of regulation is then needed to understand how regulation is interpreted by the target organizations, and to allow the organizations to incorporate social values as part of their purpose, albeit one tied to a perspective of economic success.[9] Along with this is a need then to promote broader concerns, such as compensation and rehabilitation, as part of the proper focus of business and organizational life. Where possible policies should be directly targeted at the bottom line, while providing organizations with legislative structures which can assist in reducing costs through improving safety.

The aim of this book has been to explore regulatory theory through understanding the logic of organizations as they respond to a human tragedy. The way organizations respond to tragedy, and the implications this holds for regulation, has demanded a broadening of the debate on regulation, beyond a focus purely on penalties and statutory regulations. The model proposed builds on insights of Weber and Marx and incorporates Shearing's (1993) notion of constitutive regulation. Hopefully, it provides a framework where research into regulation can be both comprehensive and grounded, and lead to policies which are both practical and robust.

[9] In addition to the material presented here, see Selznick (1992:352–4).

Appendix: Research Methods

THE research presented in this book required an understanding of each of the fifteen cases over a period of a number of years, but primarily at two stages: namely, at the time of the death; and four years later, at the time of the follow-up research which aimed to ascertain the long-term response to the death. All of the deaths occurred in 1987, at a worksite which involved more than one company. The follow-up interviews took place over a three month period in 1991.

The aim of this research was to get as broad an understanding as possible of the way companies respond to death. This entailed extensive use of coronial records, which detailed events leading up to each of the deaths, and in many cases contained documents outlining preliminary responses by some of the companies to the deaths. There was also limited access to company documents, made available to me during the interviews. The interviews were obviously of paramount importance, and were transcribed in full. I also kept a research diary which recorded telephone conversations with various company personnel, and regulatory authorities. These form the bulk of the 'formal' records. Equally as important to me in many cases was the fact I had considerable informal access to those working in the field, including regulators, safety officers and engineers working for companies outside the official sample. The insight of all of these people was invaluable in helping me glean the maximum benefit from the formal records I had at my disposal. Without their input, the analysis would have lacked considerable depth.

As is always the case with research, I encountered a number of practical problems which had to be overcome. One of the first arose in attempting to obtain accurate information regarding the identity and number of those who had died in a work related capacity. There were a number of dimensions to this problem. For example, the number of deaths considered relevant varies according to differing definitions of a work related death (Hopkins, Easson and Harrison, 1992; Polk, Haines and Perrone, 1995). 'Work related' fatalities is a contested definition. It was decided that information regarding the quantity of deaths and the identity of those who died could best be gained from relevant governmental agencies who dealt with only those deaths which had a work related capacity. Documents concerning identification of work related deaths were scattered amongst a number of different government agencies, some state and some federal, which all had a different industrial jurisdiction. The primary source of the numbers of deaths and the identity of those who died was gained from the WorkCover Authority (previously known as the Department of Labour). However, deaths which occurred in mining (apart from open cut) were obtained from the (then) Department of Industry, Technology and Resources, trucking fatalities from the Road Traffic Authority, and deaths relating to air transport and the sea were gained from the Bureau of Air Safety (a federal agency) and the Marine Board respectively. Information from these various sources indicated there was a total of 52 work related deaths in Victoria in the year under study, 1987.[1]

The interest in this research lay in fatalities resulting from multiple employer worksites, that is where there were contractual and subcontractual relationships involved in the worksite where the death occurred. Of the 52 total work related deaths for 1987 the number involving companies and other organizations (as opposed to the self employed) was 40. The total number of fatalities with multiple employer workplaces was 15. The total number of companies[2] involved in these fatalities was 37. In terms of age and sex all the people killed were male and their ages ranged from 23 to 54.

[1] This total was accurate according to available data at the time this study was undertaken. However, further investigation by a later study reveals the total to be higher (95). The reason for the difference relates to the difference in methodology. This study wrote to each government agency responsible for investigating industrial deaths and compiled a total from each of the agencies. Since the definition of work related fatality was not a central issue, it was considered that this approach was the most appropriate. The subsequent study manually went through each of the deaths for the year reported to the coroner, a number in excess of 7,000 files, searching for work related fatalities. This latter study found considerable numbers of deaths reported to the coroner but not to a regulatory body. For a report on the discrepancy see Polk, Haines and Perrone (1995).

[2] The term company is used very broadly. It includes both private and public companies, local councils, government utilities and landowners (which may include the government).

Compiling the Case-Studies

Once the identity of those who had died had been elicited from the relevant governmental agency, information regarding the circumstances surrounding the deaths was gathered primarily from the coroner's records. These records contained a rich and varied source of information including: police reports, autopsy findings, witness depositions or statements, relevant regulatory authority reports as well as a transcript of the inquest proceedings. In cases of extreme complexity, experts could be asked to provide reports and conduct independent investigations of, for example: vehicles, plant machinery or components implicated in the fatality. In other instances organizations involved undertook their own investigations, reports of their findings being made available to the coroner. Employer organizations, unions and government regulatory bodies, contacted by the researcher independently of the coroner's records, provided additional material.

This information formed the basis for case-studies which were compiled on each of the fifteen deaths. The diverse sources of information allowed some validation of important aspects of the deaths, since information was not only elicited from official organizational sources, but also eye-witnesses and union representatives. As Yin (1989) points out case-studies need to be aware of the possibility of bias if information is gained from only one source. Information from diverse sources can be used to 'test the validity' of previously gathered material.

Nonetheless, some limitations with the case-study information must be noted—the main problem being that much of the information, namely the coronial material, was originally collected as part of a legal investigation. The original purpose of the collection of the material, namely to inform a coronial inquest, may have influenced both what material was gathered and the quality of that information. The coronial process itself can be viewed as a process of negotiating truth about the 'facts' surrounding the death. In this negotiation process material considered relevant is emphasized, material deemed irrelevant is discarded or downplayed (Van Maanen and Pentland, 1994). Nonetheless, the file material could illustrate the contested nature of various 'facts' and provide a unique insight into the contextual nature of the final version of the death.

A second limitation was that the amount of information available on each case varied. Deaths involving large high-profile companies resulted in copious documentation, where deaths in small, non-unionized business contexts could be more sparsely documented. Despite both these limitations the data provided a useful starting-point, and enabled a reasonable understanding of events that led to the deaths. Further, the understanding of the cases through the coronial material generated a useful interview strategy where the interviewer had sufficient knowledge of the case that interviewees' answers could be challenged when they diverged from the coronial account.

Investigating Responses

In order to understand how the companies in the case-studies presented in chapter 3 responded to the deaths, information was gathered in two ways. First, there was some, albeit limited, information regarding the response contained in the coroner's file. The inquest can occur some months after the death takes place, and companies which come to the court can give evidence of steps they have taken to eliminate the hazard.

The majority of information concerning response was gathered through direct contact with the organizations themselves. The method here was intensive interviewing, complemented with notes of telephone conversations and the researcher's impressions of companies and other interested parties. In the event a refusal for interview was finally encountered, such notes provided valuable insights into the companies, including those elements that the companies perceived as threats. Other people providing useful information included receivers (in the event of the company going out of business), unions, and employer organizations. This information was not used as a sole indicator of their response or lack of response to the fatality, rather it was used as background information to supplement interview material on the rationalizations behind responses. Information from these 'non-participants' (Sutton, 1989) provided valuable additional information.

Semi-structured interviews were conducted with personnel from twenty-one of the organizations, with interviews ranging from one to three hours. Substantial information, covering many of the same issues raised in the interviews, was gathered in informal conversation with another seven, giving a total sample of twenty-eight organizations. Of these organizations, eleven were large and seventeen small. Nine organizations were not able to be included in the sample. Of these nine organizations, two had gone out of business and were unable to be traced. The seven remaining companies excluded from the sample were either unable or unwilling to participate.[3] Reasons for this ranged from a fear of losing insurance cover, problems of confidentiality, to personal reasons because of closeness to the victim. In this way data was available for analysis on thirteen of the fifteen fatalities. Total data collected gave rise to a total of approximately 250 pages of transcript.[4]

The aim was to interview people who had some knowledge of the fatality, preferably direct knowledge (i.e. they were employed at the time) and had knowledge of issues in the health and safety area. A range of levels of management from managing directors to administrative personnel and safety officers were interviewed, (see Table 4.1). In one case a worker safety representative was interviewed in addition to the safety officer. The strength of interviewing those with direct knowledge of the fatality was that such people would be more likely to be aware of changes that had been made, and take an interest in those changes. The weakness is that the interviewees varied in their roles in the organization which may have systematically affected responses. For this reason

[3] In two cases a number of appointments were made, but the company changed its mind on each occasion. These were counted as refusals.

[4] Due to the sensitive nature of the material, gaining access to people with adequate knowledge of effects of the fatalities was negotiated rather than the researcher being able to dictate all the parameters of the interviews. This introduces some difficulties, including the organization wanting to present the person with the 'right' perspective, as well as genuine differences in viewpoint depending on the level of management interviewed. However, given the sensitive nature of the events, trauma involved, and defensiveness on behalf of some of the companies, the researcher was not always in a position to negotiate the ideal interview. For example, one interview took place with a company that had refused to speak directly to anyone, including other companies, the coroner and regulatory bodies. All information from this company concerning the fatality, previous to this research, had been via the insurance company's lawyer. The researcher was able to secure an interview with the general manager. Room to manoeuvre to dictate who to interview in such circumstances is difficult. These restrictions aside, the data gathered allowed the researcher to enter the perspective of the organization and gain insight into both the responses, and the reasons behind those responses.

the results must be interpreted with care. However, the different roles of interviewee did not systematically correspond with different types of response. Additionally, the same roles in organizations did not equate with the same degree of power to influence the companies' actions. In some small companies, multiple roles such as safety officer, manager and so on were all performed by the owner/director. Knowledge of the fatality proved to be the most practical guide regarding choice of interviewee.

The interview schedule was drawn up in order to explore the factors highlighted by the literature and the case-studies. Questions were generated to cover the changes the organizations had made since the fatality and the influence legal considerations had on responses. Cultural issues were canvassed focusing on the role of health and safety in the organization, including the structure of safety departments and health and safety committees, as well as the priority the organization placed on safety issues. As well as the culture specifically concerned with health and safety, questions were asked concerning the philosophy of the organization concerning organizational democracy, use of 'culture shaping' programmes such as Quality Assurance and Total Quality Management. The interview also canvassed issues of the profitability of the organization, and the effect profitability had on safety. The complexities of worksites were explored as well as the responsibilities of the particular organization on particular sites. Finally, gross changes in the organization were covered such as takeover by another firm or sell off of the organization from a particular umbrella group.

The interview schedules were discussed with outside safety consultants in order to word them in such a way to have the best chance of ascertaining the real level of safety in the organization. Before each interview the relevant coroner's file was reviewed and questions were altered or supplemented in light of that information.

Interviews were considered the most appropriate primary tool in gauging response since they allowed the best opportunity to understand the 'logic' of the response by the organization by entering their world and exploring the meaning attached to events and actions (Minichiello, Arone, Timewell and Alexander, 1990; McCracken, 1988; Williamson, Karp, Dolphin and Grey,

1982). Interviews rather than surveys minimize the possibility of misunderstanding (McCracken, 1988; Spradley, 1979; Williamson et al., 1982), and give the greatest possibility of access to sensitive issues (Williamson et al., 1982). In addition, all but one interview took place at the organization concerned, which gave added insight into the work environment.

There are certain weaknesses in using interviews, however. In this case some of the cases involved considerable technical complexity, and probing of the adequacy of the response could be limited by the interviewer's knowledge. To minimize this risk, all cases were discussed with an engineer to allow the researcher some understanding of the technical issues involved, for example in the case of Resource Mining. In addition there could be misunderstanding between the researcher and the interviewee regarding behaviour and the significance of events (Williamson et al., 1982). It was for this reason that examples were requested from respondents to illustrate the connection between meaning and behaviour. Repetition of each central question was a major concern, although the researcher often deviated from the question schedule to explore issues raised by the respondent. The researcher requested concrete examples to be used to illustrate issues raised, which assisted understanding as well as 'manufacturing distance' (McCracken, 1988), that is to ensure that assumptions of common understanding were not made, so accuracy of understanding could be enhanced.

There are, of course, further limitations in using interviews as a method of understanding organizational culture. Participant observation, or some other ethnographic method aimed at seeking non-linguistic aspects of culture, would have enhanced the ability to understand the various cultures within the organizations studied. Further, culture may not be monolithic, and may vary between departments (Gross, 1978). In some instances it may be more accurately described as the sum of a number of subcultures, rather than one overarching ethos (Sinclair, 1993). Interviews are limited in that they restrict the researcher both to the written word, and the perspective of the particular interviewee. It is for this reason that this study views culture in a specific way, namely that outlined in chapter 2. As was outlined in that chapter, culture is seen as a normative device which shapes the way individuals reflect and act within their organization (Schein, 1986; Calori and Sarnin, 1991). Interviews are an appropriate method to gain an understanding of the normative assumptions which mould behaviour, in this case the assumptions in question were those which lay behind reactions to the deaths, and assumptions which allowed rationalizations on the death itself.

Culture as described in this way can be seen as separate from, but related to, behaviour. Culture provides the normative assumptions which lie behind behaviour. For safety, this means an individual manager acts reflexively according to the culture of the company. Safety culture as typically described involves safety consciousness, a commitment to continuous improvement in the area of safety and a philosophy of 'safety first', frowning upon cutting corners which impinge on safety and so on (Braithwaite, 1995; Quinlan and Bohle, 1991; Hopkins, 1995). For such a culture to live, it has to exist in the everyday relationships between individuals in the company, and form the well spring from which their decisions are made. The culture of the company thus provides rationalizations for the indvidual to behave in a safety conscious manner.

One other concept requires further elaboration, namely the process by which 'contribution' was ascertained. The definition of contribution used here was broad, in order to anticipate possible responses that could have been made to improve safety. An organization was said to have contributed if the fatality had occurred, at least in part, because of their action or failure to act. In other words, the fatality could have been avoided if the company had acted, or not acted, in a particular way which was consistent with their role on site. An example here is Arcade. Arcade contributed to the death in not insisting safety harnesses were used correctly on its site, the warehouse construction, where it had overall control. The definition of contribution does not imply, however, that the organization bears sole responsibility for what occurred. As was clear again from the case-studies, many of the fatalities occurred as a result of a number of events coming together at the same time. In the case of Nagel Constructions, the case involving building of a sports stadium, four of the five organizations involved in the death were considered to have contributed to the fatality. Only the electricity commission, which had given extensive instructions to the council regarding the dangers of building under power lines, was exempt.[5] Leafytown Council contributed in that it did not insist on the moving of the crane. Nagels was responsible in that it did not ensure adequate supervision of the erection of the steel, and use of proper equipment. Daytons and Service Cranes contributed in that they foresaw the danger of the crane and chose to do nothing. Daytons contributed further in that the owner discontinued supervising the erection of the steel. Contribution may also have been either large or small. In both the case of Arcade and Nagel the contribution was fairly major; however, it was also considered that Hoefschtede Mines contributed to the fatality of the delivery driver who had a heart attack, by failing to erect a sufficiently large barrier to prevent vehicles driving over the road edge into the quarry. In this case, though, the contribution is minor.

The data collected in this study was seen primarily as a heuristic device (Mills, 1963). That is, the primary aim of this research is to comprehend a particular social world, being in this study to understand the relationships between individuals, organizations and their environment which affect the responses made to a human tragedy, a workplace death. In line with that tradition this research contends that data cannot be divorced either from specific theory (Gouldner, 1971) or indeed from a broad 'world view' (Kuhn, 1962). This does not diminish the importance of the data as it is understood that theorizing 'in a vacuum' may lead to intriguing theories, but ones which bear little relevance to or shed light on the way the world works (McCarl Nielson, 1988). However, this does recognize that interpretation brings with it certain hazards, such as the researcher imposing order which distorts understanding, in order to make a particular theory 'fit' (Williamson et al., 1982). Counteracting this is the way the data itself challenges prior assumptions both of the researcher and of the theory and at times appears to defy the imposition of any structure or order. It is in the process of reflection and analysis of the complexity of the data that distance can be created from the 'specifics' surrounding the cases, as well as distance from biases the researcher may have held going into the data collecting process.

[5] The electricity commission in this case did not have a contractual relationship with the other organizations on site and so was not included in the sample. It is used here to illustrate the line between contribution and non-contribution to fatalities.

Ironically it may well be the data which is most challenging to the researcher's preconceived ideas, wherein lies the greatest theoretical promise (Kuhn, 1962). After all, qualitative research is primarily about reconstructing and discovering categories, not testing prior hypotheses (McCracken, 1988). In terms of this research, it was found that the key to future directions in regulatory theory lay in aspects of the data which fit neither current regulatory theory, nor the researcher's suspicions upon entering the research.[6] In the words of Grant McCracken qualitative research 'does not survey the terrain, it mines it' (McCracken, 1988:17).

[6] Despite my theoretical knowledge, my suspicions upon entering the research process at a 'gut' level revolved around notions of organizations avoiding responsibility and of investigators trapped through regulatory capture and unable to see the degree of negligence of the companies involved.

Bibliography

Ackroyd, S. and Crowdy, P. (1990) 'Can Culture be Managed? Working with "Raw" Material: The Case of English Slaughtermen' *Personnel Review* 19:5:3–13.

Anderson, T. (1993) 'Financial Deregulation: Why did Competitive Markets Fail?' *Journal of Australian Political Economy* 31:57–73.

AS 3901—1987 *Quality Systems for Design/Development, Production, Installation and Servicing* Standards Australia.

AS 3902—1987 *Quality Systems for Production and Installation* Standards Australia.

Atkinson, J. (1994) *GATT: What do the poor get?* Background Report 5, Fitzroy, Community Aid Abroad.

Aubert, V. (1952) 'White Collar Crime and Social Structure', *American Journal of Sociology* 58:3:263–71.

Axelrod, R. (1984) *The Evolution of Cooperation* New York, Basic Books.

Ayres, I. and Braithwaite, J. (1991) 'Tripartism: Regulatory Capture and Empowerment' *Law and Social Inquiry* 16:3:435–96.

Ayres, I. and Braithwaite, J. (1992) *Responsive Regulation: Transcending the Deregulation Debate* New York, Oxford University Press.

Bachrach, P. and Baratz, M. S. (1970) *Power and Poverty in Theory and Practice* New York, University Press.

Bardach, E. and Kagan, R. (1982) *Going by the Book: The Problem of Regulatory Unreasonableness* Philadelphia: Temple University Press.

Barlow, H. D. (1993) 'From fiddle factors to networks of collusion: Charting the waters of small business crime' *Crime, Law and Social Change* 20:319–37.

Battin, T. (1991) 'What is this Thing called Economic Rationalism' *Australian Journal of Social Issues* 26:4:294–307.

Battin, T. (1992) 'A Case of Mistaken Identity: A Reply to Dollery' *Australian Journal of Social Issues* 27:3:213–14.

Bendix, R. (1977) *Max Weber: An Intellectual Portrait* Berkeley, University of California Press.

Benson, M. L. (1984) 'The Fall from Grace: Loss of Occupational Status as a Consequence of Conviction for a White Collar Crime' *Criminology* 22:4:573–93.

Benson, M. L. (1985) 'Denying the Guilty Mind: Accounting for Involvement in White Collar Crime' *Criminology* 23:583–607.

Bergman, D. (1991) *Deaths at Work: Accidents or Corporate Crime* Workers Educational Association, London Hazards Centre.

Berle, A. A. and Means, G. C. (1967) (First published 1932) *The Modern Corporation and Private Property* (Revised Edition) New York, Harcourt Brace and World, Inc.

Berman, P. (1992) 'The Quality View' *Flight Deck* April.

Biggins, D. R., Phillips, M. and O'Sullivan, P. (1991) 'Benefits of Worker Participation in Health and Safety' *Labour and Industry* 4:1:138–59.

Blumer, H. (1978) 'Methodological Principles of Empirical Science' in N. K. Denzin (ed.) *Sociological Methods: A Sourcebook* New York, McGraw-Hill Book Company, 29–44.

Bradmore, D. (1993) 'Sales and Marketing' in R. Collins (ed.) *Effective Management* New Zealand, CCH International, 365–96.

Braithwaite, J. (1978) 'An Exploratory Study of Used Car Fraud' in P. Wilson and J. Braithwaite (eds.) *Two Faces of Deviance: Crimes of the Powerless and Powerful* Brisbane, University of Queensland Press.

Braithwaite, J. (1982) 'Enforced self regulation: A new strategy for corporate crime control' *Michigan Law Review* 80:1466–507.

Braithwaite, J. (1984) *Corporate Crime in the Pharmaceutical Industry*, London, Routledge and Kegan Paul.

Braithwaite, J. (1985) *To Punish or Persuade: Enforcement of Coal Mine Safety* Albany, State University of New York Press.

Braithwaite, J. (1989) *Crime, Shame and Reintegration* Sydney, Cambridge University Press.

Braithwaite, J. (1991) 'Policies for an Era of Regulatory flux' in B. Head and E. McCoy *Deregulation or Better Regulation?* Centre for Australian Public Sector Management, Brisbane, Macmillan, 21–34.

Braithwaite, J. (1993) 'Responsive Business Regulatory Institutions' in C. A. J. Coady and C. J. C. Sampford (eds.) *Business Ethics and the Law* Sydney, The Federation Press, 83–92.

Braithwaite, J. and Grabosky, P. (1985) *Occupational Health and Safety Enforcement in Australia: A Report to the National Occupational Health and Safety Commission* Australian Institute of Criminology.

Brockway, G. P. (1993) *The End of Economic Man* (Revised) New York, W. W. Norton and Company.

Bucy, P. H. (1991) 'Corporate Ethos: A Standard for Imposing Corporate Criminal Liability' *Minnesota Law Review* 75:1095–184.

Burke, T., Maddock, S. and Rose, A. (1993) 'How Ethical is British Business? An analysis of the sensitivity of senior managers and other professionals to ethical issues in business', Research Working Paper Series 2 No. 1, Faculty of Business, Management and Social Studies, University of Westminster.

Calori, R. and Sarnin, P. (1991) 'Corporate Culture and Economic Performance: A French Study' *Organization Studies* 12:1:49–74.

Carson, K. and Hennenberg, C. (1990) 'Social Justice and the Workplace: The political economy of health and safety laws' *Social Justice* 16:124–40.

Carson, K. and Johnstone, R. (1990) 'The Dupes of Hazard: Occupational Health and Safety and the Victorian Sanctions Debate' *Australian and New Zealand Journal of Sociology* 26:1:126–40.

Carson, W. G. (1970) 'White Collar Crime and the Enforcement of Factory Legislation' *British Journal of Criminology* 10:383–98.

Cartwright, D. (1990) 'What Price Ethics' *Leadership and Organizational Development Journal* 11:3:28–31.

Chan, J. (1992) *Doing Less Time: Penal Reform in Crisis* Sydney, Institute of Criminology.

Chua, T. and Wei Ling, W. (1993) 'Help! is there a way out?' *Asian Labour Update* 12:1–8.

Clinard, M. and Yeager, P. (1980) *Corporate Crime* New York, Free Press.

Coffee, J. C. (1981) ' "No Soul to Damn: No Body to Kick": An Unscandalized Inquiry into the Problem of Corporate Punishment' *Michigan Law Review* 79:386–459.

Cohen, S. (1988) 'The Object of Criminology: Reflections on the New Criminalization' in *Against Criminology* New Brunswick, Transaction Books, 235–76.

Cooper, R. (1990) 'Organization/Disorganization' in J. Hassard and D. Pym (eds.) *The Theory and Philosophy of Organizations* London, Routledge, 167–97.

Coulton, R., McCulloch, A. and Noble, R. (1990) *The Social Dimensions of Occupational Health and Safety* Wentworth Falls, Social Science Press.

Cox, E. (1995) *A Truly Civil Society* Sydney, ABC Books.

Cressey, D. R. (1953) *Other People's Money: The Social Psychology of Embezzlement* New York, Free Press.

Cressey, D. R. (1986) 'Why Managers Commit Fraud' *Australian and New Zealand Journal of Criminology* 19:195–209.

Croall. H. (1989) 'Who is the White Collar Criminal?' *British Journal of Criminology* 29:2:157–74.

Crowe, M. P. (1986) 'Hardwood logging accidents and counter-measures for their reduction' *Australian Forestry* 49:1:44–55.

Davis, K. and Harper I. (1993) *Privatisation: The Financial Implications* Sydney, Allen and Unwin.

Dawson, C. and Lewelling, J. (1991) 'Level Playing Fields: International Standards, Product Certification, and the Global Marketplace' *Regulation* Summer, 25–9.

Dent, J. F. (1991) 'Accounting and Organizational Cultures: A Field Study of the Emergence of a New Organizational Reality' *Accounting, Organizations and Society* 16:8:705–32.

Di Maggio, P. and Powell, W. (1991) *The New Institutionalism in Organizational Analysis* Chicago, University of Chicago Press.

Ditton, J. and Duffy, J. (1983) 'Bias in the Newspaper Reporting of Crime News' *British Journal of Criminology* 23:2:159–65.

Dollery, B. (1992) 'What is This Thing Called Economic Rationalism?: Comment' *Australian Journal of Social Issues* 27:3:209–12.

Donaldson, L. (1985) *In Defence of Organization Theory: A Reply to the Critics* London, Cambridge University Press.

Drucker, P. F. (1992) *Managing for the Future* Oxford, Butterworth-Heinemann.

Eaton, M. and Stilwell, F. (1993) 'Ten Years Hard Labour' *Journal of Australian Political Economy* 31:89–105.

Ewer, P., Hampson, I., Lloyd, C., Randford, J., Rix, S. and Smith, M. (1993) *International Best Practice? A Critical Guide* Leichhardt, NSW, Pluto Press.

Fenichel, O. (1946) *The Psychoanalytic Theory of Neurosis*, London, Routledge and Kegan Paul.

Field, S. and Jorg, N. (1991) 'Liability and Manslaughter: should we be going Dutch?' *Criminal Law Review* March, 156–71.

Fisse, B. (1983) 'Reconstructing Corporate Criminal Law: Deterrence, Retribution, Fault, and Sanctions' *Southern California Law Review* 56:1141–245.

Fisse, B. (1990) *Howard's Criminal Law* Fifth Edition, Sydney, The Law Book Company Ltd.

Fisse, B. (1991) 'The Attribution of Criminal Liability to Corporations: A Statutory Model' *Sydney Law Review* September, 277–97.

Fisse, B. and Braithwaite, J. (1983) *The Impact of Publicity on Corporate Offenders* Albany, State University of New York Press.

Fisse, B. and Braithwaite, J. (1988) 'Accountability and the Control of Corporate Crime: Making the Buck Stop' in M. Findlay and R. Hogg (eds.) *Understanding Crime and Criminal Justice* Sydney, The Law Book Company Ltd. 78–92.

Fisse, B. and Braithwaite, J. (1993) *Corporations. Crime and Accountability* Melbourne, Cambridge University Press.

Fisse, B. and French, P. A. (1985) *Corrigible Corporations and Unruly Law* San Antonio, Trinity University Press.

Foerschler, A. (1990) 'Corporate Criminal Intent: Toward a Better Understanding of Corporate Misconduct' *California Law Review* 78:1287–311.

Foucault, M. (1980) 'Truth and Power' in *Power/Knowledge: Selected Interviews and Other Writings 1972–1977* edited by C. Gordon, New York, Pantheon Books, 109–133.

Friedman, M. (1962) *Capitalism and Freedom* Chicago, University of Chicago Press.

Friedman, M. (1988) 'The Social Responsibility of Business is to increase its Profits' in T. Beauchamp and N. Bowie (eds.) *Ethical Theory and Business* Eaglewood Cliffs, Prentice Hall, 87–91.

Fukuyama, F. (1995) *Trust: The Social Virtues and the Creation of Prosperity* London, Hamish Hamilton.

Galbraith, J. K. (1973) *Economics and the Public Purpose* London, Andre Deutch.

Garland, D. (1990) *Punishment and Modern Society: A Study in Social Theory* Oxford, Clarendon Press.

Geis, G. (1967) 'The Heavy Electrical Equipment Antitrust Cases of 1961' in M. Clinard and R. Quinney (eds.) *Criminal Behaviour Systems* New York, Holt, Rinehard and Winston.

Geis, G. and Meir, R. F. (1977) *White Collar Crime* New York, Free Press.

Gill, S. and Law, D. (1988) *The Global Political Economy: Perspectives, Problems and Policies* London, Harvester Wheatsheaf.

Glasbeek, H. and Rowland, S. (1979) 'Are Injuring and Killing at Work Crimes?' *Osgoode Hall Law Journal* 17:3:506–94.

Gouldner, A. W. (1971) *The Coming Crisis of Western Sociology* London, Heinemann.

Grabosky, P. (1983) 'Hidden Violence: Death and Injury in the Australian Workplace' *Labour Forum* 5:2:14–16.

Grabosky, P. (1989) *Wayward Governance: Illegality and its Control in the Public Sector* Canberra, Australian Institute of Criminology.

Grabosky, P. (1994a) 'Beyond the Regulatory State' *Australian and New Zealand Journal of Criminology* 27:2:192–7.

Grabosky, P. (1994b) 'Green Markets: Environmental Regulation by the Private Sector' *Law and Policy* 16:4:419–48.

Grabosky, P. and Braithwaite, J. (1986) *Of Manners Gentle: Enforcement Strategies of Australian Business Regulatory Agencies* Melbourne, Oxford University Press in association with the Australian Institute of Criminology.

Grabosky, P. and Sutton, A. (1989) *Stains on a White Collar: Fourteen Studies in Corporate Crime or Corporate Harm*, Annandale, The Federation Press.

Gray, R. H. (1990) 'Business Ethics and Organisational Change' *Leadership & Organizational Development Journal* 11:3:12–21.

Gross, E. (1978) 'Organizations as Criminal Actors' in Paul Wilson and John Braithwaite *Two Faces of Deviance: Crimes of the Powerless and the Powerful* St Lucia, University of Queensland Press, 199–213.

Gunningham, N. (1984) *Safeguarding the Worker: Job Hazards and the Rule of Law* London, The Law Book Company Limited.

Gunningham, N. (1991) 'Private Ordering, Self Regulation and Futures Markets: A Comparative Study of Informal Social Control' *Law and Policy* 13:4:297–326.

Gunningham, N. (1993) 'Beyond Command and Control: Towards Flexible and Cost Efficient Business Regulation' in C. A. J. Coady and C. J. C. Sampford *Business Ethics and the Law* Sydney, The Federation Press, 93–112.

Gunningham, N., Johnstone, R. and Rozen, P. (1996) 'Enforcement Measures for Occupational Health and Safety in New South Wales: Issues and Options', unpublished report to the New South Wales Government.

Habermas, J. (1976) *Legitimation Crisis* Cambridge, Polity Press.

Haines, F. (1990) 'Injuries should not be ignored' *Legal Service Bulletin* 15:4:178–9.

Haines, F. (1993) 'The Show Must Go On: The Response to Fatalities in Multiple Employer Workplaces' *Social Problems* 40:4:547–63.

Haines, F. (1994) 'The Use and Effectiveness of Prosecution in the Industrial Safety Context: Interrogating the Punish/Persuade Debate', in R. Johnstone (ed.) *Occupational Health and Safety Prosecutions in Australia: Overviews and Issues* Centre for Employment and Labour Relations Law Occasional Monograph Series, No. 1, University of Melbourne, 39–51.

Haines, F. and Polk, K. (1990) 'Consequences of the Unsafe Workplace: on the need for an unambiguous prosecution of workplace negligence', paper presented at the Australian Law and Society Conference, Griffith University, December.

Haines, F. and Sutton, A. (1997) 'Crime Prevention and White Collar Crime: Some Lessons for Regulatory Theory' in P. O'Malley and A. Sutton (eds.) *Crime Prevention in Australia* Sydney, The Federation Press, 138–63.

Harvey, D. (1989) *The Condition of Postmodernity* Cambridge, Blackwell.

Hassard, J. and Pym, D. (eds.) (1990) *The Theory and Philosophy of Organizations: Critical Issues and New Perspectives* London, Routledge.

Hawkins, K. (1990) 'Compliance Strategy, Prosecution Policy and Aunt Sally' *British Journal of Criminology* 30:4:444–66.

Hayward D. and Salvaris, M. (1994) 'Rating the States: Credit Rating Agencies and the Australian State Governments' *Journal of Australian Political Economy* 34:1–26.

Head, B. (1991) 'Regulation and Deregulation' in Brian Head and Elaine McCoy (eds.) *Deregulation or Better Regulation?* South Melbourne, Macmillan, 1–8.

Hill, F. M. (1986) 'Quality Circles in the UK: A Longitudinal Study' *Personnel Review* 15:3:25–34.

Hilmer, F. (1993) See Independent Committee of Enquiry.

Hopkins, A. (1988) 'Plant size and accident rates, a response to Tombs' *Industrial Relations Journal* 19:251–3.

Hopkins, A. (1989a) 'Social Values in Occupational Health and Safety Law' *Legal Studies Forum* 13:2:135–50.

Hopkins, A. (1989b) 'Crime without Punishment: The Appin Mine Disaster' in P. Grabosky, and A. Sutton *Stains on a White Collar: Fourteen*

Studies in Corporate Crime or Corporate Harm, Annandale, The Federation Press, 160–74.

Hopkins, A. (1989c) 'Death at Kellogs' in P. Grabosky and A. Sutton *Stains on a White Collar: Fourteen Studies in Corporate Crime or Corporate Harm*, Annandale, The Federation Press, 175–90.

Hopkins, A. (1994a) 'Patterns of Prosecution' in R. Johnstone (ed.) *Occupational Health and Safety Prosecution in Australia: Overviews and Issues*, Centre for Employment and Labour Relations Law Occasional Monograph Series, No. 1, University of Melbourne, 2–12.

Hopkins, A. (1994b) 'Making Prosecutions more Effective' *Occupational Health and Safety Prosecutions in Australia* Centre for Employment and Labour Relations Law Occasional Monograph Series, No. 1, University of Melbourne, 22–38.

Hopkins, A. (1995) *Making Safety Work: Getting Management Commitment to Occupational Health and Safety* St Leonards, Allen and Unwin.

Hopkins, A. and Palser, J. (1987) 'The Causes of Coal Mine Accidents' *Industrial Relations Journal* 18:1:26–49.

Hopkins, A., Easson, H. and Harrison, J. (1992) 'The legal response to work death fatalities in NSW in 1984' *Australian and New Zealand Journal of Criminology* 25:2:135–55.

Horne, D. (1992) *The Trouble with Economic Rationalism* Newham, Scribe.

Hutton, W. (1996) *The State We're In* London, Vintage.

INDECS (1992) *State of Play 7: The Australian Economic Policy Debate* St Leonards, Allen and Unwin.

Independent Committee of Inquiry (1993) *National Competition Policy*, Report to Australian Governments, Chairman: Professor F. G. Hilmer, Canberra, AGPS, February.

Industry Commission (1994) *Workers Compensation in Australia* Report No. 36, Canberra, Australian Government Printer Service.

Industry Commission (1995) *Work, Health and Safety: Inquiry into Occupational Health and Safety* Report No. 47 (2 Volumes), Canberra, Australian Government Printer Service.

ISO 9001—*Quality systems—Model for quality assurance in design/development, production, installation and servicing* International Organization for Standardization.

ISO 9002—*Quality systems—Model for quality assurance in production and installation* International Organization for Standardization.

Jackall, R. (1988) *Moral Mazes: The World of Corporate Managers* New York, Oxford University Press.

James, C. (1993) 'Social Processes and Reporting or Non-Reporting' in Michael Quinlan (ed.) *Work and Health: The Origins, Management and Regulation of Occupational Illness* South Melbourne, Macmillan, 33–56.

James, P. (1992) 'Reforming British Health and Safety Law: a framework for discussion' *Industrial Law Journal* 24:2:83–105.

Jamrozik, A. (1991) *Class, Inequality and the State* South Melbourne, Macmillan.

Johnstone, R. (1994) 'The Court and the Factory: The Legal Construction of Occupational Health and Safety Offences in Victoria', Unpublished Ph.D. thesis.

Kiel, H. (1989) 'Partners in Crime' *Legal Service Bulletin* 14:6:254–7.

Kolko, G. (1963) *The Triumph of Conservatism* New York, Free Press of Glencoe.

Kolko, G. (1965) *Railroads and Regulation* Princeton, Princeton University Press.

Kroeber, T. C. (1969) 'The Coping Functions of the Ego Mechanism' in R. W. White (ed.) *The Study of Lives: Essays on Personality in Honour of Henry Murray* New York, Atherton Press, 178–98.

Kuhn, T. S. (1962) *The Structure of Scientific Revolutions* Chicago, University of Chicago Press.

Leonard, W. and Weber, M. (1977) 'Automakers and Dealers: A Study of Criminogenic Market Forces' in G. Geis and R. Meier (eds.) *White Collar Crime: Offences in Business, Politics and the Professions,* New York, Free Press.

Leroy, X. (1992) 'Corporate Ethics: Tomorrow's Decisionmakers Speak Out' *Fortune* July 27.

Lukes, S. (1974) *Power: A Radical View* London, Macmillan.

Macaulay, S. (1969) 'Non-contractual relations in business' in Vilhelm Aubert (ed.) *Sociology of Law* Harmondsworth, Penguin.

MacIntyre, A. (1984) *After Virtue: A Study in Moral Theory* 2nd Edition, Notre Dame, Ind., University of Notre Dame Press.

MacIntyre, A. (1995) 'The Virtues, The Unity of a Human Life, and the Concept of a Tradition' in D. T. Goldberg (ed.) *Ethical Theory and Social Issues: Historical Texts and Contemporary Readings* 2nd Edition, Fort Worth, Harcourt Brace, 188–97.

Maitra, P. (1993) 'Internationalisation of Production and Capitalism's Dilemma', paper presented at the Second International Conference on Development and Future Studies, 13–15 December, The Conference Centre, Edith Cowan University, Perth, Western Australia.

March, J. and Simon, A. (1958) *Organizations* New York, John Wiley and Sons.

Marvel, H. P. (1977) 'Factory Regulation: A Reinterpretation of Early English Experience' *The Journal of Law and Economics* 20:379–402.

Marx, K. (1976) *Capital: Volume 1* London, Penguin.

Mathews, J. (1985) *Health and Safety at Work: A Trade Union Safety Representatives Handbook* Sydney, Pluto Press.

McCarl Nielson, J. (ed.) (1990) *Feminist Research Methods: Exemplary Readings in the Social Sciences* Colorado, Westview Press. Introduction, 1–25.

McCracken, G. (1988) *The Long Interview* Newbury Park, Sage Publications.

McLaughlin, Y. (1993) 'Total Quality Management' in R. Collins (ed.) *Effective Management* New Zealand, CCH International, 397–422.

Mills, C. W. (1963) 'Two Styles of Social Science Research' in *Power, Politics and People: The collected essays of C. Wright Mills* edited with an introduction by Irving Louis Horowitz, New York, Oxford University Press, 553–67.

Minichiello, V., Aroni, R., Timewell, E. and Alexander, L. (1990) *In-Depth Interviewing: Researching People* Melbourne, Longman Cheshire.

Mintzberg, H. (1990) 'The Manager's Job: Foklore and Fact' *Harvard Business Review* March April, 163–76.

Moore, C. A. (1987) 'Taming the Giant Corporation? Some Cautionary Remarks on the Deterrability of Corporate Crime' *Crime and Delinquency* 33:2:379–402.

Morgan, G. (1986) *Images of Organization* Beverley Hills, Sage.

Morris, P. (1992) House of Representatives Standing Committee on Transport, Communications and Infrastructure *Ships of Shame: Inquiry into Ship Safety* Canberra, Australian Government Printing Service.

Nichols, T. (1989) 'On the analysis of size effects and "accidents"—a further comment' *Industrial Relations Journal* 20:62–5.

Nichols, T. (1994) 'Industrial accidents as a means of withdrawal from the workplace according to the Tavistock Institute of Human Relations: A re-examination of a classic study' *British Journal of Sociology* 45:3:387–406.

Occupational Health and Safety Act 1985 (Vic.).

O'Connor, J. (1973) *The Fiscal Crisis of the State,* London, St James Press.

Offe, C. (1984) *Contradictions of the Welfare State* Cambridge Mass., MIT Press.

Pearce, F. (1973) 'Crime, Corporations and the American Social Order' in I. Taylor and L. Taylor (eds.) *Politics and Deviance* Baltimore, Penguin, 13–41.

Pearce, F. and Tombs, S. (1990) 'Ideology, Hegemony and Empiricism: Compliance Theories of Regulation' *British Journal of Criminology* 30:4:423–43.

Pearce, F. and Tombs, S. (1992) 'Realism and Corporate Crime' in R. Matthews and J. Young *Issues in Realist Criminology* London, Sage Publications, 13–41.

Perrone, S. (1993) 'Workplace Fatalities in Victoria: The Adequacy of Prosecution and the Political Influences on the Decision to Prosecute', paper presented to the 9th annual conference of the Australian and

New Zealand Society of Criminology, Women's College, Univesity of Sydney.

Perrow, C. (1984) *Normal Accidents: Living with High Risk Technologies* New York, Basic Books.

Perrow, C. (1986) *Complex Organizations: A Critical Essay* 3rd Edition, New York, McGraw Hill.

Pettigrew, A. (1985) *The Awakening Giant: Continuity and change in ICI* London, Blackwell.

Polk, K. and Stone, W. (1994) 'Public perceptions of white collar crime: a replication and extension', paper presented to the 10th annual conference of the Australian and New Zealand Society of Criminology, The University of New South Wales, 27–30 September.

Polk, K., Haines, F. and Perrone, S. (1993) 'Homicide, Negligence and Work Death: The Need for Legal Change' in Michael Quinlan (ed.) *Work and Health: The Origins, Management and Regulation of Occupational Illness* South Melbourne, Macmillan.

Polk, K., Haines, F. and Perrone, S. (1995) 'Work Death in Victoria, 1987–1990: An Overview' *Australian and New Zealand Journal of Criminology* 28:2:178–92.

Poulantzas, N. (1978) *State, Power, Socialism* London, Verso.

Pritchard, B. (1994) 'Finance Capital as an Engine of Restructuring: The 1980's Merger Wave' *Australian Journal of Political Economy* 33:1–20.

Pusey, M. (1991) *Economic Rationalism in Canberra: A Nation Building State Changes its Mind* Melbourne, Cambridge University Press.

Quinlan, M. (1993) 'The Industrial Relations of Occupational Health and Safety' in Michael Quinlan (ed.) *Work and Health: The Origins, Management and Regulation of Occupational Illness* South Melbourne, Macmillan, 140–69.

Quinlan, M. (1996) 'Managing Occupational Health and Safety in a Changing Environment' in R. Johnstone (ed.) *New Directions in Occupational Health and Safety Prosecutions: The Individual Liability of Corporate Officers, and Prosecutions for Industrial Manslaughter and Related Offences* Centre for Employment and Labour Relations Law Working Papers, University of Melbourne, 22–8.

Quinlan, M. and Bohle, P. (1991) *Managing Occupational Health and Safety in Australia: A Multidisciplinary Approach* South Melbourne, Macmillan.

Raphael, B. (1993) 'The Prevention of Post-Traumatic Stress Reactions', Conference Proceedings of Division of Workplace Health and Safety (Queensland) Conference on Occupational Violence 10–12 February, St Lucia, University of Queensland.

Reasons, C., Ross, L. and Paterson, C. (1981) *Assault on the Worker: Occupational Health and Safety in Canada,* Toronto, Butterworths.

Reed, M. I. (1992) *The Sociology of Organizations: Themes, Perspectives and Prospects* London, Harvester Wheatsheaf.

Rees, J. V. (1988) *Reforming the Workplace: A Study of Self-Regulation in Occupational Safety* Philadelphia, University of Pennsylvania Press.

Rees, J. V. (1994) *Hostages of Each Other: The Transformation of Nuclear Safety since Three Mile Island* Chicago, University of Chicago Press.

Regulation Reform (1992) *Principles for Occupational Regulation* Victorian Government Policy on Occupational Regulation, Department of Small Business, Government of Victoria.

Reiner, I. and Chatten Brown, J. (1989a) 'When it is not an Accident but a Crime: Prosecutors get tough with OSHA Violations' *Northern Kentucky Law Review* 17:1:83–103.

Reiner, I. and Chatten-Brown, J. (1989b) 'Deterring Death in the Workplace: The Prosecutor's Perspective' *Law, Medicine and Health Care* 17:23–31.

Review of Occupational Health and Safety in Australia (1990) Report by the review Committee to the Minister for Industrial Relations, Australian Government Printing Office, November.

Robens, Lord (1972) *Report of the Committee on Safety at Work 1970–1972* HMSO, London.

Robson, M. (1982) *Quality Circles: A Practical Guide* Aldershot, Gower.

Ross, E. A. (1907) (Reprinted 1977) 'The Ciminaloid' in G. Geis and R. F. Meier (eds.) *White Collar Crime* New York, Free Press.

Rowbothom, S. and Mitter, S. (1994) *Dignity and Daily Bread: New forms of organising among poor women in the Third World and First* London, Routledge.

Savas, E. (1987) *Privatisation: The Key to Better Government* New York, Chatham House.

Schein, E. H. (1986) *Organizational Culture and Leadership* San Francisco, Jossey Bass.

Scholtz, J. T. (1984a) 'Deterrence, co-operation, and the ecology of regulatory enforcement' *Law and Society Review* 18:179–224.

Scholtz, J. T. (1984b) 'Voluntary Compliance and Regulatory Policy' *Law and Policy* 6:385–404.

Selznick, P. (1992) *The Moral Commonwealth: Social Theory and the Promise of Community* Berkeley, University of California Press.

Shearing, C. D. (1989) 'Decriminalizing Criminology: Reflections on the Literal and Tropological Meaning of the Term' *Canadian Journal of Criminology* April, 169–78.

Shearing, C. D. (1993) 'A Constitutive Conception of Regulation' in P. Grabosky and J. Braithwaite (eds.) *Business Regulation and Australia's Future* Canberra, Australian Institute of Criminology.

Sherman, L. (1993) 'Defiance, Deterrence and Irrelevance: A Theory of the Criminal Sanction' *Journal of Research in Crime and Delinquency* 30:4:445–73.

Sinclair, A. (1992) 'Organizational Culture Cures for Bad Business Ethics', University of Melbourne Graduate School of Management Working Paper No. 6, June.

Sinclair, A. (1993) 'Improving Ethics through Organizational Culture: A Comparison of Two Approaches' in C. A. J. Coady and C. J. C. Sampford *Business Ethics and the Law* Sydney, The Federation Press, 128–48.

Sitkin, S. B. and Bies, R. J. (1994a) 'The Legalization of Organizations: A Multi-Theoretical Perspective' in S. B. Sitkin and R. J. Bies (eds.) *The Legalistic Organization* California, Sage.

Sitkin, S. B. and Bies, R. J. (eds.) (1994b) *The Legalistic Organization* London, Sage.

Slapper. G. (1992) 'Crime without conviction' *New Law Journal* February 14.

Smirchich, L. (1983) 'Concepts of Culture and Organizational Analysis' *Administrative Sciences Quarterly* 28:339–58, September.

Spradley, J. P. (1979) *The Ethnographic Interview* New York, Holt Reinhart and Wilson.

Standards Australia (1991) *Catalogue and Subject Index of Australian Standards and Other Products.*

Stilwell, F. (1993) *Economic Inequality: Who gets what in Australia* Leichhardt, Pluto Press.

Stone, C. (1975) *Where the Law Ends: The Social Control of Corporate Behaviour* New York, Harper and Row.

Stone, C. (1987) 'Corporate Regulation: The Place of Social Responsibility' in B. Fisse and P. French (eds.) *Corrigible Corporations and Unruly Law* San Antonio, Trinity University Press, 13–38.

Sutherland, E. (1940) 'White Collar Criminality' *American Sociological Review.*

Sutherland, E. (1983) (First published 1949) *White Collar Crime: The Uncut Version* New Haven, Yale University Press.

Sutton, A. (1983) 'Company Crime in New South Wales, A Sociological Perspective', Unpublished Ph.D. thesis.

Sutton, A. (1994) 'Crime Prevention: Promise or Threat?' *Australian and New Zealand Journal of Criminology* 27:1:5–20.

Sutton, A. and Wild, R. (1980) 'Investigating Company Fraud: Case Studies from Australia' in G. Geis and E. Stotland (eds.) *White Collar Crime: Theory and Research* London, Sage.

Sutton, A. and Wild, R. (1988) 'Small Business: White-Collar Villains or Victims?' in Mark Findlay and Russell Hogg (eds.) *Understanding Crime and Criminal Justice* North Ryde, The Law Book Company.

Sutton, R. I. (1989) 'Reactions of Non Participants as Additional Rather than Missing Data: Opportunities for Organizational Research' *Human Relations* 42:5:423–39.

Sykes, G. M. and Matza, D. (1976) (First published 1957) 'Techniques of Neutralization: A Theory of Delinquency' in Rose Giallombardo (ed.) *Juvenile Delinquency* Third Edition, New York, John Wiley and Sons.

Sykes, T. (1994) *The Bold Riders* St Leonards, Allen and Unwin.

Terry, G. R. *A Guide to Management* Homewood, Learning Systems Company.

Textile, Clothing and Footwear Union of Australia (1995) *The hidden cost of Fashion: Report on the National Outwork Information Campaign*, March (Report available from the Textile, Clothing and Footwear Union).

Thomas, J. (1995) 'Organisations of the future are taking shape' *Professional Update* The Official Journal of the Association of Professional Engineers, Scientists and Managers, Australia, March, 5:2:15.

Tombs, S. (1988) ' "The causes of coal-mine accidents" worker autonomy and the myth of the small firm' *Industrial Relations Journal* 19:248–51.

Tombs, S. (1991) 'Injury and Death in the chemical industry: decentring the accident prone victim' *Industrial Crisis Quarterly* 5:59–75.

Turner, B. (1976) 'The Organizational and Interorganizational Development of Disasters' *Administrative Science Quarterly* 21:3:378–97.

Turner, B. (1992a) 'Stepping into the same river twice: learning to handle unique management problems', Middlesex University Inaugural Lectures 2.

Turner, B. (1992b) 'Organizational Learning and the Management of Risk', paper presented to the British Academy of Management Conference, Bradford Management School, 14–16 September.

Van Maanen, J. and Pentland, B. T. (1994) 'Cops and Auditors: The Rhetoric of Records' in S. B. Sitkin and R. J. Bies (eds.) *The Legalistic Organization* California, Sage.

Vaughan, D. (1982) 'Towards Understanding Unlawful Organizational Behaviour' *Michigan Law Review* 80:1377–402.

Viscusi, W. K. (1992) *Fatal Tradeoffs: Public and Private Responsibilities for Risk* New York, Oxford University Press.

Von Ebers, D. (1986) 'The Application of Criminal Homicide Statutes to Work-Related Deaths: Mens Rea and Deterrence' *University of Illinois Law Review* No. 3:969–99.

Walzer, M. (1990) 'The Communitarian Critique of Liberalism' *Political Theory* 18:1:6–23.

Weber, M. (1946) 'The Meaning of Discipline' in H. H. Gerth and C. Wright Mills (eds.) *From Max Weber: Essays in Sociology* New York, Oxford University Press.

Weber, M. (1951) *The Religion of China* Translated by H. H. Gerth with an Introduction of C. K. Yang, New York, Free Press.

Weber, M. (1972) *Basic Concepts in Sociology* Translated with an Introduction by H. P. Secher, New Jersey, The Citadel Press.

Weber, M. (1974) *The Protestant Ethic and the Spirit of Capitalism* Translated by Talcott Parsons, London, Unwin University Books.

Weber, M. (1978) *Max Weber: Selections in translation* Edited by W. C. Runciman and translated by E. Matthews, London, Cambridge University Press.

Weber, M. (1991) *From Max Weber: Essays in Sociology* Edited with an Introduction by H. H. Gerth and C. Wright Mills, with a new Preface by Bryan S. Turner, London, Routledge.

Wells, C. (1988) 'The Decline and Rise of English Murder: Corporate Crime and Individual Responsibility' *Criminal Law Review* December, 788–801.

Wells, C. (1993) 'Corporations: Culture, Risk and Criminal Liability' *Criminal Law Review* August, 551–66.

Wettenhall, G. (1988) 'Deaths in the workplace: The double standard' *Australian Society* 7:11:14–16.

Williamson, J. B., Karp, D., Dolphin, J. R. and Gray, P. S. (1982) *The Research Craft* Boston, Little, Brown and Co.

Wiltshire, K. (1991) 'Privatisation, Regulation and the Public Interest: Britain and Australia' in Brian Head and Elaine McCoy (eds.) *Deregulation or Better Regulation?* South Melbourne, Macmillan, 35–47.

Yeager, P. (1987) 'Structural Bias in Regulatory Law Enforcement: The Case of the U.S. Environmental Protection Agency' *Social Problems* 34:4:330–44.

Yin, R. K. (1989) *Case Study Research* Beverley Hills, Sage.

Young, E. (1989) 'On the Naming of the Rose: Interests and Multiple Meanings as Elements of Organizational Culture' *Organization Studies* 10:2:187–206.

Index